Ivo Mijnssen

THE QUEST FOR AN IDEAL YOUTH IN PUTIN'S RUSSIA I

Back to Our Future!
History, Modernity, and Patriotism according to *Nashi*, 2005-2013

With a foreword by Jeronim Perović

ibidem-Verlag
Stuttgart

Bibliografische Information der Deutschen Nationalbibliothek
Die Deutsche Nationalbibliothek verzeichnet diese Publikation in der
Deutschen Nationalbibliografie; detaillierte bibliografische Daten sind im
Internet über http://dnb.d-nb.de abrufbar.

Bibliographic information published by the Deutsche Nationalbibliothek
Die Deutsche Nationalbibliothek lists this publication in the Deutsche Nationalbibliografie;
detailed bibliographic data are available in the Internet at http://dnb.d-nb.de.

Cover Picture: The main stage of the International Youth Forum at Lake Seliger
in summer 2010 © Ivo Mijnssen.

Second, Revised and Expanded Edition

∞

Gedruckt auf alterungsbeständigem, säurefreien Papier
Printed on acid-free paper

ISSN: 1614-3515

ISBN-13: 978-3-8382-0368-3

© *ibidem*-Verlag
Stuttgart 2014

Alle Rechte vorbehalten

Das Werk einschließlich aller seiner Teile ist urheberrechtlich geschützt. Jede Verwertung außerhalb der engen Grenzen des Urheberrechtsgesetzes ist ohne Zustimmung des Verlages unzulässig und strafbar. Dies gilt insbesondere für Vervielfältigungen, Übersetzungen, Mikroverfilmungen und elektronische Speicherformen sowie die Einspeicherung und Verarbeitung in elektronischen Systemen.

All rights reserved. No part of this publication may be reproduced, stored in or introduced into a retrieval system, or transmitted, in any form, or by any means (electronic, mechanical, photocopying, recording or otherwise) without the prior written permission of the publisher. Any person who does any unauthorized act in relation to this publication may be liable to criminal prosecution and civil claims for damages.

Printed in Germany

Soviet and Post-Soviet Politics and Society (SPPS)
ISSN 1614-3515

General Editor: Andreas Umland,
Kyiv-Mohyla Academy, umland@stanfordalumni.org

Commissioning Editor: Max Jakob Horstmann,
London, mjh@ibidem.eu

EDITORIAL COMMITTEE*

DOMESTIC & COMPARATIVE POLITICS
Prof. **Ellen Bos**, *Andrássy University of Budapest*
Dr. **Ingmar Bredies**, *FH Bund, Brühl*
Dr. **Andrey Kazantsev**, *MGIMO (U) MID RF, Moscow*
Dr. **Heiko Pleines**, *University of Bremen*
Prof. **Richard Sakwa**, *University of Kent at Canterbury*
Dr. **Sarah Whitmore**, *Oxford Brookes University*
Dr. **Harald Wydra**, *University of Cambridge*

SOCIETY, CLASS & ETHNICITY
Col. **David Glantz**, *"Journal of Slavic Military Studies"*
Dr. **Marlène Laruelle**, *George Washington University*
Dr. **Stephen Shulman**, *Southern Illinois University*
Prof. **Stefan Troebst**, *University of Leipzig*

POLITICAL ECONOMY & PUBLIC POLICY
Prof. em. **Marshall Goldman**, *Wellesley College, Mass.*
Dr. **Andreas Goldthau**, *Central European University*
Dr. **Robert Kravchuk**, *University of North Carolina*
Dr. **David Lane**, *University of Cambridge*
Dr. **Carol Leonard**, *University of Oxford*
Dr. **Maria Popova**, *McGill University, Montreal*

FOREIGN POLICY & INTERNATIONAL AFFAIRS
Dr. **Peter Duncan**, *University College London*
Dr. **Taras Kuzio**, *Johns Hopkins University*
Prof. **Gerhard Mangott**, *University of Innsbruck*
Dr. **Diana Schmidt-Pfister**, *University of Konstanz*
Dr. **Lisbeth Tarlow**, *Harvard University, Cambridge*
Dr. **Christian Wipperfürth**, *N-Ost Network, Berlin*
Dr. **William Zimmerman**, *University of Michigan*

HISTORY, CULTURE & THOUGHT
Dr. **Catherine Andreyev**, *University of Oxford*
Prof. **Mark Bassin**, *Södertörn University*
Prof. **Karsten Brüggemann**, *Tallinn University*
Dr. **Alexander Etkind**, *University of Cambridge*
Dr. **Gasan Gusejnov**, *Moscow State University*
Prof. em. **Walter Laqueur**, *Georgetown University*
Prof. **Leonid Luks**, *Catholic University of Eichstaett*
Dr. **Olga Malinova**, *Russian Academy of Sciences*
Dr. **Andrei Rogatchevski**, *University of Glasgow*
Dr. **Mark Tauger**, *West Virginia University*
Dr. **Stefan Wiederkehr**, *BBAW, Berlin*

ADVISORY BOARD*

Prof. **Dominique Arel**, *University of Ottawa*
Prof. **Jörg Baberowski**, *Humboldt University of Berlin*
Prof. **Margarita Balmaceda**, *Seton Hall University*
Dr. **John Barber**, *University of Cambridge*
Prof. **Timm Beichelt**, *European University Viadrina*
Dr. **Katrin Boeckh**, *University of Munich*
Prof. em. **Archie Brown**, *University of Oxford*
Dr. **Vyacheslav Bryukhovetsky**, *Kyiv-Mohyla Academy*
Prof. **Timothy Colton**, *Harvard University, Cambridge*
Prof. **Paul D'Anieri**, *University of Florida*
Dr. **Heike Dörrenbächer**, *DGO, Berlin*
Dr. **John Dunlop**, *Hoover Institution, Stanford, California*
Dr. **Sabine Fischer**, *SWP, Berlin*
Dr. **Geir Flikke**, *NUPI, Oslo*
Prof. **David Galbreath**, *University of Aberdeen*
Prof. **Alexander Galkin**, *Russian Academy of Sciences*
Prof. **Frank Golczewski**, *University of Hamburg*
Dr. **Nikolas Gvosdev**, *Naval War College, Newport, RI*
Prof. **Mark von Hagen**, *Arizona State University*
Dr. **Guido Hausmann**, *University of Freiburg i.Br.*
Prof. **Dale Herspring**, *Kansas State University*
Dr. **Stefani Hoffman**, *Hebrew University of Jerusalem*
Prof. **Mikhail Ilyin**, *MGIMO (U) MID RF, Moscow*
Prof. **Vladimir Kantor**, *Higher School of Economics*
Dr. **Ivan Katchanovski**, *University of Ottawa*
Prof. em. **Andrzej Korbonski**, *University of California*
Dr. **Iris Kempe**, *"Caucasus Analytical Digest"*
Prof. **Herbert Küpper**, *Institut für Ostrecht Regensburg*
Dr. **Rainer Lindner**, *CEEER, Berlin*
Dr. **Vladimir Malakhov**, *Russian Academy of Sciences*

Dr. **Luke March**, *University of Edinburgh*
Prof. **Michael McFaul**, *US Embassy at Moscow*
Prof. **Birgit Menzel**, *University of Mainz-Germersheim*
Prof. **Valery Mikhailenko**, *The Urals State University*
Prof. **Emil Pain**, *Higher School of Economics, Moscow*
Prof. **Oleg Podvintsev**, *Russian Academy of Sciences*
Prof. **Olga Popova**, *St. Petersburg State University*
Dr. **Alex Pravda**, *University of Oxford*
Dr. **Erik van Ree**, *University of Amsterdam*
Dr. **Joachim Rogall**, *Robert Bosch Foundation Stuttgart*
Prof. **Peter Rutland**, *Wesleyan University, Middletown*
Prof. **Marat Salikov**, *The Urals State Law Academy*
Dr. **Gwendolyn Sasse**, *University of Oxford*
Prof. **Jutta Scherrer**, *EHESS, Paris*
Prof. **Robert Service**, *University of Oxford*
Mr. **James Sherr**, *RIIA Chatham House London*
Dr. **Oxana Shevel**, *Tufts University, Medford*
Prof. **Eberhard Schneider**, *University of Siegen*
Prof. **Olexander Shnyrkov**, *Shevchenko University, Kyiv*
Prof. **Hans-Henning Schröder**, *SWP, Berlin*
Prof. **Yuri Shapoval**, *Ukrainian Academy of Sciences*
Prof. **Viktor Shnirelman**, *Russian Academy of Sciences*
Dr. **Lisa Sundstrom**, *University of British Columbia*
Dr. **Philip Walters**, *"Religion, State and Society"*, Oxford
Prof. **Zenon Wasyliw**, *Ithaca College, New York State*
Dr. **Lucan Way**, *University of Toronto*
Dr. **Markus Wehner**, *"Frankfurter Allgemeine Zeitung"*
Dr. **Andrew Wilson**, *University College London*
Prof. **Jan Zielonka**, *University of Oxford*
Prof. **Andrei Zorin**, *University of Oxford*

* While the Editorial Committee and Advisory Board support the General Editor in the choice and improvement of manuscripts for publication, responsibility for remaining errors and misinterpretations in the series' volumes lies with the books' authors.

Soviet and Post-Soviet Politics and Society (SPPS)
ISSN 1614-3515

Founded in 2004 and refereed since 2007, SPPS makes available affordable English-, German- and Russian-language studies on the history of the countries of the former Soviet bloc from the late Tsarist period to today. It publishes between 5 and 20 volumes per year, and focuses on issues in transitions to and from democracy such as economic crisis, identity formation, civil society development, and constitutional reform in CEE and the NIS. SPPS also aims to highlight so far understudied themes in East European studies such as right-wing radicalism, religious life, higher education, or human rights protection. The authors and titles of all previously published manuscripts are listed at the end of this book. For a full description of the series and reviews of its books, see www.ibidem-verlag.de/red/spps.

Editorial correspondence & manuscripts should be sent to: Dr. Andreas Umland, DAAD, German Embassy, vul. Bohdana Khmelnitskoho 25, UA-01901 Kyiv, Ukraine. e-mail: umland@stanfordalumni.org

Business correspondence & review copy requests should be sent to: *ibidem*-Verlag, Leuschnerstr. 40, D-30457 Hannover, Germany; tel.: +49(0)511-2622200; fax: +49(0)511-2622201; spps@ibidem-verlag.de.

Book orders & payments should be made via the publisher's electronic book shop at: www.ibidem-verlag.de/red/SPPS_EN/

Authors, reviewers, referees, and editors for (as well as all other persons sympathetic to) SPPS are invited to join its networks at www.facebook.com/group.php?gid=52638198614 www.linkedin.com/groups?about=&gid=103012 www.xing.com/net/spps-ibidem-verlag/

Recent Volumes

106 Anna Dost
Das russische Verfassungsrecht auf dem Weg zum Föderalismus und zurück
Zum Konflikt von Rechtsnormen und -wirklichkeit in der Russländischen Föderation von 1991 bis 2009
Mit einem Vorwort von Alexander Blankenagel
ISBN 978-3-8382-0292-1

107 Philipp Herzog
Sozialistische Völkerfreundschaft, nationaler Widerstand oder harmloser Zeitvertreib?
Zur politischen Funktion der Volkskunst im sowjetischen Estland
Mit einem Vorwort von Andreas Kappeler
ISBN 978-3-8382-0216-7

108 Marlène Laruelle (ed.)
Russian Nationalism, Foreign Policy, and Identity Debates in Putin's Russia
New Ideological Patterns after the Orange Revolution
ISBN 978-3-8382-0325-6

109 Michail Logvinov
Russlands Kampf gegen den internationalen Terrorismus
Eine kritische Bestandsaufnahme des Bekämpfungsansatzes
Mit einem Geleitwort von Hans-Henning Schröder und einem Vorwort von Eckhard Jesse
ISBN 978-3-8382-0329-4

110 John B. Dunlop
The Moscow Bombings of September 1999
Examinations of Russian Terrorist Attacks at the Onset of Vladimir Putin's Rule
ISBN 978-3-8382-0388-1

111 Андрей А. Ковалёв
Свидетельство из-за кулис российской политики I
Можно ли делать добро из зла? (Воспоминания и размышления о последних советских и первых послесоветских годах)
With a foreword by Peter Reddaway
ISBN 978-3-8382-0302-7

112 Андрей А. Ковалёв
Свидетельство из-за кулис российской политики II
Угроза для себя и окружающих (Наблюдения и предостережения относительно происходящего после 2000 г.)
ISBN 978-3-8382-0303-4

113 Bernd Kappenberg
Zeichen setzen für Europa
Der Gebrauch europäischer lateinischer Sonderzeichen in der deutschen Öffentlichkeit
Mit einem Vorwort von Peter Schlobinski
ISBN 978-3-89821-749-1

For Jessy

Contents

Preface		9
Foreword by Jeronim Perović		13
I	**Introduction**	17
II	**Background and Context**	25
	Focal Points and Sources	26
	The Soviet Collapse as Dislocation	28
	Dislocation in Youth Politics	32
	A New Order	36
	Securitization in Contemporary Russia	38
	Cultural Memory, Commemoration and Hegemony	41
	The 60th Anniversary of Victory	44
	Soviet and Russian Political Identities	49
III	**Russia's Youth, the Orange Revolution, and Nashi**	53
	Orange Revolution	54
	The Orange Revolution and Russia	56
	Taking Back the Streets	59
	Our Victory	62
	Patriotic Education	66
	The Manifesto	72
	Foreign Enemies	77
	Domestic Enemies	81
	Unusual Fascists	85
	Nashi after the Orange Revolution	90

IV	Remember! Nashi and the Bronze Soldier	97
	History, National Identity and Ethnic Tension	98
	The Bronze Soldier	102
	Nashi and the First Protests	105
	Bronze Nights	107
	Events at the Estonian Embassy	110
	The International Dimension	114
	Aftermath	119
	Victory Day 2007 and Beyond	124
V	Seliger: The Foundry of Modernization	133
	Seliger: The Early Years	134
	Participant Observation at Seliger	138
	International Youth Forum Seliger 2010	140
	Difficult Beginnings	143
	The Songs of Seliger	145
	Leisure and Discipline	152
	Lectures	155
	Sharing Sessions	159
	The World Outside	162
	A Happy Ending?	168
VI	Conclusions	177
	Bibliography	187
	Index	211
	Appendix I: Brochure «*Neobyknovennyi Fashizm*»	215
	Appendix II: Instruction Manual «*Neskol'ko Neudobnykh Voprosov Rossiiskoi Vlasti*»	228

Preface

My interest in Nashi began with the organization's first demonstration in 2005: the fact that a youth organization had used the commemoration of the Great Patriotic War to mobilize young Russians was very surprising to my Western European mind. Young people in Switzerland are more soporific than energetic when discussions or lessons in school turn to historical issues.

In Russia, however, war memory is held sacred by a vast majority of the population and continues to serve an important societal and political function. That a state-sponsored youth movement would use this memory as the basis of its identity is thus less surprising than it first seemed. The goal of this book is to show the role that war memory played for Nashi and its link to various aspects of the movement's identity concepts and ideology.

I developed *Back to Our Future* out of a Masters thesis at the University of Basel, submitted in 2010. Since then, I have revised and translated the book, added a chapter and new materials. I did research for this book in St. Petersburg, Moscow, at Lake Seliger, at Stanford University, in Zürich, Bern and Basel.

After finishing the book in August 2012, the opportunity arose to publish a second, revised and extended edition of the book in late 2013. The new edition includes current developments, some minor corrections and an improved index at the end. By covering Nashi's development from 2005-2013, the book now contains the organization's entire history, as it was disbanded in early 2013. Other state-sponsored youth organizations have taken Nashi's place, and new ones will undoubtedly be founded when the need arises to demonstrate unity and youth support for the Putin regime. It is my hope that this book – in conjunction with the parallel volume written by my colleague Jussi Lassila – will also continue to contribute to a better understanding of youth politics in Russia in the future.

I first want to thank my Russian friends and colleagues who have helped me understand Russian politics better. Danila Korogodskii hosted me in St. Petersburg and provided me with an astute and critical view on his country. Alla Lapidus guided me through the challenges of working in the Russian National Library, and Sergei Simonov, editor of *politgramota.ru*, took a lot of time to explain the intricacies of Russia's youth politics to me. I want to thank the two Nashi commissars, who spoke to me so openly, for their valuable insights into the organizations inner workings. This book would have been much less rich without my participation in the «International Youth Forum Seliger 2010». In spite of all its problematic aspects, I want to thank the organizers of the forum for inviting international students to the beautiful shores of Seliger. It was, however, the Russian volunteers who acted as unpaid mediators and translators between internationals and Russians who deserve the highest praise. I am particularly grateful to Dima, Masha and Polina.

I did a lot of work on this book during my year as a Visiting Scholar at the Center for Russian, East European and Eurasian Studies at Stanford University (CREEES). I am grateful to Professor Emeritus Abbott Gleason and Professor Norman Naimark for making this year possible, and to Rob Wessling, Bob Crews, Karen Haley and Van-Anh Nguyen for the continued support at the Center.

The graduate students at CREEES and in Russian and Eastern European History made sure I felt welcome on campus. I want to thank Markian Dobczansky and Dan Heller for reading drafts of chapters. Jussi Lassila read the entire manuscript and gave me very useful feedback. Anna Whittington did a tremendous job editing the book «European style» and making sure my German did not get in the way of readable English prose. I am also grateful for series editor Andreas Umland's formatting work.

This project began and ended in Switzerland. Professor Emeritus Heiko Haumann was a great first reader of my MA-thesis, and Professor Jeronim Perovic deserves thanks for being a second reader and writing the foreword. Last but not least, Dr. Philipp Casula has for the past five years been a wonderful colleague and critic of my work.

At different times, this work absorbed me heavily. I therefore want to thank my family. My parents Daniela and Pete read early drafts of the thesis, and my brother Remo was an amazing study partner during the summer of 2009. My wife Jessy, finally, not only read multiple drafts of the English manuscript but also made sure I could focus on my work *and* not get too absorbed by it. Without her, life would be much less fun.

Ivo Mijnssen
Zürich, January 2014

Foreword

On 7 May 2012, Vladimir Putin was inaugurated as President of the Russian Federation, reclaiming the office he held from 2000 to 2008 and resuming the mantle of power that he had never fully relinquished to Dmitry Medvedev. Looking back at past achievements, he declared in his inaugural speech that we «strengthened our country and returned our dignity as a great nation», so that the «world has seen Russia risen anew». The new Russia Putin intends to build is a Russia looking back. The dignity restored means a correction of past errors, the biggest of which Putin sees in the decision to dissolve the Soviet Union, an event that he once described as the «greatest geopolitical catastrophe» of the 20th century. While Putin recognizes that a return to Soviet times is impossible, he promised in his inaugural speech to make Russia the «leader and centre of gravity for the whole of Eurasia». He has the country's «great past» and its «hundreds of years of history» in mind, thus, if not explicitly, holding up the imperial era as a model for the future.

Russia's still considerable military, political and economic weight, as well as its crucial importance as an energy supplier to Europe, mean that the West cannot afford to ignore developments in this country. Either way Russia turns will affect stability and security on the Eurasian continent. Russia's actions in the recent past, repeatedly cutting energy supplies to costumers west of its borders, invading Georgia in August 2008 with disproportionate use of force, suppressing free media, and cracking down on political opposition all clearly point toward a less cooperative Russia when dealing with the West, a more aggressive Russia when defending interests in its near abroad, and a more authoritarian system domestically. Yet if most would agree that Russia has become more assertive under Putin's leadership, few understand the ideological and sociopolitical underpinnings of this development. If official rhetoric and behavior tell only half of the story at best, then it is necessary to take a deep look into society itself.

Ivo Mijnssen chose to do precisely this when he examined the Russian youth organization called The Democratic Anti-Fascist Youth Movement 'Nashi'.

Nashi, which means «Ours» in English translation, was founded in 2005 and claimed several tens of thousands of members in dozens of Russian regions at the peak of its existence during 2005-07. Although a large organization, it is certainly not to be compared with Soviet youth organizations, such as the «Young Pioneers», or «Komsomol», with memberships in the tens of millions. In fact, many Russians are not even aware of Nashi's existence, as opinion polls show. Yet because Nashi is an organization initiated and founded directly by the Kremlin, as is widely acknowledged today in the literature, looking into its organizational structure, slogans, manifestos, and actions help to better understand state ideology and goals. What politicians like Putin might not find suitable to utter publicly, the leaders of Nashi, the so-called «commissars», never hesitate to do.

Nashi was founded with a clear purpose: To prevent a Russian repeat of Ukraine's 2004 Orange Revolution. Nashi's task was to mobilize youth in support of the government, ensuring that people loyal to Putin controlled the streets, thus preventing a scenario in which a mass movement was able to overthrow the existing regime. Nashi draws its legitimacy from Russia's heroic past, namely the war against Nazi Germany, or what Russians call the «Great Patriotic War». Nashi sees itself as a defender of homeland and history. Nashi defines all of what it considers Russia's foes today, be these international organizations, NGOs, individuals, states or internal opposition groups, to be «fascist», equating them with the Soviet Union's enemies in WWII.

Over two decades have passed since the collapse of the Soviet Union. To an entire generation of young people, this mighty empire seems already a thing of a distant past. A majority of young Russians in Moscow, St. Petersburg or Nizhny Novgorod profess similar values, and share the same interests as young people in Rome, Paris or Berlin. Most are apolitical and seek to pursue their individual happiness. Yet, as the example of the youth movement Nashi demonstrates, the Russian state under Putin has long recognized the vast strategic resource that young people represent in building a new Russia, and the government has put considerable effort into forming a «patriotic» youth with visions similar to those of Putin's strong and united country over the past decade. In fact, since the founding of Nashi in 2005, Russia has seen other state-initiated efforts to create youth organizations. It is in these organizations where some of the new leaders of tomorrow's Russia are being formed. And it is thus essential to understand these organizations better, if we are to understand the Russia not only of the present, but also of the future.

Ivo Mijnssen's book is the more fascinating since it not only includes an analysis of existing literature and various types of documents but also the author's own experience as a participant in a Nashi summer camp in 2010 on Lake Seliger. The author thus traveled a long road, physically and figuratively. What he started in 2008-09 as a MA-thesis at the University of Basel, he now presents in a much enlarged and revised version in book-form. I thank Ivo for taking the extra time and effort in order to make his results available to a larger audience. The Western reader will enter a world largely unknown, and I am sure he will appreciate it as he will gain much needed insight into the way Russia «ticks» on many different levels.

Jeronim Perović
University of Zurich

I Introduction

«History is the succession of generations. Each generation is faced with the choice of either disappearing unnoticed or changing the world. Today, we, the generation of young Russians, are facing this choice.» (Nashi 2005a)

On 15 May 2005 a new organization appears in the spotlight of Russia's political stage: the Democratic Anti-Fascist Youth Movement (*Molodezhnoe Demokraticheskoe Antifashistskoe Dvizhenie*) Nashi (*Ours*). Founded just one month earlier, Nashi gathers 60'000 young people shortly after Victory Day, in a show of solidarity with the veterans of the Great Patriotic War[1] – and with Vladimir Putin. The demonstrators have a clear message: Russia's youth is patriotic and values the country's historical achievements. Russia's youth is loyal to Putin and ready to take on the challenges facing the country. Two weeks later, Putin receives a delegation of Nashi-«commissars» – the organization's cadres – in the Kremlin. The meeting demonstrates the president's blessing for the youth movement. Putin appears to support Nashi's aim of carrying out a «revolution», a revolution that will put a patriotic new elite in power, one that «believes in the future of Russia» (Nashi 2005a).
Fortunately for the Russian government, Nashi's revolution is with, not against Putin. Since he stands for returning Russia to its rightful status as a global great power, Nashi argues, he deserves the support of Russia's patriotic youth. Only a powerful and modern Russia can maintain its sovereignty in a globalized system of ruthless competition and safeguard the freedom of its people, writes Nashi. Russia must be an open and innovative country that buttresses its position not by military might, but because of the «attractiveness of Russian culture, its way of life, its political, economic and social system» (ibid.).

---

[1] This name is used in Russia to designate World War II. World War II started on 1 September 1939 with the German invasion of Poland, whereas the Great Patriotic War began on 22 June 1941 with the German invasion of the Soviet Union (Operation Barbarossa). Both ended with the German surrender on 8/9 May 1945.

Despite the clear affinity between the Kremlin and the patriotic-minded youth organization, both go to great lengths to avoid the impression that the organization is state-run, presenting it instead as a grassroots initiative (Kashin 2005c). Nonetheless, the relationship between Nashi and the authorities is close from the start. The organization was able to make large-scale use of the government's «administrative resources»: mass demonstrations in Russia did not take place without official blessing in 2005.

Nashi-founder Vasilii Iakemenko was a former official in the Presidential Administration with a history of founding pro-Kremlin movements: his previous project was the organization Idushchie Vmeste (*Going Together*). Another early driving force was Vladislav Surkov, architect of Sovereign Democracy, which discursively combines Russia's democratic development with a strong emphasis on safeguarding the country's national sovereignty.

The Kremlin's willingness to mobilize tens of thousands of young Russians shows that the authorities took the threat of an Orange Revolution very seriously. Nashi was only the largest of a number of newly founded pro-Kremlin youth organizations.[2] Political scientists disagree on the extent to which the Ukrainian events endangered the Putin regime. Robert Horvath believes that Russia faced a potentially revolutionary situation in 2005 (Horvath 2011: 2). Viktor Eremin argues that Nashi's demonstrations were merely meant to show to the opposition the mobilization potential of pro-Kremlin youth groups (Eremin 2007: 3).[3]

Nashi was founded to stabilize Russia's political system and to take back the streets from opposition demonstrators. Journalist Maksim Sokolov called Nashi the Kremlin's «Iron Soldiers» (*zheleznyi frunt*) (Sokolov 2005), and Ivan Bol'shakov, political scientist and liberal politician, termed them «storm troopers» (Bol'shakov 2006: 120). These polemic descriptions of Nashi nonetheless pinpoint a major problem of the organization – the propensity for violence among parts of its activists. However, they are neither analytically profound, nor do they account for Nashi's ability to attract large numbers of youth

---

2   Other organizations founded in 2005 included the Young Guard (*Molodaia Gvardiia*), founded by the party of power United Russia (*Edinaia Rossiia*), and the Locals (*Mestnye*).
3   The Russian government defines youth as the age group between 14 and 30 years (Pravitel'stvo Rossiiskoi Federatsii 2006). This corresponds to the Soviet definition. Young Soviet citizens joined the Komsomol at 14 and left it at 30.

or its longevity. Nashi played an important political role long after its main goal – the prevention of an opposition coup during the presidential elections of 2008 (Nashi 2011b) – was fulfilled.

A more analytical line of research sees Nashi as a vehicle for official youth politics. As the Putin administration has traditionally kept a tight lid on political expression, these authors maintain, Nashi serves as a kind of valve to channel popular discontent in a controlled fashion (Robertson 2009: 545). Sergei Balmasov defines Nashi as a «puppet youth movement» (Balmasov 2006: 21) of the Kremlin, and Sergei Gavrov considers their actions to be political theater (Gavrov 2006: 353). Philosopher Pavel Gurevich writes that Nashi is an «imitation» of youth politics (Gurevich 2005: 24). This strand of research argues that the Russian government is unable or unwilling to provide youth with avenues of upward social mobility and political participation. The authors place the emergence of Nashi in the context of Russian politics, without, however, conducting an in-depth investigation of this context.

Aside from promising upward social mobility, Nashi directs potential aggression among youth against real and imagined enemies that block activists' – and Russia's – success. These «enemies» were repeatedly the target of verbal and physical attacks by Nashi. Dmitrii Andreev conceptualizes this channeled discontent as «managed passion» (*upravliaemaia passionarnost'*):

> «For the impassioned (*passionarii*), some kind of an enemy is absolutely vital. Or not even so much an enemy as some kind of a negative example, an object of anti-imitation (*ob"ekta antipodrazhaniia*), a strong idea of what one does not want to be under any circumstances.» (Andreev 2006: 50)

«Ours»' sense of shared identity thus relies to a significant extent on a shared opposition against those who are «not us».

Only a handful of scholars have published more profound analyses of Nashi. Liubov Borusiak was the first to scrutinize the organization's ideological foundations (Borusiak 2005). Ulrich Schmid focuses on Nashi's political function. He points to the discursive connection between war memory and the fight against a vague «fascist» enemy (Schmid 2006: 14). This connection plays an important role for the analysis in this book as well.

Douglas Buchacek's MA thesis on Nashi (Buchacek 2006) focuses on Nashi's mobilization mechanisms and ideology. He convincingly analyzes Nashi's early publications but rarely contextualizes them further.

All of these publications came out within a year of Nashi's foundation. Since 2006, interest in the movement has waned considerably, with some scholars predicting the organization's inevitable decline as early as 2008 (Heller 2008). The important exceptions are Maya Atwal and Jussi Lassila, who wrote their dissertations about Nashi.[4] Both negotiate the tension between its status as a vehicle for the promotion of official policies in the youth sphere and the organization's independent maneuvering space. Atwal's article tracks Nashi's development since 2008 and provides an important framework for understanding the movement's continued existence. According to her, Nashi refocused its activities in the economic realm and achieved a modicum of independence from the government (Atwal 2009: 756). Lassila believes that Nashi has to fulfill a difficult balancing act between propagating a government platform and providing its activists with a means of expression appropriate to the youth sphere. He highlights the importance of Nashi's performative acts in creating emotional attachment to official ideology among youth (Lassila 2012a: 110ff.). As an important actor in the sphere of youth politics, Nashi conveys a government-sponsored political identity to young Russians. This book analyzes Nashi and its ideas in the context of Russian politics and youth politics in particular, tracking the organization's development from 2005 to 2012. The book principally analyzes Nashi's discourse at three specific points in its history, localizing it in the political environment of contemporary Russia. These three «focal points» (Hansen 2006) include Nashi's founding in 2005, its actions in the «memory wars» with Estonia in 2007, and the «International Youth Forum 2010» at Lake Seliger.

The foundation of Nashi and its discursive underpinning, I maintain, cannot be understood separately from the values and worldviews of the Putin government. Nashi reflects government-sponsored efforts to stabilize the field of politics and official values following the 1990s and the collapse of the Soviet Union.[5] The most important demands in this official discourse are a strong

---

[4] Atwal's dissertation is as of yet unpublished, her published article is discussed below. Lassila defended his PhD-thesis in 2011. The ibidem-Verlag published it in a revised version along with my book (see Lassila 2012b).

[5] The assumed existence of a hegemonic project under Putin means neither that he alone articulated this project, nor that it originated with him. Instead, the Putin regime coopted various discourses and demands. Moreover, there is considerable continuity between the politics of Yeltsin's second administration and Putin's (Bacon

Russian state anchored in its heroic history, a modern economy, global great power status, and a society united against its enemies. Nashi conveys these demands to a youthful audience.

Nashi thus offers to its activists a political identity, a historical genealogy, a sense of belonging to a community, and, possibly, a career. An idealized narrative of the Great Patriotic War plays a crucial role as a discursive template to make sense of the current situation in Russia. It has contributed significantly to state-sponsored attempts at consolidating youth politics and Russia's national identity. As will be shown, its mobilizing power is considerable, especially in times of perceived threat.

However, the most important moments of Nashi's discourse remain in tension with one other – particularly with regards to Russia's position in the world: warlike imagery of the world suggests an exclusive focus on defending the country, while a modern economy demands a degree of openness. Moreover, Nashi promises its supporters self-realization and simultaneously demands submission to a highly hierarchical system. These contradictions are a great problem for Nashi's professed goal of turning Russia into a country that is internationally competitive. The contradictions in Nashi's discourse thus threaten to undermine its goals. At the same time, the variety of goals and demands in Nashi's discourse – and in the ideology of Sovereign Democracy on which much of it is based – is the precondition for mobilizing a broad cross-section of Russia's youth. The analysis of the effects of these contradictions thus plays an important role in this book.

Background and Context, the first chapter, provides the methodological and theoretical framework of analysis. This includes the basic terms of Ernesto Laclau and Chantal Mouffe's discourse analysis and of the politics of history and memory. I then discuss Barry Buzan and Ole Wæver's concept of securitization, complemented by an analysis of the historical background of the Putin regime, which focuses on the government's attempts to stabilize the political situation after the Soviet collapse and the chaos of the 1990s.

---

et al. 2006: 183). Putin has articulated and embodied these efforts in the most consistent and convincing fashion.

The second chapter, *Russia's Youth, the Orange Revolution, and Nashi*, turns to Russia in 2005. Nashi's founding occurred as a direct consequence of Ukraine's 2004 Orange Revolution, which deeply affected Russian politics. The analysis in this chapter shows that official discourse presented the Orange Revolution as threatening the stability of Russia's political system. Government agencies and Russian political scientists wanted to safeguard the patriotism and political reliability of a young generation often perceived as exposed to harmful (Western) influences and in need of guidance. The stabilization and *securitization* (Buzan, Wæver and de Wilde 1998) of the youth sphere through the foundation of Nashi became a crucial political task.

The promotion of an idealized, mythologized narrative of the Great Patriotic War was a key component of programs for the youth's patriotic education. Nashi presented itself as standing at the forefront of a struggle to build a Russia anchored in its historical identity and ready to face present and future challenges. The war myth became a template through which to interpret the ambitions and obstacles on Russia's path to great power status. Drawing on historical parallels, Nashi identified enemies that threatened Russia's statehood and subsumed them under the signifier «fascist». Combined with Vladislav Surkov's ideology of Sovereign Democracy, the war myth provided a hegemonic response to the political instability of early 2005.

The conflict over the removal of the «Bronze Soldier » in Tallinn, Estonia is the subject of chapter three, *Remember! Nashi and the Bronze Soldier*. The riots after the Estonian government's removal of the Soviet war memorial from downtown Tallinn on 26 and 27 April 2007 were one of the few instances in which conflicting interpretations of World War II turned violent. In the aftermath, Nashi picketed the Estonian embassy in Moscow and attacked the ambassador.

Analysis of Nashi's online publications reveals the role the war myth played as a template for interpreting the political conflict with contemporary Estonia. Nashi discursively equated the supporters of the National Socialists in World War II with the contemporary Estonian state and thus evoked a sense of immediate threat to present-day Russia: both were subsumed under the term «fascist». This threat perception led to the securitization of memory, which legitimized drastic measures by Nashi.

In chapter four, *The Foundry of Modernization*, the focus shifts to the International Youth Forum Seliger 2010, which the Russian government and Nashi organized. Seliger is a further «focal point» for Nashi. Nashi calls the camp its «foundry of modernization» and has steadily extended both its size and the scope of participants.

The organizers first opened the secretive camp to foreign participants in 2010. As a participant observer, I was able to study the manner in which official Russian identity concepts were conveyed to an international audience. The war myth and the moment of unity against Russia's enemies played a smaller role than the themes of modernity, international cooperation, and Sovereign Democracy. Nonetheless, the organizational structure of the camp and unofficial documents still revealed strong securitizing moments: the demand for openness and modernization was undermined by a perceived need to maintain control.

II Background and Context

A study of Nashi is inevitably also a study of the official political sphere[6] in Russia. Since I, like many others, argue that Nashi is a government project, it is necessary to analyze the political background of the regime that created Nashi. This chapter therefore contextualizes the emergence and consolidation of the Putin regime in Russia. I argue that Nashi's worldviews and values are part of a broader project during Vladimir Putin's first two terms: the stabilization of Russia's political system and the articulation of an official, government-sponsored political identity.

This book analyzes the process of political stabilization primarily on a discursive level, through the concepts of *dislocation* and *hegemony* developed by Ernesto Laclau und Chantal Mouffe (Laclau and Mouffe 2001). The notion of *securitization* (Buzan, Wæver and de Wilde 1998) is another key concept for understanding Russian politics before and under Putin. A special section of this chapter provides an introduction into Russian youth politics.

Possibly the most striking feature of this process has been Putin's skillful use of symbolic politics, analyzed in the chapter's final section. His government has placed strong emphasis on historical continuity. The commemoration of the Great Patriotic War has been at the center of efforts to foster pride in Russian culture and Russian statehood. Analysis of the official war narrative reveals how this commemoration has served Putin's project.

This chapter thus serves two purposes. On one hand, it introduces the theoretical and methodological framework of this book. On the other, it applies the theoretical framework to analyze changes in Russia's political identity since the collapse of the Soviet Union and the politics of history as it relates to the commemoration of the Great Patriotic War.

---

6 I use the word «official» to mean «state-sponsored» discourses and identities, in which the state is strongly involved. Naturally, many other societal processes in Russia are not controlled by the state. To describe these would go beyond the scope of this book. I would thus like to caution readers of considering the aspects described here as representative for «Russian society». Because Nashi is a government sponsored, project, this book also focuses on the spheres in which the state is the central actor.

Focal Points and Sources

This book predominantly analyzes Nashi's publications as well as speeches and position papers from Vladimir Putin and Vladislav Surkov. Putin's utterances on Russian politics and Russian identity, as well as his speeches commemorating the Great Patriotic War, have received wide attention – both on the international stage and in Russia. Because Nashi has repeatedly emphasized that it is loyal to Putin specifically, his statements can be considered programmatic for the organization.

Vladislav Surkov, currently an advisor to Vladimir Putin after a brief fall from official grace following his dismissal as Deputy Prime Minister, is a less public figure. For a long time, many considered the former Deputy Head of the Presidential Administration and architect of the ideology of Sovereign Democracy to be the *eminence grise* of Russian politics. His ideas have not only been discussed extensively among political scientists and in the press but have also made their way into Putin's policy speeches. In 2006, Putin officially endorsed Sovereign Democracy as the government's official ideology (Edinaia Rossiia 2006). Furthermore, Surkov played a decisive role in the founding of Nashi. He was present at the organization's secret inaugural meeting in the spa town of Solnechnogorsk in late February of 2005 (Loskutova 2008: 260). Texts on the organization's website (www.Nashi.su) serve as the main source for this analysis of Nashi's ideas and worldview. Lassila understands these online writings as the crystallization of Nashi's voice (Lassila 2012a: 106). Though they do not constitute official government positions, the analysis in the following chapters shows that they contain many of the same discursive demands. Nashi's website confirms the organization's close connection to official discourse: Nashi's former «ideology» section contained speeches, articles and presentations by Putin and Surkov (Nashi 2009a).[7]

In spite of this closeness, it remains important to distinguish between Nashi and official discourse. One might say that Nashi provides a window into offi-

---

[7] Nashi's new website, launched after 2009, no longer contains an ideology section. Instead, the organization's views are featured on a sub-site called «Nasha Positsiia»: It contains more than 100 articles written by pro-Kremlin pundits and officials, most of them on current political affairs. This may indicate that the tight ideological grounding of Nashi's early years has given way to a broader variety of issues and positions. Nonetheless, Putin and Surkov remain central figures.

cial discourse and adapts this discourse for the youth sphere. This transfer leads to a change in style and to contradictions, since government policy is not always well suited to mobilize youth. Lassila thus writes, «pro-Kremlin youth movements truly struggle with cogent expressions for their political ideologies.» (Lassila 2012a: 138) This struggle and the contradictions it engenders are an important topic in my book.

To complement the discourse analysis, I conducted two interviews with Nashi-commissars from St. Petersburg and Moscow. Within Nashi's hierarchy, commissars are the cadres. They wear a special pin with the organization's logo and undergo a vetting process that lasts two years. Commissars thus have privileged access to knowledge about Nashi and are treated as experts for the purposes of this book. The interviewees provide information about Nashi's decision-making processes and routines that other, more official documents cannot. These interviews address two major difficulties in studying Nashi: secrecy about its inner workings and its hierarchical structure. The information it releases to the public is thus adapted to the organization's political needs and not necessarily objective. Due to the sensitive nature of some of the interview material, I use pseudonyms («Andrei» and «Marina») instead of their real names.

The interview with the St. Petersburg commissar (Andrei) was conducted in person during a research trip to the city in spring of 2009. It followed the form of a guided expert interview (Meuser and Nagel 1994: 123f.). I asked a number of general questions that satisfied my scientific interest, at the same time giving Andrei room to develop his narrative. Conversations with the second expert (Marina) took place over a period of multiple months – in person in Moscow, and through online chats.

The interviews are primarily used to clarify facts and to illustrate how individuals within Nashi appropriate the organization's ideas. The selection of experts is by no means representative, and not all of their opinions necessarily represent Nashi's official positions. Their information is thus contextualized and contrasted with more official sources whenever possible (Kassner und Wassermann 2005: 109).

Chapter 4 on the «International Youth Forum Seliger 2010» makes use of a larger variety of materials than the parts that precede it. I gathered these materials as a participant observer during the youth forum. They include representations of official discourse in popular culture, thus providing hints about the reproduction of political identities in a broader cultural realm (Hansen 2006: 64). Specific methodological challenges will be addressed separately in chapter 4. Finally, this book uses a wide variety of secondary sources to locate Nashi within the context of contemporary Russian politics.

I cannot address all aspects of Nashi's history and discourse. Instead, I use three case studies to illustrate important events and moments. In her methodological chapter on discourse analysis, Lene Hansen suggests that researchers focus their attention on time frames and issues that illustrate political processes in a «crystallized» fashion (Hansen 2006: 78). I selected three such «focal points», the subjects of subsequent chapters: the organization's founding in the aftermath of Ukraine's 2004 Orange Revolution, its response to the relocation of Tallinn's Soviet war memorial in 2007, and Nashi's summer camp at Lake Seliger in 2010. Based on these three case studies, I analyze the various moments of Nashi's discourse and show which of them are emphasized over others in various contexts. First I expound on the historic and political background that made the emergence of Nashi possible. The best starting point is the collapse of the Soviet Union.

The Soviet Collapse as Dislocation

The collapse of the Soviet Union marked the disappearance of a multinational empire whose influence had stretched from Eastern Europe to Central Asia and beyond. This signified a drastic reduction of Moscow's sphere of influence and territory and a crisis in Russian identity. Even though ethnic Russians had not possessed their own national institutions during Soviet times, they played the leading political and cultural role in the USSR. Geoffrey Hosking even goes so far as to argue that Russian identity equaled Soviet identity in many regards (Hosking 2006: 2).

A discussion of the relation between Soviet and Russian identity would go beyond the scope of this book and has been discussed extensively elsewhere.[8] For the purposes of this book, this loss serves as a point of departure

---

8   Hirsch, F. 2005. *Empire of nations: Ethnographic knowledge and the making of the Soviet Union.* Ithaca: Cornell University Press; Martin, T. 2001. *The Affirmative Ac-*

for understanding contemporary Russian political identities and their historical foundation.

To grasp this loss and its compensation theoretically, I use Ernesto Laclau and Chantal Mouffe's terminology. Their discourse theory allows for a dynamic conception of social identities. Laclau and Mouffe see societies and nations not as natural, objectively existing entities, but rather as the results of discursive articulations. They draw their political terminology from Antonio Gramsci and their notion of discourse from Michel Foucault. Swiss historian Philipp Sarasin located Foucault's notion of discourse as existing between things and words. Discourse is an entity with its own rules and elements that attributes meaning to items and statements within a specific societal context (Sarasin 2003: 34). According to Laclau and Mouffe, writes sociologist Urs Stäheli, discourses construct «realities» by arranging various elements in such a way as to form a significant whole (Stäheli 2001: 198). Practices and actions only become meaningful when embedded in a discourse and connected to other signifiers. Similarly, identities are not preexistent but socially and politically constructed.

Laclau and Mouffe call this «unfixity» of identities *dislocation*. Identities remain perennially unstable and are only temporarily arranged within a discourse, to create a measure of stability: «Any discourse is constituted as an attempt to dominate the field of discursivity, to arrest the flow of differences, to construct a centre.» (Laclau and Mouffe 2001: 112). This «centre» is constructed by arranging various discursive moments in a chain of equivalence around so-called «nodal points» – «privileged signifiers that fix the meaning of a signifying chain» (ibid.). These nodal points tie the different moments of a discourse together and provide it with a coherent meaning.

When this combination is successful, one can speak of a hegemonic discourse. A hegemonic discourse describes the world in a new, convincing manner by articulating and connecting norms, values and perceptions (Torfing 1999: 302). It presents a worldview that enjoys widespread acceptance within a social collective.

---

tion Empire: Nations and Nationalism in the Soviet Union, 1923-1939. Ithaca: Cornell University Press; Slezkine, Y. 1994. «The USSR as a Communal Apartment, or How a Socialist State Promoted Ethnic Particularism». *Slavic Review* 53, 2. 414-452.

A hegemonic operation is always the result of discursive dislocation, as it stabilizes an entity that is inherently unstable. Laclau and Mouffe, however, attach a second meaning to dislocation: concrete events and political demands that undermine the stability of a hegemonic discourse because the latter cannot absorb and arrange them as part of the dominant worldview (ibid.: 301). Put simply, dislocations are discursive moments deeply at odds with the predominant values in a society.

German sociologist Philipp Casula argues that the demands and events that could not be articulated within Soviet discourse contributed significantly to the Union's collapse (Casula 2010: 249). Demands for economic and social reforms beyond the socialist framework, declining living standards, the disaster at Chernobyl and Eastern European and Baltic states' drive for national independence contradicted the dominant Soviet worldview. Official Soviet discourse presented socialism as the most progressive system in the world, as superior to capitalism, and as the home of a multitude of «brotherly» nations. Even if some Soviet citizens, particularly in the late USSR, had a critical and even cynical attitude towards official declarations, a different system was unimaginable for the vast majority.

According to Alexei Yurchak, Mikhail Gorbachev began the «deconstruction of Soviet authoritative discourse» by suggesting that the answer to the USSR's economic and social problems might lie outside of socialist ideology and the Communist Party (Yurchak 2006: 291f.). His reforms, and particularly *glasnost'* (*openness*), broke the hegemonic power of Soviet discourse and the Communist Party. In Laclau's terms, Soviet discourse was dislocated by Gorbachev's reform plans, which could not be convincingly connected with other «socialist» discursive moments.

The government's decision not to use military force to maintain the Eastern European satellite states within the socialist system in 1989 and the worsening economic and political situation in the USSR finally provoked an attempted coup d'état by anti-reform Communists in 1991. The failure of the August coup, however, led to the establishment of a sovereign Russian state and sealed the fate of the Soviet Union. Political collapse followed discursive dislocation.

The Russian state that emerged in the 1990s lacked stable political and territorial foundations. Politicians struggled to articulate a common political identity. To a certain extent, this was intentional: the market ideology promoted aggressively by Russian reformers in the early Yeltsin period led to a limitation of the state's involvement in social, political and economic affairs. Many considered any attempt to articulate and promote an official political identity to be reminiscent of Soviet methods and thus potentially totalitarian (Molchanov 2005: 19).

At the same time, Russians were faced with a dramatic deterioration of living standards. Chechnya declared independence in 1994, and the unsuccessful and costly war that followed demonstrated the Russian army's severe limitations. The treaty of Khasaviurt, which provided Chechnya with de-facto autonomy, contributed to a widespread sense that the Russian state was losing control over large parts of the country. The collapse of the ruble in 1998, which resulted in the vast number of Russians losing their savings, constituted a further dislocation.

Official government discourse presented Russia as a democratic country with a market economy, yet this discourse failed to provide a unifying national idea.[9] Other discourses were simultaneously competing for hegemony. Olga Malinova identifies two main blocks: the «Democrats» around Yeltsin, and the «Popular-Patriotic Opposition» (Malinova 2009: 97). While the former, dominated by supporters of liberal market reforms, corresponded more or less to official government discourse, the latter united Communists and right-wing forces: «They combined traditional communist rhetoric with criticism of liberalism and Westernism, and included some elements of Russian nationalism of the imperial type» (ibid.: 101).

Both discourses struggled to reach an audience beyond their constituency. Russia's political identity therefore remained unsettled. No shared political language seemed available in the 1990s (Urban 1998: 570). It was a period during which no hegemonic discourse emerged capable of fixing the dislocated signifier of the Russian nation in a convincing and widely accepted manner.

---

9   In 1996, the government even organized an official competition to promote a new «Russian idea», with little lasting effect (Breslauer and Dale 1997).

Dislocation in Youth Politics

The discursive and social dislocations of the Soviet collapse affected Russia's youth and youth politics. An explanation of Nashi's emergence necessarily includes a description of Soviet and post-Soviet youth politics. For Douglas Blum, the socialization of youth is central to any political identity: «youth is a useful proxy for national identity more broadly, inasmuch as it is a particularly sensitive area of collective identity formation.» (Blum 2007: 3)

Russians born approximately between 1980 and 1990 – those that led the youth protests that will be discussed in chapter 2 (Danilin 2006: 23) – experienced the Soviet collapse and the 1990s at a particularly sensitive age. They also witnessed the transition from a rather strict system of socialization in the Soviet Union to the almost total liberalization of the youth sphere.

In the USSR, children joined obligatory state organizations when they became *Little Octobrists* at seven years of age. At ten, they became members of the *Pioneers*. When they were 14, they graduated into the *All-Union Leninist Young Communist League* (*Komsomol*), in which young adults stayed until the age of 28. At that point, they were able to apply for admission into the Communist Party. The function of the Komsomol was to inspire in youth as a whole the same dedication to the USSR already exhibited by the «avantgarde». (Pilkington 1994: 65)

Socialization happened through educational measures, excursions and leisure activities. Young Soviet citizens were tested annually on their knowledge of Communist ideas and history. Furthermore, youth organizations celebrated rituals that marked important steps in a young person's life, such as ascension into the Komsomol, the reception of a Soviet passport, or entrance into the army (Binns 1980: 174). The Komsomol conveyed Soviet values to youth and prepared the future cadres of the Communist Party.

The role of the Komsomol grew steadily in the years after World War II. Aside from its socializing role, the Komsomol «patrolled» the boundaries of socialist morality. When some Soviet youth – called «stiliagi» – began growing their hair out and wearing eccentric clothing under the influence of Western music in the late 1950s, Komsomol patrols agitated against them and raided illegal parties (Pilkington 1994: 69).

The societal diversification that took place particularly under Leonid Brezhnev began to blur the lines of Soviet ideology. Technological innovations promoted by the Soviet leadership increasingly connected the country with the rest of the world through radio and television. Simultaneously, official discourse condemned the influence of «bourgeois» Western ideas on Soviet youth. Soviet ideology struggled with the influence of Western popular culture (Yurchak 2006: 288f.).[10] The leadership took various measures to cope with this influence: attempts to reconsolidate the youth sphere – not the least of which was the promotion of an official narrative of the Great Patriotic War – coexisted with the toleration of a limited number of «informal» youth organizations (Kupriianova 2002: 3).[11]

This pressure for the de-monopolization of the youth sphere was linked to the Komsomol's reduced effectiveness as a career ladder because the older generation clung to power:

> «Increasingly educated citizens sought an outlet for their intellectual and material ambitions, only to be frustrated by the lack of free speech in the Soviet system, the often insurmountable official barriers to international travel and the lack of career opportunities in a country where the leadership, at many levels, grew old but never retired.» (Bacon 2002: 18)

One of the goals of Gorbachev's reforms was to break this gridlock. The Komsomol's monopoly came under increasing criticism. Its managers were accused of minding their interests instead of representing those of the youth. The Komsomol had become a behemoth, with 41 million members in 1982 and hundreds of associated enterprises, schools, camps, publishing houses, and tourist agencies (Pilkington 1994: 129, 163). It attempted to coopt many of the informal youth organizations that began to sprout everywhere and tried to change its political direction. Ultimately, though, the Komsomol became immersed in the same centrifugal processes that led to the Soviet Union's dissolution.

---

10 For a case study of the Ukrainian city of Dnepropetrovsk, see: Zhuk, S. 2010. *Rock and Roll in the Rocket City: the West, Identity and Ideology in Soviet Dnieprope-trovsk, 1960-1985*. Washington, D.C.: Woodrow Wilson Center Press.

11 On youth policies in the late Soviet Union, see Nina Tumarkin's book (Tumarkin 1994) and also: Brunstedt, J. 2011: «Building a Pan-Soviet Past: The Soviet War Cult and the Turn Away from Ethnic Particularism». *The Soviet and Post-Soviet Review* 38. 149-171; Ward, C. 2009. *Brezhnev's Folly: The Building of BAM and Late Soviet Socialism*, Pittsburgh: University of Pittsburgh Press.

The 1990s witnessed the collapse of state-sponsored youth structures in Russia. As discussed above, this dissolution was partially an intended consequence of the government's neoliberal reforms. Many officials saw the disbandment of patriotic education as essential for leaving behind the «totalitarian» past. Instead of conveying official values to youth through compulsory organizations, the post-Soviet Russian state shed its responsibility for the socialization of youth. This process of disengagement, however, was chaotic:

> «Youth policy was in abeyance, consisting of a mixture of archaic or incoherent legislation which was hastily thrown together at the time of the Soviet collapse. (...) Meanwhile, the previous system of institutional oversight and social welfare had disintegrated, leaving the younger generation unsupervised and adrift.» (Blum 2007: 110)

The education system deteriorated, state-sponsored youth leisure activities ceased to be available, and youth were often left on their own. The quick collapse of youth organizations and after-school programs left a void.[12]

Young people were particularly affected by the social crises of the 1990s. The dissolution of family structures and the economic dislocation as a result of unemployment and alcoholism had the strongest impact on children and youth because of their dependent status (Williams et al. 2003: 43). The situation has, however, improved under Putin. In 1998, for example, youth unemployment was at 27.7%. Since then, it has dropped to 17 percent (Indexmundi 2011). Still, the vast majority of jobs are poorly paid and concentrated in big cities. Especially the provincial youth continues to suffer from a lack of opportunity.

Various researchers have tried to describe this first post-Soviet generation, and most emphasize its ambiguous political identity. In her study of teenagers in the mid-1990s, Fran Markowitz describes a pragmatic and skeptical youth that longs for stability, without feeling nostalgia for Soviet times (Markowitz 2000: 195, 218). The teenagers she interviewed were born in 1980:

---

12 Some youth organizations tried to fill the gap: The Russian Youth Council (*Rossiiskii Soiuz Molodezhi*) was founded in 1990 and works with more than 1 million young people in 73 regions (Rossiiskii Soiuz Molodezhi 2009). Over 400'000 societal organizations in Russia are active in various fields (Rozhnov 2005: 33). The main problem, however, is the fact that these organizations are mostly active in the urban centers.

«[S]ixteen-year-olds in 1995 and 1996 let me know at virtually every juncture that they were neither inspired nor defeated, not happy or sad, encouraged or frustrated, creative or rebellious. What they were was busy with completing their education and preparing for adulthood.» (ibid.: 171).

Williams, Chuprov and Zubok analyze this generation through the concept of «risk». The unstable political and social situation in Russia exposed its youth to numerous dangers and increased the risks it confronted in its development. Post-Soviet youth had to adapt to general uncertainty and did so by rejecting the values of the older generation (Williams et al. 2003: 186).

This brief description of the first post-Soviet generation shows a youth that has been confronted with a large number of challenges and risks, but also opportunities. The Soviet collapse put official youth politics in disarray. A formerly strict system of state-sponsored youth socialization was almost totally dissolved. This loss of control gave rise to anxieties among Russian educators and social scientists. Particularly those formerly responsible for youth socialization criticized the state's withdrawal from youth politics.

Many of them believe today that the post-Soviet generation of young Russians grew up in a spiritual vacuum (Bacon et al. 2006: 108). As we will see in the next chapter, this has led to demands to strengthen youth's patriotic education. The majority of Russian educators believe that the state should play a leading role in the socialization of youth (Blum 2007: 117).

On a discursive level, the liberalization of the youth sphere dislocated the Soviet discourse on youth, which attributed the central role in the socialization and near constant supervision of youth to the state. The chaotic youth politics of the 1990s were widely perceived as a loss of control over the young generation. As a result, a large number of voices called for a state-led consolidation of the youth sphere by the late 1990s.

On the political level, analogous calls for a stronger state role became louder. A so-called «Statist» discourse emerged in the second half of the 1990s (cf. Tsygankov 1997). The Statist discourse included elements of both the «Democratic» and the «Popular-Patriotic» discourse, with a particular emphasis on strengthening state capacity and a call to restore order in politics and the economy. This demand for «order» (*poriadok*) became a central signifier in Russian politics (Urban 1998: 973).

A New Order

On 31 December 1999, Boris Yeltsin announced the largely unknown Vladimir Putin as his successor. His program resonated with a large part of the population, which welcomed a strong and seemingly uncorrupt leader (Shevtsova 2005: 71). Almost from the beginning, Putin's popularity exceeded that of other politicians and institutions significantly (Schröder 2009: 85).

The new president presented himself as a competent manager. Putin appeared as capable of bridging the gap between Democrats, Communists and Nationalists. He seemed to stand above partisan politics:

> «It is partly against the background of the weakening of the polarised left/right spectrum in the late 1990s that the conservative discourse was first articulated in the election campaign of 1999-2000, marked by the emergence of the figure of Putin as a challenger to both the national-patriotic 'left' and the pro-Western 'right'.» (Prozorov 2005: 124)

Putin's «conservatism» combined liberal market policies, patriotic rhetoric and an emphasis on historical continuity.[13] He continued the liberal economic reforms of the Yeltsin era and identified Russia's competitiveness on the international stage as a high priority in his foreign policy.

On the international stage, Russia assumed a more assertive role. Richard Sakwa calls the combination of greater Russian ambitions and its willingness to work within the existing world order «great power pragmatism». This meant «joining the world, but on Russia's terms, not as a supplicant but as an equal, retaining Russia's own identity and defending its interests». (Sakwa 2008: 378)

According to Vera Tolz, Putin's vision for a Russian political identity was not revolutionary but combined familiar elements:

> «Putin stressed that in no way did he envisage the introduction of a new state ideology. For Putin, the 'Russian idea' is the combination of (unspecified)

---

[13] Putin called the collapse of the Soviet Union «the greatest geopolitical catastrophe of the century» (*quoted in*: Associated Press 2005). This statement articulated the widespread feelings of nostalgia for the Soviet Union. Simultaneously, the Putin regime took measures to cultivate national symbols and connect them to the Russian state: The Soviet national anthem was reintroduced, albeit with new lyrics. The imperial double-headed eagle was resurrected as the emblem of the Russian state, the red flag as the symbol of the Russian Army. This combination of imperial and Soviet symbolism served to reendow Russia's political identity with a sense of historical continuity.

panhuman values and such traditional *rossiiskie* values as patriotism – a feeling of pride in one's country, its achievements and its history, *derzhavnost'* (Russia as a great power), and *gosudarstvennost'* (statism, a belief in a strong state that ensures order and is at the forefront of progressive reforms).» (Tolz 2004: 170)

The strengthening of Russian statehood and the demand that Russia reclaim its rightful position as a great global power are discursive nodal points in a hegemonic project embodied and promoted by Putin. It was supposed to compensate for the dislocation of Russian weakness after the collapse of the USSR and should thus not be seen as «the majestic unfolding of an identity but the response to a crisis» (Laclau and Mouffe 2001: 7).

To a large extent, this consolidation happened by defining clearly what Russia was *not*, by identifying opponents and enemies. Stäheli writes that for Laclau and Mouffe, identities are politically created:

«Soziale und kulturelle Identitäten lassen sich nicht aus einer ihnen zugrunde liegenden Instanz ableiten, sondern werden durch diskursive Artikulationsprozesse hergestellt. Jede Identität wird in Abgrenzung zu anderen Identitäten erzeugt und trägt von sich aus keine Bedeutung.» (Stäheli 2001: 197)[14]

The identities articulated within discourses, then, only attain meaning by distinguishing themselves from what they are not. In Laclau and Mouffe's words, they distinguish themselves from a *constitutive outside*. As a discourse articulates *elements* into *moments*, it endows the latter with specific meaning. This definition of a signifier is a political decision that excludes other options, since each signifier could theoretically be defined in a variety of ways (Torfing 1999: 69). Laclau and Mouffe call this potential multiplicity of meanings *overdetermination*. It lies at the heart of their concept of identity: identities remain contingent because their nodal points have various possible definitions (Laclau and Mouffe 2001: 104). In order to fix the meaning of an identity temporarily, a discourse pushes competing definitions beyond its own boundaries – into the *constitutive outside*. The constitutive outside is both the condition for the emergence of a hegemonic identity and for its subversion:

---

14 «Social and cultural identities are not derived from some essence that is inherent to them. They are produced by discursive processes of articulation. Each identity is produced through its distinction from other identities and does not have meaning in and of itself.»

> «The constitutive outside is a discursive exteriority that cannot be related to the moments within the discourse (...), as it has the form of a radical alterity, which threatens and disrupts the discursive system (...). The constitutive outside is an outside which blocks the identity of the inside, but it is nonetheless a prerequisite for the construction of the identity of the inside. The constitutive limits of a discourse are constructed in relation to the threatening outside.»
> (Torfing 1999: 299)

As will be discussed greater detail in the following chapter, Putin presented Russia as a country brought to the brink of ruin by constitutive outsides, including «irresponsible politicians», «oligarchs» and «terrorists» (Putin 2008b). In order to fight these constitutive outsides, the Russian government began a second war in Chechnya. Oppositional «Oligarchs» like Mikhail Khodorkovsky and Boris Berezovskii were jailed and forced into exile. A recentralization of the political system took place as the Putin administration put obstacles in the way of oppositional parties wanting to compete in elections. In order to construct a «power vertical», the Kremlin began to appoint regional governors instead of having them elected after 2005.

The Putin regime presented these measures as contributions to strengthening Russian statehood. That some did not meet democratic standards and violated the rule of law was accepted as a necessary means for imposing order and stability (Perovic and Casula 2009: 24). This process of political and social «normalization» (Sakwa 2004: 43) is a distinctive feature of Putin's tenure as the president: stability is imposed from above, and political problems are presented as too grave for ordinary politics.

After Vladimir Putin took power in 2000, the country experienced a period of political, social and economic consolidation and centralization. This «normalization» allowed the country to overcome the chaos and disintegration of the 1990s at the price of curtailed political freedoms.

Securitization in Contemporary Russia

Putin's method of political stabilization in Russia matches Barry Buzan, Ole Wæver und Jaap de Wilde's concept of *securitization*. Their theory aims at extending the definition of security beyond the military context. They define securitization as a discursive operation by which a conflict or a threat is presented as existential to a referent object – usually the state, the nation or the people as a whole.

> «The special nature of security threats justifies the use of extraordinary measures to handle them. The invocation of security has been the key to legitimizing the use of force, but more generally it has opened the way for the state to mobilize, or to take special powers, to handle existential threats. Traditionally, by saying 'security,' a state representative declares an emergency condition, thus claiming a right to use whatever means are necessary to block a threatening development.» (Buzan, Wæver and de Wilde 1998: 21)

The invocation of security thus justifies the figurative (or literal) declaration of a state of emergency that legitimizes the use of extraordinary means of defense.[15] A key discursive operation towards securitizing a political issue is its removal from the arena of regular politics by declaring it to be «a special kind of politics or above politics» (ibid.: 23). Only a select group of managers, experts or generals are considered competent to address the issue.

The success of a discursive securitization operation depends on the approval of public opinion. The public has to be convinced that the problem in question in reality threatens the security of the state or society. The operation depends on a convincing narrative – «a plot that includes existential threat, point of no return, and a possible way out» (ibid.: 33). Without such a narrative, the securitization operation is unlikely to be accepted.

Buzan, Wæver and de Wilde caution against the excessive application of a securitization framework, however. They remind readers that a securitization operation can at best achieve a stabilization of conflicts by means of effective state intervention. This intervention does not solve the conflict. The solution of conflicts is only possible through «desecuritization – the shifting of issues out of emergency mode and into the normal bargaining processes of the political sphere» (ibid.: 4).

Under Putin, a number of political issues were stabilized through securitization in the early 2000s. Edwin Bacon and his co-authors see the concept of securitization as the analytical key to the rationale of political decision-making under Putin. They identify two aspects of this process. On one hand, they

---

15 Such operations are not limited to Russia. An example for the securitization of political issues was the reaction to the terror attacks in New York on 11 September 2001 in the USA. See: Kelstrup 2004.

write, officials who had made their careers in the secret service and the military (*siloviki*) extended their power under Putin (Bacon et al. 2006: 1). On the other, the Russian government has defined a number of issues and areas – the Chechen conflict, religion, some sectors of the economy as well as non-governmental organizations – as subject to securitization (ibid.: 23).

For the purposes of this book, securitization serves as an important analytical tool to explain the discursive form of political operations under Putin. Buzan and his co-authors see a crucial role for securitization in the stabilization of collective and political identities (Buzan, Wæver and de Wilde 1998: 23). The stabilization of Russia's political identity under Putin took place against the background of a major identity crisis and a sense of insecurity about the boundaries of the Russian nation, which provided fertile ground for the politics of securitization.

These politics of securitization utilizes an antagonistic logic, identifying and neutralizing a constitutive outside through extraordinary measures. Securitization works in a situation of immediate threat. However, securitization as a political rationale simultaneously creates a problem for Russia's self-definition as a democratic country and a constructive partner on the international stage. Democratic institutions and international partnerships necessitate the acceptance of different positions and the negotiation of these differences in a political process. The logic of securitization, on the other hand, tends to suppress alternatives.

Chantal Mouffe suggests a distinction between agonistic and antagonistic worldviews (Mouffe 2005): an agonist is a legitimate opponent, while an antagonist is an enemy with whom reconciliation is rarely possible by peaceful means. In order to construct an agonistic relationship, the opponents would agree on a set of shared rules that both adhere to and settle their differences within this system (Torfing 1999: 255). Official Russian discourse often accuses domestic and foreign enemies of the state of not playing by the rules and intending to weaken the country. The state's fight against them discursively legitimizes undemocratic and violent measures.

Cultural Memory, Commemoration and Hegemony

I consider the unified presentation of national symbols and Russia's history to be a central aspect of Putin's hegemonic project of strengthening statehood. A hegemonic discourse constitutes a reaction to dislocation. The elements it rearranges, however, do not derive exclusively from this dislocation. Instead, discourses rearrange and articulate elements that have been present in a society prior to the dislocation. In Laclau's words: «[t]he acceptance of a discourse depends on its credibility, and this will not be granted if its proposals clash with the basic principles informing the organization of a group.» (Laclau 1990: 66) Laclau, however, remains rather vague as to where to find these basic organizational principles.

The Russian case under Putin shows the important role that historical elements play in the emergence of a hegemonic discourse. A large body of research suggests that the identity of a society is strongly tied to collective or cultural memory.[16] Egyptologist Jan Assmann defines cultural memory as

«alles Wissen, das im spezifischen Interaktionsrahmen einer Gesellschaft Handeln und Erleben steuert und von Generation zu Generation zur wiederholten Einübung und Einweisung ansteht.» (Assmann 1988: 9)[17]

Cultural memory is therefore a kind of archive that «stores» significant past events, people and places. The values, worldviews and attitudes of a society emerge from cultural memory. It is the basis for social identities: «[t]he core meaning of any individual or group identity, namely a sense of sameness over time and space, is sustained by remembering.» (Gillis 1994: 3) Exactly what is remembered varies from society to society.

In Russia, the most powerful historical symbol is the Great Patriotic War. Anyone who has been to Russia notices the enormous role World War II still

---

[16] The number of studies published in the last two decades on the connection between memory and identity is large. Many of them have developed Maurice Halbwachs' concept of collective memory (Halbwachs 1985): Assmann, A. and D. Harth, eds. 1991. *Kultur als Lebenswelt und Monument*. Frankfurt a.M.: Suhrkamp; Assmann, J. 1999. *Das kulturelle Gedächtnis. Schrift, Erinnerung und politische Identität in frühen Hochkulturen*. München: C.H. Beck Verlag; Fentress, J. and C. Wickham. 1992. *Social Memory: New Perspectives on the Past*. Oxford: Blackwell Publishers; Welzer, H., ed. 2001. *Das soziale Gedächtnis: Geschichte, Erinnerung, Tradierung*. Hamburg: Hamburger Edition.

[17] «[A]ll knowledge that guides actions and experiences within the specific interactive framework of a society and is used repeatedly to instruct and teach each successive generation.»

plays in individual memories and the public space. The people in the former USSR made enormous sacrifices in the war against the National Socialists: approximately 27 million Soviet citizens died, 70'000 villages, towns and cities were destroyed, and countless veterans returned with physical and psychological wounds. The Soviet Union faced the brunt of Nazi Germany's war machine and defeated it «against almost universal expectation» (Overy 1998: 327). Civilians' and soldiers' experience of the war in Leningrad and Stalingrad and countless lesser-known places in the Soviet Union is beyond anyone's power of imagination, and yet the Red Army prevailed.[18]

Still today, the veterans of the Great Patriotic War enjoy almost universal reverence in Russia: children bring them flowers on Victory Day on 9 May, they receive preferential treatment in public institutions, and the maltreatment of veterans by officials causes public outrage (Mijnssen 2009: 300). Victory Day (*Den' Pobedy*) remains the most widely observed holiday in Russia and is observed by the vast majority of Russians. The historian Iurii Afanas'ev goes so far as to state that the Great Patriotic War occupies a central position in almost all discourses in contemporary Russia (Afanas'ev 2009a).

War memory, however, fulfills not only a central societal but also a political role. As the Russian state suffers from a «poverty of symbols» (Dubin 2007), the victory over the National Socialists remains one of the few truly unifying and powerful symbols. This poverty is a consequence of the dislocations of the 1990s. With the collapse of the Soviet Union, most signifiers, values and symbols that were linked to socialism lost their meaning.[19]

Cultural memory and commemoration are closely tied to politics. The fundamental question is, in Alon Confino's words: «[w]ho wants whom to remember

---

[18] The following books are among the interesting examples of current historiography on the war: Beevor A. and V. Grossman. 2005. *A Writer at War: Vasily Grossman with the Red Army 1941-1945*. London: The Harvill Press; Hellbeck, J. 2013. *Die Stalingrad Protokolle: Sowjetische Augenzeugen berichten aus der Schlacht*. Frankfurt a.M.: Fischer Verlag; Kropachev, S. 2011. *Von der Lüge zur Aufklärung: Verluste durch 'Grossen Terror' und Krieg in der sowjetischen und russischen Historiografie*. Berlin: Metropol; Stahel, D. 2013. *Operation Typhoon: Hitler's March on Moscow, October 1941*. New York: Cambridge University Press.

[19] The anniversary of the October Revolution, for instance – until 1991 the most important holiday in the Soviet Union – disappeared from the list of holidays in post-Soviet Russia. The new holidays that the Russian government tried to institute, such as Independence Day on 12 June or Constitution Day on 12 December, have failed to catch on (Smith 2002: 91ff.).

what, and why?» (Confino 1997: 1393). Ultimately, the answer to this question depends on the power relations in a society. The dominant historical narrative is the outcome of negotiations between multiple groups, one of which is the state (Winter and Sivan 1999: 31). It is a process that often involves the suppression of alternative versions of historical events and produces a highly selective narrative that highlights some aspects at the expense of others.

Various authors have used the Gramscian notion of hegemonic struggle to describe the process of shaping cultural memory (Ashplant, Dawson and Roper 2000; König 2008; Meyer 2008: 178). The politicization of memory and commemorations is particularly pronounced in the case of war memory:

«This hegemonic framing of memory is a selective process in which the nation-state exercises its power to recognize and incorporate within its national narrative only certain war memories, whilst others are officially marginalized or forgotten.» (Ashplant, Dawson and Roper 2000: 53)

This process of articulating a hegemonic narrative of war events was particularly difficult in post-Soviet Russia. The ritualized official commemorations of the war – parades, national mourning –, which are crucial practices for shaping cultural memory (Assmann 1999: 19), ceased for a good part of the 1990s. The meaning of the Soviet victory was contested as more information became available about its costs. While Soviet official discourse in the Brezhnev era had ignored the negative aspects of the war entirely, producing an idealized and mythologized narrative, Mikhail Gorbachev actively promoted filling in the «blank spots» of history. He believed that a truthful examination of the past would provide new legitimacy to a stagnating political system (Sherlock 2007: 18). The new facts and publications that had become available through *glasnost'* shattered many myths (Overy 1998: 326) and contributed significantly to the collapse of Soviet political identity and the subversion of the system's legitimacy.[20]

---

20 For example, the Soviet public learned that the NKVD, not the Germans, had shot 22'000 members of the Polish intellectual and military elite in the forests of Katyn, in Belarus and the Soviet Union. Other disclosures included the extent of the pre-war purges among the Red Army's leadership and the existence of Stalin's order 227. This order, titled «Not a step back!» (*Ne Shagu Nazad!*), allowed the NKVD to shoot deserters and repress their families. Order 270 provided the legal basis for the arrest and mass deportation of prisoners of war as «traitors».

The commemoration of historical events provides social groups and nation-states with a sense of social cohesion (Olick 2008: 157), and a hegemonic narrative of the past is an important element of a country's national identity.[21] It is thus necessary to further investigate the central role that the commemoration of the Great Patriotic War has played under Putin.

The emphasis on historical continuity has endowed the Russian state not only with a new set of symbols but also an official genealogy of past achievements. «Anchoring Russian national identity in the Soviet past is a genealogical feature of Putin's regime,» writes Professor of EU-Russia Studies at the University of Tartu Viacheslav Morozov (Morozov 2008: 159). The Great Patriotic War has become a kind of «foundation myth» (Sherlock 2007: 8) on which Russia's official political identity is based.

Under Putin, then, the Great Patriotic War began to occupy a more privileged place in the public sphere than under Yeltsin. Six to eight percent of broadcasting time on state-controlled television is allotted to movies, documentaries and reports related to World War II – a number that increases significantly before major holidays like 9 May (Gudkov 2005: 61). Putin followed veterans' organizations in calling for a more «balanced» approach to the history of the war. The promotion of patriotism in official media also increased Russians' pride in victory: Lev Gudkov cites a survey, according to which the number of Russians who said they were proud of Russia's achievements in the Great Patriotic War rose from 44 percent to 87 percent between 1996 and 2003. This number has remained consistently high since then.

The 60th Anniversary of Victory

The commemoration of the war reached an unprecedented level of intensity in the run-up to the celebrations of the 60th anniversary of victory on 9 May 2005.[22] The main festivities between 8 and 10 May included concerts for vet-

---

21 On the notion of commemoration, consider also John Gillis' definition: «Commemorative activity is by definition social and political, for it involves the coordination of individual and group memories, whose results may appear consensual when they are in fact the product of processes of intense contest, struggle, and, in some instance, annihilation.» (Gillis 1994: 5)

22 The 60th anniversary of the end of World War II inspired a number of important publications on the subject. The journals *Osteuropa* (4-6) and *Neprikosnovennyi Zapas* (40) published a special issue called *Kluften der Erinnerung*. Other works

erans, meetings and, for first time since the collapse of the Soviet Union, the military parade on 9 May.

It is worthwhile to take a closer look at Putin's Victory Day allocution, which combined the main nodal points of official discourse. Analysis of the speech demonstrates the central position that the commemoration of the war occupies in the official sphere of contemporary Russia. For our purposes, the address and its ritual context provided a blueprint for Nashi's commemoration of the war in terms of style and content.

The speech underlined not only Russia's demand for great power status (*derzhavnichestvo*) in the world, but also painted it as an active and equal partner in the international community. Putin highlighted the unity of the Russian people and their partnerships with post-Soviet and western nations, and he provided an elaborate narrative of the war. Historical continuity lay at the heart of the address as the president drew analogies between past and present global threats. It thus articulated the nodal points of hegemonic discourse.

Moreover, the speech was embedded in a thoroughly organized and elaborate, symbolically charged ritual, an example that Nashi would follow. The arrangements of the Victory Parade staged historical continuity quite literally: young soldiers of the Red Army wore uniforms from the Great Patriotic War, and war veterans rode through Red Square in historic trucks.

In his speech, Putin, surrounded by the heads of state of major Western countries, noted that 60 years had passed since the «great Victory» (*velikaia Pobeda*), which had brought «peace» and «the triumph of justice». He then

---

published in recent years include: Biess, F. and R.G. Moeller, ed. 2010. *Histories of the Aftermath: The Legacies of the Second World War in Europe*. New York & Oxford: Berghahn Books; Bomsdorf, F. and G. Bordiugov, eds. 2005. *60-letie Okonchaniia Vtoroi Mirovoi i Velikoi Otechestvennoi: Pobediteli i Pobezhdennye v Kontekste Politiki, Mifologii i Pamiati*. Moskva: Fond Fridrikha Naumanna; Bonner, W. and A. Rosenholm, eds. 2008. *Recalling the Past – (Re)constructing the Past: Collective and Individual Memory of World War II in Russia and Germany*. Helsinki: Kikimora Press; Friess, N. 2010. *Nichts ist vergessen, niemand ist vergessen? Erinnerungskultur und kollektives Gedächtnis im heutigen Russland*. Potsdam: Universitätsverlag Potsdam; Kurilo, O., ed. 2006. *Der zweite Weltkrieg im deutschen und russischen Gedächtnis*. Berlin: Avinus Verlag; Martens, S. and J. Echternkamp, eds. 2007. *Der Zweite Weltkrieg in Europa: Erfahrung und Erinnerung*. Paderborn: Ferdinand Schöningh. On the role of war memory in contemporary Russia, see also: *Otechestvennye Zapiski* 4/2008.

celebrated the day of «victory of good over evil and of freedom over tyranny» (Putin 2008a: 291).

Putin's words illustrate the elevated status of Victory Day. At the end of his speech, he called Victory Day a «holy day», thereby building on the quasi-religious position that victory had occupied in Soviet times (Kämpfer 1994: 335), using the same elevated and formulaic language to talk about victory that had been used by Soviet leaders in the 1960s (Gudkov 2005: 62).

Despite the sixty years that had passed since 1945, Putin explained, the deeds of the victors had not been forgotten and the dead were still mourned. He expounded on the scale of the war, which affected 61 countries and 80 percent of the world population and acknowledged the support of the European and American allies: «we never divided the victory into ours and theirs» (ibid.: 292). Above all, however, he highlighted the Soviet Union's particular sacrifice, leaving no doubt that it suffered the bulk of the casualties and destruction: «the most ruthless and decisive events – the events that determined the drama and the outcome of this inhuman war – unfolded on the territory of the Soviet Union.» (Putin 2008a: 291),

On the one hand, this statement addresses a widespread opinion in contemporary Russia that the Soviet contribution to victory over Nazi Germany is not sufficiently acknowledged. Many American and European history books highlight D-Day, the French Resistance and the Battle of Britain and pay much less attention to the campaign in the East. The United States did not physically enter the war against Germany until 6 June of 1944 and ignored Stalin's repeated demands for the opening of a second front. They did, however, supply the USSR with military hardware and aid through the Lend-Lease program. Putin's speech thus presents a counterhegemonic war narrative in an international setting.

On the other hand, the Soviet victory against Germany is used to bolster the demand for a strong and respected global position for Russia. The present world order, reliant on peace, justice, dialogue and tolerance, Putin went on to explain, resulted from Soviet and Russian sacrifice. The defeat of the «inhuman» German aggressors and National Socialist ideology created the preconditions for a more peaceful and humane international system.

Now that the Cold War is over, Putin continues, «we have made significant strides toward the lofty goal of ensuring peace and calm in Europe.» (ibid.: 293) However, this world order is also threatened. Putin draws a direct parallel between the signifiers *fascism* and *terrorism*:

> «History teaches nations to do their best, not to ignore the emergence of new deadly doctrines, the origins and environment in which new threats evolve. (…) In the face of today's real *terrorist threats*, we must remain faithful to the memory of our fathers. We must defend the world order based on security and justice, a new culture of relations which does not allow for a repetition of cold or hot wars.» (ibid.: 292f., *emphasis added*)

This emphasis on terrorism as a common enemy of both the West and Russia lies at the basis of Russia's great power pragmatism. Russia's foreign policy in the mid-2000s sought shared interests with Western countries. Opposition to terrorism provided a common bond (Morozov 2008: 162). The attacks in the United States on 11 September 2001, the bombings of apartment buildings in Russian cities in September 1999 (which Putin used to justify the second invasion of Chechnya), the spate of terrorist acts in Moscow and Beslan in 2004 and the bombings in London made the war against terrorism a high priority for all involved states.

For the articulation of a shared identity as an international community, with Russia as a partner, the signifier *terrorism* became the constitutive outside. Terrorism, according to Putin and other world leaders, undermines the global order («based on security and justice»), it is a «deadly doctrine». The historical parallel with National Socialism underlines that no agonistic relationship with terrorists is possible, as they are intent only on destruction and mass murder.

Terrorism mainly functions to signify a vaguely defined opposite of the international community. The antagonist *terrorism* discursively justifies actions against various groups of perceived enemies and conceals the differences within the «international community».[23] By 2005, however, in the aftermath of

---

23 An example of such a disagreement over the definition of anti-terrorist actions was the repeated Western criticism over human rights violations in Russia's «war against terrorism» in Chechnya. Russia was repeatedly castigated by the US government and condemned by the European Court of Human Rights (Russian Justice Initiative 2011).

the Orange Revolution and the political fights over the US-invasion of Iraq, the anti-terror coalition was already showing signs of strain.

These are recognizable between the lines of Putin's Victory Day speech. When he addresses the exact nature of the values that Russia is defending, he defines them as «the right of every state to choose its path of development independently», as well as «international dialogue and co-operation» (Putin 2008a: 293). These words are directed at the United States and its attempts to gain a foothold in the post-Soviet space. They are also reminiscent of the doctrine of Sovereign Democracy, discussed in greater depth in the next chapter. Essentially, Putin underlines the necessity of supplementing democracy with a strong state.

Putin's speech also hints at tensions in relations between Russia and its neighbors in post-Soviet space. According to Putin, the memory of shared sacrifice unites Russia and its neighbors:

> «All peoples, all republics of the former USSR, suffered their own irreparable losses. Grief reached every household, touched every family. That is why 9 May is a sacred day for all nations in the Commonwealth of Independent States. We are united by our anguish, our memory and our duty to future generations. And we must pass on to those who will come after us the spirit of historic connection, common aspirations and common hope.» (ibid.: 292)

The notion that the united Soviet peoples attained victory has been part of the Soviet war narrative since Stalin's victory speech in 1945.[24] This narrative is, however, incapable of expressing the differing interpretations of the World War in post-Soviet and Eastern European states after the end of the USSR.

Most notably, Putin speaks of the Commonwealth of Independent States, rather than the states of the former Soviet Union. The Baltic States, which never joined the CIS, are explicitly exempted. Chapter 3 explores the differing narratives of the war in Russia and the Baltic States in greater detail. For now, it is sufficient to say that the Estonian and Lithuanian presidents declined Putin's invitation to come to Moscow on 9 May (Pääbo 2008: 20).

Even within the CIS, however, interpretations of the war are not homogenous. Ukrainian president Viktor Yushchenko, for example, initially declined the invi-

---

24 One must add that Stalin's «toast to the Russian people» from 24 May already contained a hierarchy of heroism, with the Russian people as the «most outstanding nation of all the nations forming the Soviet Union».

tation but nevertheless attended under pressure from veteran groups (Lozowy 2005: 3). The question of how to unite the Soviet narrative and the commemoration of Ukrainian resistance groups has led to heated conflicts on Ukraine's domestic political scene and to tensions with Russia.

Putin's proclaimed unity within post-Soviet space represents a demand rather than a convincing description of the world. The political circumstances of the commemoration of the 60th anniversary of Victory reveal the depth of these rifts on the international political stage (Sakwa 2008: 225).

Soviet and Russian Political Identities

The political tensions point to a major problem inherent in using the commemoration of the Great Patriotic War as the basis for a post-Soviet Russian identity: the war narrative, as reinvigorated by Putin, is modeled strongly after the war narrative that emerged in the Brezhnev era. The plot, topoi and associated values recall those of the 1960s very closely – minus the Communist ideology:

> «Fascists expected to enslave our people in an instant. In fact, they counted on destroying the country. Their plans failed. The Soviet army first stopped the Fascists outside of Moscow. And over the three subsequent years, it managed not only to resist the assault but also to force the enemy back into his lair.» (Putin 2008a: 291f.)

Nashi copied this narrative almost verbatim. A brief comparison with Leonid Brezhnev's speech on 8 May 1965 in honor of Victory Day reveals clear parallels. The events between 1939 and 1941, when the USSR and Nazi Germany were allied, receive no mention. The Red Army's colossal casualties in the early days of the war are mentioned only in passing. These were the result of the massive German onslaught, but also of the purged Red Army's unpreparedness for war and the grave mistakes of the leadership. Brezhnev speaks only vaguely of «conditions that were unfavorable for us and favorable for the enemy» (Brezhnev 1965: 9). Other parallels include the notion of enslavement and annihilation (ibid.) and of victory signifying the triumph of «humanism over barbarity» (ibid.: 6). In both discourses, the «fascists» play the role of the constitutive outside.

The major difference – aside from the fact that Brezhnev only mentioned 20 million casualties instead of 27 million – lies in the identity of the people who attained victory. Brezhnev mentions «the Soviet People» 38 times in his speech. The Soviet People includes all nationalities of the former USSR and is thus a signifier that stands for the unity of the entire empire. Neither the Soviet People nor the kind of unity it signifies exists in contemporary Russia. The war narrative, according to Amir Weiner, «outlived the polity» to which it originally applied (Weiner 1996: 639). Today, the former Soviet peoples have taken recourse to a variety of conflicting war narratives.

As a template for Russian identity, the war narrative is both convincing and deeply flawed. It is convincing because official discourse can tap into «templates of memory» that anchor Russian identity in deeper strata of cultural memory (Ashplant, Dawson and Roper 2000: 34). The commemoration of the Great Patriotic War enjoys profound popular acceptance, and by honoring this memory, the state presents itself as a preserver of the country's historical identity in a time of rapid change. Secondly, it recalls a sense of national unity and purpose that many see as lacking today (Sherlock 2007: 166).

Thirdly, and crucially, the commemoration works with templates from the Brezhnev era (1964-1982). This means that it evokes not only the war, but also the Brezhnev era itself. Many Russians see this era not as a time of stagnation but a kind of «golden era» (Dubin 2007: 5). The population enjoyed a modest degree of wealth, the housing problem that had plagued millions during the first decades of the Soviet Union was mostly solved, and the Soviet government no longer conducted campaigns of mass repression and destruction. Furthermore, the USSR was at the peak of its power. In its idealized form, the Brezhnev era Soviet Union was «a global power with a strong technologically advanced economy» (Sherlock 2007: 161). The articulation of the war myth in contemporary Russia evokes the same notions of unity and global power that the Brezhnev era symbolizes for many.

If Morozov is correct in stating that the Putin regime bases Russia's political identity on the past, one problem remains: «Anchoring Russian national identity in the Soviet past does not help in solving one of the crucial problems of contemporary Russia – that of the boundaries of the political community.» (Morozov 2008: 174). The war myth contributes to this problem, as it articulates a community that no longer exists.

Today, Russia finds itself enmeshed in complicated conflicts within the post-Soviet space over the interpretation of the outcome of World War II. The political use of the war narrative as a basis for Russia's post-Soviet identity contributes to conflicts with its neighbors. Within Russia, however, it serves as a tool to mobilize support on the domestic political stage.

Framed in discourse-analytical terms, the commemoration of the Great Patriotic War is a crucial moment of Putin's hegemonic project to consolidate Russian identity. The war and the Soviet victory are presented in a highly idealized and mythologized form. Putin and other government figures deploy it to serve the Russian state's contemporary political interests (Andreev and Bordiugov 2005: 47).

Laclau's unique definition of «myth» applies well to the commemoration of the war in contemporary Russia. A myth is a surface on which any number of demands can be inscribed (Laclau 1990: 63). At the same time, the myth presents itself as an objective fullness: «Thus, the effectiveness of myth is essentially hegemonic: it involves forming a new objectivity by means of the re-articulation of the dislocated elements. Any objectivity, then, is merely a crystallized myth.» (ibid.: 61). Like all hegemonic projects, however, the myth is a reaction to dislocation: «[t]he mythical space is constituted as a critique of the lack of structuration accompanying the dominant order.» (ibid.: 62)

As the mythical space is located on a different discursive plane, it does not necessarily describe what conditions are like but what they should be like. At the same time, the myth discursively naturalizes this desired state. Compare Laclau's definition to Roland Barthes' classic formulation: A myth functions on two levels – as a message and as a statement (Barthes 1964: 105). It thus expresses a desire but presents this desire as an objective description of reality. Martin Müller illustrates this naturalization of demands for a «strong Russia» at MGIMO (Moscow State Institute of International Relations):

> «In accordance with the character of a myth, the position of a strong Russia often appears naturalised. (…) Raising Russian strength largely goes as an unquestioned assumption underlying foreign policy analysis. The loyalty to the Russian state is seldom openly addressed in classes but is implicit in many statements.» (Müller 2009a: 208)

In the context of the war myth, then, demands for a strong, modern and unified Russian state with great power status, for historical continuity and a decisive stance against the country's enemies become a template through which contemporary Russia is presented. Through this template, threats to Russian statehood are articulated alongside visions of a strong Russian community capable of withstanding them. It thus compensates for the insecurities about Russia's position in the world: the country's isolation in post-Soviet space, its lack of international competitiveness, and recurrent international criticism of democratic shortcomings.

While this myth thus fosters elements of patriotism, it contains the potential for frustration and conflict if interpreted too literally: «these notions can only represent ideal states, unattainable in an imperfect world; given the nature of the social and geopolitical relations, they must always remain unfulfilled.» (Smith 1999: 66) If interpreted too literally, the myth fails as a hegemonic project because its description of the world loses its plausibility. In this case, the war myth leads to a tendency of blaming the gap between expectations and «reality» on the machinations of Russia's enemies.

A political identity based on a myth is not especially sustainable: «for longer or shorter periods they [myths] have a certain relative elasticity beyond which we witness their inexorable decline.» (Laclau 1990: 67)

The myth of the Great Patriotic War emerged with particular strength at a time of perceived unrest among youth. In the Brezhnev-era, the Komsomol played a leading role in implementing a program of «patriotic education» to convey socialist and patriotic values to youth. I argue that the reemergence of the myth in 2005, at a time of major social upheaval, was no coincidence. The next chapter addresses these upheavals and the government response to them. As will be seen, the foundation of the youth organization Nashi was one of the most important measures to consolidate the political identity of Russia's youth.

III   Russia's Youth, the Orange Revolution, and Nashi

The years 2004-2005 were a period of political instability in Russia. In 2004, a wave of terrorist attacks had occurred: The hostage taking in Beslan's Secondary School Number One and the Russian security forces' storming of the building left over 300 hostages dead. Two blasts in the Moscow metro in February and August of 2004 and the bombings of two airplanes by terrorists from the Caucasus killed hundreds of Russians. The attacks contradicted Putin's repeated claim that Chechnya and the Caucasus had been «normalized» (Cornell 2005) and left a deep sense of insecurity among Russian citizens.
Politically, the reelection of Vladimir Putin on 14 March 2004 coincided with a dramatic rise in political protests against the government. Prime Minister Mikhail Fradkov monetized services such as free public transport and medical services, mostly used by pensioners, and introduced tuition at Russian universities. On 12 February 2005, 250'000 people all over Russia participated in an «All-Russian Day of Protest» against the monetization (Danilin 2006: 189).
As time went on, the protests began to outgrow specific sectional grievances and were becoming a platform for broader opposition against the government and the Putin regime:

> «As the agitation was joined by youth activists and leading political figures, the slogans shifted from narrow economic complaints to explicitly political demands for the resignation of the government. (…) For the first time, Putin's carefully cultivated image as a national savior was under assault.» (Horvath 2011: 8)

Some troubling signs indicated growing rifts within the political elite. Dmitrii Rogozin led his nationalist and originally pro-Kremlin Rodina party in a hunger strike against the monetization and demanded the resignation of the government. Former Prime Minister Mikhail Kasianov, dismissed because of his criticism of Putin's handling of the Khodorkovsky case, attacked the government's economic policies. Already in January 2004, a number of prominent figures founded the umbrella organization *Committee 2008*. Among them were former chess champion Garry Kasparov, former deputy Prime Minister Boris Nemtsov, former speaker of the State Duma Vladimir Ryzhkov, and Irina Khakamada, one of the leaders of the Union of Right Forces (*Soiuz Pravikh Sil* – SPS). The stated goal of this loose alliance was to keep Putin from installing a successor when his term ran out in 2008. It had little in common except for its opposition to Putin's and government's policies.

Nonetheless, the Russian government feared that a latently discontented electorate might support oppositional forces: because of popular outrage about the monetization reforms, for example, the Pensioners' Party won more than twenty percent of votes in regional elections in Magadan (Il'iushchenko 2005). In the capitals, numerous anti-government protests took place.

Observers were struck by the extent to which Russia's youth – previously considered apolitical and passive – began to play an important role in the organization of street protests against the government's social reforms. Youth groups of the National Bolshevik Party (NBP – *Natsional-Bol'shevistskaia Partiia*), and the umbrella organization Oborona (*Defense*), founded by the youth wings of the liberal parties Iabloko and the SPS, took to the streets with radical slogans and spectacular actions.

Nashi emerged from this moment of political instability. As I show in this chapter, its creation represented an attempt by the Russian government to create a patriotic youth movement. This movement was to physically contain youth protests, provide an offer for identification to young Russians and mobilize them in support for government projects.

Orange Revolution

Signs of youth dissatisfaction with government policies became particularly threatening to the Putin regime in connection with one specific event: the street protests in Ukraine that became known as the «Orange Revolution».[25]

---

25 The «Orange Revolution» has been analyzed in numerous books and publications. Among them is a five-volume collection of essays entitled *Aspects of the Orange Revolution*, published by ibidem-Verlag. Other publications include: Åslund, A. and M. McFaul. 2006. *Revolution in Orange: The Origins of Ukraine's Democratic Breakthrough*. Washington: Carnegie Endowment for International Peace; D'Anieri, P. 2010. *Orange Revolution and Aftermath: Mobilization, Apathy, and the State in Ukraine*. Baltimore: Woodrow Wilson Center Press; Pogrebinskii, M. 2005. *«Oranzhevaia» Revoliutsiia: Versii, Khronika, Dokumenty*. Kiev: Optima.

The series of revolutions and regime changes in Serbia and Georgia had unsettled the Russian government, but it considered the Ukrainian case to be particularly serious. Ukraine and Russia have been closely connected to each other through numerous political, cultural and economic ties for centuries. The rapid collapse of the regime of Leonid Kuchma, independent Ukraine's second president, showed the Russian government how quickly a seemingly stable political system could unravel.

The revolution in Kiev was sparked by electoral fraud. Viktor Yanukovich, the designated successor to president Kuchma, was declared the winner of the elections against oppositional candidate Viktor Yushchenko, even though independent exit polls had indicated a clear victory for Yushchenko. The resulting mass protests, which lasted two weeks, started on 22 November. At least 100'000 to 300'000 people protested on Independence Square (*Maidan Nezalezhnosti*, often shortened *Maidan*) in central Kiev, and additional mass demonstrations took place in other cities, mostly in Western Ukraine (Copsey 2005: 102f.). The protesters demanded a repeat of the elections and engaged in largely peaceful means of civil disobedience, setting up a tent city in downtown Kiev. On 3 December, the Supreme Court ordered a re-run of the second round of the election, which Yushchenko won with 52 percent of the vote, a result largely in line with earlier exit polls.

Socially, the protests were based on disaffection about the political and economic situation in the country, mainly among young, urban Ukrainians. Volodymyr Yevtukh dates the emergence of the Ukrainian protest movement to the parliamentary elections of 2002. The electoral fraud only acted as a trigger (Yevtukh 2005: 16). The organizers were highly skilled in mobilizing masses of youth through modern communication technologies and the effective use of symbols: the color of the protest movement was orange, and participants received orange ribbons, flags and posters (ibid.: 23).

Pora (*It is time*), the youth organization that coordinated the protests in Kiev, had received training in nonviolent resistance from activists formerly involved in regime changes in Serbia and Georgia. Furthermore, some international foundations and non-governmental organizations had contributed financially to the Orange Revolution. These contributions were relatively small: Pora received 130'000 dollars in total from Freedom House, the Canadian Interna-

tional Development Agency, and the German Marshall Fund of the United States. Pora's total financing amounted to 1.56 million dollars, and it received an additional 6.5 million dollars in donations in kind – all of which came from domestic sources (Demes and Forbrig 2006: 97f.). Fredo Arias-King, who studied the international connections of the «Orange» movement, concludes:
«despite rhetoric by the Kremlin and conspiracy theorists, the Ukrainian Orange Revolution was mostly the result of domestic factors combined with an ever growing mass of outraged citizens, and not plotting by 'dark forces' from abroad.» (Arias-King 2007a: 45)

The Orange Revolution caused political shock waves in Russia (Horvath 2011: 8). The leading political role of youth in the Orange Revolution raised the question of whether Russian youth might attempt a similar revolution.

The Orange Revolution and Russia

Not surprisingly, official interpretations of the Orange Revolution in Russia frame the events in Ukraine almost exclusively in terms of threat. Fundamentally, the Orange Revolution is interpreted as a western-led coup: the limited international assistance and Western endorsement of Yushchenko led pro-Kremlin political scientists to argue that the only result of the Orange Revolution was the replacement of a pro-Russian by a pro-Western elite (Il'inskii 2005: 44).

It would, however, be too simple to discount this interpretation as government manipulation of public opinion. To a certain extent, it is based on deep-seated popular frames of interpretation: the view of the Orange Revolution as directed against Russia is widespread *and* exploited politically by the Russian government.

The fact that pro-Western governments took power first in Georgia and then in Ukraine meant that both countries sought greater distance from Russia. Public opinion in Russia felt this distance acutely: in a survey by the Public Opinion Foundation among 1500 respondents in January 2006, almost 60 percent said that the relations between Ukraine and Russia had worsened as a result of the Orange Revolution and the so-called «gas war» (Stiftung Öffentliche Meinung 2006: 15).

For many Russians, Ukrainians are part of a common Slavic people. A Levada-Center survey in November 2004 revealed that more than two thirds of all

Russians do not consider Ukraine to be a country «abroad» (Levada-Zentrum 2004: 17). The fact that many Russians still today – half affectionately and half condescendingly – call Ukraine «Little Russia» (*Malaia Rossiia*) reflects this attitude. According to Ukrainian historian Serhii Plokhy, the idea that Ukrainian statehood is part of a conspiracy against Russia has its roots in the early 19th century (Plokhy 2008: 6).

One of the more extreme interpretations of the Orange Revolution by a mainstream political scientist in Russia echoes this conspiratorial interpretation. According to Aleksei Mukhin, director of the Center for Political Information, the colored revolutions in the post-Soviet space form part of an American and British conspiracy to scale Russia back to the status of a regional power (Mukhin 2006: 7). By using the slogans of democratization and the fight against corruption, the CIA tries to contain Russia, writes Mukhin. A «war of secret services» is taking place in the post-Soviet space, in which «spin-doctors» (*polit-tekhnologi*) engineer revolutions and uprisings (ibid.: 10f.). The plan of the United States is to build a wall: «[t]his wall is movable – in truth it can only be moved towards the center – towards Moscow» (ibid.: 12).[26]

Vladislav Surkov provides a more moderate interpretation of the events in Kiev but reaches similar conclusions. In his article «Natsionalizatsiia Budushchego» (*The Nationalization of the Future*), he describes Ukraine as a state that never had sovereignty in its history. According to Surkov, Ukraine was always under the influence of various «patrons» (*pokroviteli*) that changed periodically in «amusing 'revolutions'». He states that the Orange Revolution is a further example of such a «revolution»[27], leading to a «democracy that is guided from outside» (Surkov 2006b).

Western «double standards» on democracy threaten to delegitimize democracy as such, maintains Surkov and mentions the violence in Iraq and secret U.S. prisons as examples (Surkov 2006a: 75). These double standards apply to Ukraine insofar as Surkov considers the means by which Yushchenko

---

26   Serguei Alex Oushakine considers conspiracy theories to be an important part of post-Soviet nationalism in Russia (Oushakine 2009).

27   In virtually all speeches and papers on the Orange Revolution by pro-Kremlin authors, the word revolution is put in quotes. This is to emphasize the view that the Orange Revolution was merely an elaborately orchestrated coup without any popular support. Mukhin drives this point home by claiming that «Hollywood producers» had fabricated the Orange Revolution (Mukhin 2006: 5).

came to power illegal – it was «an unconstitutional 'orange' coup» (ibid.). Pavel Danilin, a political scientist and expert on youth politics close to the Kremlin and to Nashi, focuses his criticism on the revote, which was an «absolutely unlawful procedure» (Danilin 2006: 172).

For Surkov, the Orange Revolution followed a well-rehearsed script:
> «How this is done is well known: you weaken values, declare the state to be ineffective, provoke internal conflicts. It is all part of the same 'orange' technology. (…) Now that they have managed to carry this out in four countries, why shouldn't they try in a fifth? (…) Our foreign friends could try to repeat it in the future.» (Surkov 2006a: 79)

After Serbia, Georgia, Kyrgyzstan and Ukraine, Russia is the next country, where «foreign friends» will attempt a «revolution». Surkov labels «Colored Revolutions» as means of «soft absorption» (*miagkoe pogloshchenie*) and considers them to be one of four primary threats to Russia's sovereignty: the other three are terrorism, a war with another great power and a stagnant economy (ibid.: 65ff.).

The central role of the Orange Revolution in Surkov's threat assessment is noteworthy. The signifier «Orange Revolution» works as a kind of constitutive outside, posing an immediate threat to the Russian state. «Soft absorption» encompasses both domestic and foreign enemies working against the state and the fear of this state's inherent weakness. «Soft absorption» as an antagonistic force in Laclau and Mouffe's sense thus subverts the stable Russian political identity articulated in official discourse and shows how such an identity is always undermined by what it excludes (Torfing 1999: 86).

At the same time, however, the antagonism the Russian state supposedly faces legitimizes political actions as a hegemonic response to the dislocation of identity. Expressed within a securitization framework, Surkov's narrative includes «existential threat, point of no return, and a possible way out» (Buzan, Wæver and De Wilde 1998: 32f.). The threat has been articulated, and the point of no return was reached with Ukraine's Orange Revolution. The possible way out and consolidation of the discursive and political order would comprise measures that included the founding of Nashi.

Taking Back the Streets

A crucial precondition for the Orange Revolution was a split in the political elite, when former Prime Minister Viktor Yushchenko broke with Leonid Kuchma. However, a critical factor for the revolution's success was the fact that troops of the Ministry of the Interior were unwilling and possibly unable to use all the repressive means at their disposal against large numbers of protesters in downtown Kiev (Arel 2005: 326f.).

Government figures in Russia, first and foremost Surkov and political scientist Gleb Pavlovskii, understood this fact well. In an interview with the Russian newspaper *Nezavisimaia Gazeta*, Pavlovskii expressed concern that Russia was not ready to fight off the «combination of the domestic weakening of the political system and external pressure» that had led to the Orange Revolution. There was only one way to safeguard Russia's political system: «[we must] develop the specific know-how for the prevention of revolutions, develop, if necessary, the 'counter-revolutionary' features of our political authorities (*vlast'*) and our society» (*quoted in*: Samarina 2004).

Surkov elaborates this demand. Even though he considers the likelihood of an Orange Revolution in Russia to be «1 in 100», he calls for decisive action: «[W]e must be ready to respond [to any revolutionary attempt] peacefully and within the boundaries of the law. The street must be ours, in Moscow as well as in other large cities» (Surkov 2006a: 78). This goal can only be reached if «a nationally oriented elite» takes charge (ibid.: 69).

In early 2005, Vasilii Iakemenko started secretly touring Russian educational institutions. He and his brother Boris had founded an earlier pro-Kremlin youth organization, Idushchie Vmeste), which was then struggling from numerous scandals and waning mobilizational power (see Lassila 2012b). It had achieved considerable international notoriety when activists of the organization tore up the novelist Vladimir Sorokin's books and disposed of them in a huge toilet bowl in downtown Moscow (Buchacek 2006: 19). Nonetheless, Pavel Danilin, the editor-in-chief of *kremlin.org* and a member of the pro-Kremlin think-tank «Foundation for Effective Politics», called Vasilii Iakemenko the most capable founder of youth movements in contemporary Russia (Danilin 2006: 218).

Iakemenko's secret speech in front of students at the College for Economics and Law in Kursk was leaked to the newspaper *Moskovskii Komsomolets*. He started his presentation by stating: «[m]y name is Vasilii. I am 33 years old, and my function is very simple. I go to towns in 20 regions, (…) and I am trying to find kindred spirits (*edinomyshlenniki*).» (Moskovskii Komsomolets 2005). The political situation as laid out by Iakemenko was dramatic: Ukraine had already become an American colony, and Russia was next. Russia was incapable of competing in the global economy, and the Americans were founding organizations – he singled out the NBP – that were supposed to do what Pora had done in Ukraine. An adequate response was urgent: Iakemenko recruited cadres for a «movement» called «Nashi» (ibid.).

These «commissars» had to take a map of their city, continued Iakemenko, and mark on it any square that could hold more than 200 people. Each activist was to put his name on one public place and take charge of it. A secret staff center would coordinate Nashi's activities in every city.

Nashi was not only supposed to become active in the event of major protests but also fulfill a policing function. Iakemenko quotes the example of drug use: If Nashi was present on public squares, it could detain drug users, which would create a positive image in the media. Commissars' training was equally crucial. Educational institutions would be created in which commissars would learn to «fight the enemy»:

> «Three times a week, (…) for three hours, you will go to these activities. They will teach you PR, creativity, the basics of leadership, the art of oratory, technologies of guiding mass actions, and you will learn about everything that is going on in the world.» (ibid.)

Trained in this way, Iakemenko promised, the Nashi-commissars would become the vanguard of a new national elite and part of a shadow cabinet that would be established parallel to official power structures in 2006.

In 2008, when Nashi had helped to forestall an Orange Revolution in Russia during the elections – which the official discourse repeatedly presented as the main part of the «Orange» plan – the commissars would help elect a new president. Furthermore, they would fill the 450 seats of a parliamentary structure that paralleled the Duma. Iakemenko believed that Nashi would attain a well-trained membership of 200'000 to 300'000 within three years, compared to which the Komsomol was mere «child play and crap (*otstoi*)» (ibid.).

Iakemenko thus laid out an offer for participation in revolutionary change to an educated young audience – provided it helped forestall an Orange Revolution. Though not everybody present was apparently convinced of all of Iakemenko's fantastic promises, the new movement gained considerable momentum.

Andrei, whom I interviewed in St. Petersburg in 2009, was one of Nashi's earliest recruits. Andrei says that he was approached already in November 2004 and asked whether he was interested in helping to create a new youth movement. He had been working at a youth center and had coordinated patriotic education programs. Among other tasks, he led a so-called «druzhina» made up of young people, a kind of citizen patrol that assisted the police in keeping order in specific neighborhoods.[28] Nashi recruited Andrei because of his know-how for keeping order in the streets of St. Petersburg:

> «Why was my experience important for Nashi? Because Nashi was a response to the events in Ukraine. Honestly, I believe there was considerable fear in Russian society and among the elite because it was obvious that the political projects that the Russian spin-doctors had set up in Ukraine were ineffective. And the political technologies our opponents – primarily the USA – had used, were much stronger.»

Andrei describes his motivation to join Nashi as follows: «I am a patriot. I love my country. (…) I support the state that founded Nashi. I joined the project because of a sense of responsibility.»

According to Andrei, the organizers conducted research in various focus groups and then decided to call the project «Nashi» (*Ours*). The name not only evokes traditional notions of community and home but also has an interesting history: the nationalist journalist and filmmaker Aleksandr Nevzorov founded the first youth movement called Nashi in 1991 and made a well-known film by the same name about Soviet soldiers stationed in the restive Baltic States. The movement was politically close to the National Salvation Front, which opposed Yeltsin's reforms and advocated for the restoration of the Soviet Union (Hahn 1994: 311).

---

28 The «druzhiny» date back to Tsarist times. In the Soviet Union, the youth organization Komsomol used these kinds of patrols after World War II to enforce Communist morality. They had a reputation for harassing non-conformist youth like the «stiliagi» (Pilkington 1994: 70).

Although the contemporary Nashi movement has no direct connections to its predecessor, its founders were aware of the historical parallel. While Nashi does not demand a return to Soviet times, the movement openly flirts with Soviet symbols: cadres are called «commissars»[29], and Nashi's website ends with the web domain *.su* (Soviet Union) instead of *.ru* (Borusiak 2005: 24).[30] Nashi's official founding congress took place on 15 April 2004 in the concert hall of the Russian Academy of Sciences, with 687 delegates from more than 20 regions in attendance. Andrei Fursenko, Russia's minister of education and science, attended the event (Tsentr Politicheskoi Informatsii 2005: 6), lending the movement an official stamp of approval.[31] Nashi was born.

Our Victory

Exactly one month later, on 15 May, Nashi made its debut on the streets of Moscow. Its first action was a masterpiece of planning and political propaganda, aided by the large-scale use of administrative resources. The militia closed off Leninskii Prospect the night before, effectively cutting off the Southwest of Moscow from the center, causing huge traffic problems on Moscow's congested roads (Kashin 2005d). Two thousand buses with activists from different parts of the country arrived in the morning and dropped off 60'000 young people on Gagarin Square, where they began to march towards Kaluzhskaia Square. Between these two points, the organizers set up a stage. The mass of Nashi activists stretched over two kilometers (Nashi 2005e).

All participants wore matching white t-shirts that said «OUR Victory» (*NASHA Pobeda*) on the front and had the words to the Russian national anthem printed on the back. The young people were marching to the beat of military

---

[29] In Nashi's hierarchy, the «commissars», mostly students between twenty and thirty years of age, are the cadres. The second category of Nashi activists are «supporters» (*storonniki*), which are only loosely associated with the movement. They can join Nashi at age 16 (Buchacek 2006: 41).

[30] «Igor», a commissar that Jussi Lassila interviewed, claims that Nashi picked the web domain «.su» for pragmatic reasons. Namely, the regular domain «.ru» was already taken. Furthermore, Igor claims that a «.su» domain was more expensive, which was considered to be more prestigious (Lassila 2012b: 199).

[31] It appears that Vladislav Surkov did not personally attend the event. Nonetheless, numerous activists testify that he had been involved with the organization from the beginning – behind the scenes (cf. Kashin 2005a).

songs from the Great Patriotic War and chanted «Rossiia! Rossiia!» (Nashi 2005c). A sea of flags waved over the crowd. Some of them showed the Russian tricolor, but most of them featured a white cross on a red background –Nashi's flag: «Nashi uses red and white symbols because red is the color of our heroic past. White symbolizes our free future, but the actual design of our flag, the cross, refers to the Andreevskii-flag[32],» explained Vasilii Iakemenko (ibid.).

The symbolic unification of past and present, a major theme of Putin's speech on Victory Day six days earlier (see chapter 1), was the main goal of the event. In front of the big stage, the 60'000 participants met 1'000 veterans. Viktor Azarov, the head of the Veterans' Committee in Moscow Oblast', addressed Nashi after a minute of silence for the fallen:

> «Today, we hand Russia over to you. Now you shall fight for Russia, the country for which millions of heroes fell. They died so you could live. You too should live not just for yourself, but also for the country, for Russia, for future generations. You shall never give up the country for anybody. Because a person has only one native land – there will never be another.» (*quoted in*: Nashi 2005d)

Then, «in lieu of the entire young generation», the Nashi commissar Aleksandr Gorodetskii swore an oath:

> «I, citizen of a free Russia, today take our native land from the hands of the older generation. Yesterday you fought on the front lines for freedom, liberty and a happy life: Near Stalingrad and Kursk, on the Virgin Soil and in factories. Today I continue this fight wherever my native land needs me. I take Russia in my hands and swear that I will never let new colonizers and interventionists into the country, that there will be no room for neo-fascists and their helpers, that Russia's thousand year long history will not end with us. I swear to return Russia to its former glory. I swear to make its history great again. I swear I will safeguard the memory of the generations. I swear I will protect Russia's freedom and liberty.» (ibid.)

After this ceremony, all 60'000 young activists received a bullet casing – according to Iakemenko exclusively wartime relics – with the engraving «Remember the war, save the native land (*rodina*)!» (ibid.) According to Nashi, these bullet casings were a symbol of victory in the Great Patriotic War, as

---

32 The traditional symbol of the Russian fleet dating back to Tsarist times.

they had accompanied each soldier throughout the war, until the fall of the Reichstag (Nashi 2005c).

This elaborate ceremony deserves an extended analysis. First of all, the event demonstrated Nashi's and the Russian government's mobilization capabilities to the opposition. As Sergei Belokonev, an influential Nashi commissar at the time and today the head of the Agency for Youth Affairs, declared to the journalist Oleg Kashin:[33] «[h]ere it is, the real Russian Maidan» (Kashin 2005d). Nashi demonstrated with this action that it could take control of the capital's streets if necessary, and that it had the support of the authorities in doing so. «Our Victory», approved by the authorities, required considerable financial means.[34] Moreover, police had blocked streets and arrested members of the opposition who attempted to demonstrate against Nashi. Finally, Putin's meeting with Nashi-commissars only two weeks after the event assured the movement of his personal support.

Secondly, the elaborate staging of the event – aside from the white t-shirts, there were the ubiquitous St. George ribbons, and musical and ritual aspects – shows that the Russian *polit-tekhnologi* had learned their lesson from the Orange Revolution. Viktor Eremin draws a direct parallel between the techniques of show business and this type of manifestation (Eremin 2007). Pavel Danilin maintains that particularly the younger generation of Russians – those born between 1985 and 1991 – is very brand and style conscious. He thus highlights the importance of «external markers of status (…) like little em-

---

33 Oleg Kashin and Nashi have been intimately connected since 2005. He managed to sneak into a secret meeting of future Nashi activists in February of 2005 and has since then written numerous, mostly critical, articles about Nashi.

34 The question of Nashi's financial means has never been answered conclusively, as no official numbers are available. Iakemenko has confirmed that Nashi received funds from pro-Kremlin oligarchs, and it is known that the fund of the billionaire Vladimir Potanin has repeatedly given stipends to Nashi-commissars and financial support to Nashi. Some sources in 2005 assumed that Nashi initially had a budget of 300 million dollars, which was, among others, financed by Gazprom (Tsentr Politicheskoi Informatsii 2005: 6, 9). This number, however, seems rather high and originates from Vasilii Iakemenko, who tends to exaggerate. Nonetheless, Nashi's financial resources are considerable: the first camp at Lake Seliger cost 2 million dollars (Eremin 2007: 3). It is estimated that Nashi had over 100'000 dollars a month at its disposal for measures of «patriotic education» during the first three years of its existence (Heller 2008: 3). The crucial factor for Nashi's work, however, has always been the extent of its political support: access to state television, the toleration of its protests, and meetings with Putin.

blems (*znachki*)» (Danilin 2006: 26), like ribbons and bullet casings that could be hung around the neck.

Nonetheless, the event also raised questions about the quality of this mobilization. Though journalists were not allowed near participants, some managed to secure interviews. One high school student told Kashin that he had been promised a free trip to Moscow, without knowing he would participate in this event. Veterans merely knew that they were headed to a «meeting with the youth» (Kashin 2005d). It is thus impossible to determine how many of the 60'000 young people were actually dedicated to Nashi and how many joined the demonstration out of naïveté, ignorance or a simple desire to participate in a large-scale party.

Nonetheless, the effectiveness of the event should not be underestimated. It built the kind of enthusiastic mass that Gleb Pavlovskii had demanded in reaction to the Orange Revolution (Samarina 2004). In this sense, the notion of «managed passion» describes the event very well (Andreev 2006: 49).

On the discursive level, the event articulates the nodal points of Putin's hegemonic project. «Our Victory» celebrated historical continuity: As the generation that was victorious in the Great Patriotic War is slowly dying off, the legacy is taken up by a new generation, was its message.[35] This moment of continuity combines the Soviet feats in the war, the great development projects of the post-war period («on the Virgin Soil and in factories»), and the ambitions of the new generation. There is no mention of *perestroika*, the 1990s or Stalinist terror. The historical narrative thus fits Putin's emphasis on a «balanced» approach to history.

Moreover, by calling the event «Our Victory», Nashi not only references its own name but also discursively coopts the memory of the Great Patriotic War. Nashi's self-definition as a new patriotic elite becomes grounded in the historical legacy of the generation that defeated the National Socialists, and Nashi comes to represent the entire generation of post-Soviet youth. The

---

35 Aleida Assmann would call this moment the transition from communicative to cultural memory. According to Assmann, it is during this transition that memory is particularly vulnerable to instrumentalization for political purposes: «Der Übergang vom lebendigen individuellen zum künstlichen kulturellen Gedächtnis ist allerdings problematisch, weil er die Gefahr der Verzerrung, der Reduktion, der Instrumentalisierung von Erinnerung mit sich bringt.» (Assmann 1999: 15)

«Our Victory» event – carefully staged, executed and represented – created the «new space of representation» on which the myth in Laclau's sense played out (Laclau 1990: 61). It presents a new generation that stands for a strong, triumphant and unified Russia, grounded in its own great history. Within this space, Nashi becomes the successor to the war generation.

As such, Nashi maintained, it is now stepping up to the task of fighting back and strengthening Russia's position against its enemies. Not letting «new colonizers and interventionists» into the country refers to the events in Ukraine. The passage about making Russia's history great once more refers to the weakness and dislocations of the 1990s. The transfer of the power of the war myth into contemporary politics also extends to the constitutive outside: Nashi is, after all, called an «anti-fascist» movement. This means that, just like the Russians who defeated the National Socialists, Nashi is fighting «fascists».

In 2005, Nashi began this fight with a «large-scale patriotic program». By its own account, Nashi restored 1500 war monuments and wartime graves and three victory parks. Nashi claims that over 50'000 people from 30 cities and regions participated in these activities (Nashi 2005d).

Patriotic Education

«Our Victory» shows that Nashi was not only meant to stabilize the political situation in the streets of the capital but also contribute to patriotic education and foster love for the homeland. In this way, it was to mobilize a politically ambivalent youth in support of the government.

A recent study conducted by the Levada-Center and the Swiss Academy for Development surveyed Russian youth between 15 and 29 years of age in 2006 and 2007. It finds a well-educated, largely employed generation, capable of satisfying its basic material needs. Still, working conditions and low salaries are deeply dissatisfactory (Dafflon 2009: 14). Many young Russians feel dependent on and discriminated against by the older generation and disenchanted by corruption and gaps in wealth they are powerless to bridge. The experience of the 1990s lingers on as the younger generation looks toward the future with apprehension, in spite of its improved economic situation (ibid.: 9, 44). Most distrust politicians but place confidence in Vladimir Putin.[36] Researchers found that the number of young Russians interested in politics is low in comparison to the rest of Europe – 33 percent according to a survey in June 2005 (Stiftung Öffentliche Meinung 2005: 8). Elena Omel'chenko believes that this low number reflects the belief that official politics defend the interests of the economic elite and not those of regular citizens. She found that eighty percent of young Russians were willing to participate in «useful societal work» (Omel'chenko 2006: 16f.). However, the «normalized» political system in Putin's Russia tends to distrust individual forms of social activism, fearing the political potential of grassroots activism (Henry 2006: 108).[37] Youth receive little encouragement from official channels to join NGOs. Not surprisingly, the percentage actually joining non-governmental organizations is small. The focus of youth politics then lies less on constructive youth involvement, but on making sure this section of society remains loyal to the state (Omel'chenko 2006: 18).

For Blum, the role of Nashi in strengthening patriotic sentiments among youth is clear: «From an official perspective, Nashi offers a useful vehicle for enlisting youth support for various policies, as well as for encouraging service in the army and the state bureaucracy» (Blum 2007: 135).

After studying the two most important programmatic documents informing post-Soviet youth policy – «Initsiativa Molodykh – Budushchee Rossii» (*Youth Initiative – Russia's Future*) and the Doktrina Molodezhi Rossii (*Youth Doctrine of Russia*) – Blum concludes:

> «Most importantly, all reflect a shared belief in the need for an official youth policy. Each doctrine also expressed a broad consensus about the state's obligation to intervene, in order to provide essential services for the young people – including a solid moral foundation.» (Blum 2007: 117)

For the most part, then, the vision forwarded in Russia's official youth doctrine corresponds to international standards – including the state's responsibility for youth's well being. What is different is the sense of threat. In official

---

36 More on this interesting paradox will be said below. For now, it is sufficient to say that Putin is credited for the economic upturn since 2000.

37 As was evident during the large forest fires in 2010, self-organized activism also often reveals failures of the state apparatus: since the forestry authorities and the firefighters could not contain the fires, citizens began to organize their own initiatives.

discourse, one often finds the notion of youth as a strategic resource, to be manipulated by the state or its enemies (ibid.: 125). The view of youth as a strategic resource resurfaces in official programs for youth policy, which advocate for a resubmission of youth's socialization under state control as a means of neutralizing a perceived potential for destabilization, analyzes Vladimir Lukov (Lukov 2006: 83).

Igor' Il'inskii, the dean of the Moscow University for the Humanities, expresses this attitude in particularly strong terms. According to him, youth is an element of national security and a resource in the geopolitical struggle among great powers (Il'inskii 2005: 34). Western secret services are still active in Russia, Il'inskii holds, trying to manipulate its youth, for instance through teaching materials that are sponsored by the Soros Foundation (Ibid.: 35). As the state is not taking charge of youth politics to the extent that it should, Russia's youth has become vulnerable to the machinations of Western – particularly American – agents, maintains Il'inskii. According to him, the United States wants to provoke an Orange Revolution in Russia to weaken the country and install a pro-American government – just as it had done in Serbia, Georgia and Ukraine. Russia can only be saved if the government acts now: «[i]f we can save the youth, we can save Russia. Youth is the most important resource of the nation» (ibid.: 43f).

This approach did not emerge with Putin. Boris Yeltsin signed a presidential decree that articulated the education of youth in the context of the country's defense already in 1996 (Lipkovich 2005: 91). The Komsomol's comprehensive socialization function and the interconnection of youth education and military service in the USSR show that this attitude has a long tradition.

Under Putin, the first post-Soviet federal program for patriotic education was passed. Between 2001 and 2005, «Patriotic Education of the Citizens of the Russian Federation» (*Patrioticheskoe Vospitanie Grazhdan Rossiiskoi Federatsii*) was endowed with 177.95 million Rubles (about 5.4 million dollars). The successor program received three times as much money (Blum 2007: 124). The current installment of the program, covering the period between 2011 and 2015, is endowed with 25 million dollars (Rosvoentsentr 2010).

The goal of the bills coincides entirely with arguments discussed above: «The implementation of the program will contribute to societal stability, the reconstruction of the national economy and the elevation of the country's defense-potential (*oboronosposobnost'*).» The program will make sure that citizens «fulfill their civic duties in peace and wartime». The bill deplores the upheavals of the 1990s that alienated Russia from its traditions. Furthermore, «economic disintegration», «social differentiation» and the «devaluation of spiritual values» exerted a negative influence on society:

> «Indifference, egoism, individualism, cynicism, unmotivated aggression, disrespectful behavior towards state and social institutions are very common. The prestige of military and state service is falling.» (Rossiiskaia Gazeta 2001).

Nashi's goals are very much compatible with the tasks of official patriotic education. They include:

> «to strengthen socially meaningful patriotic values, views and convictions in society, in the consciousness and feelings of citizens. (…) Respect for Russia's culture, history and traditions, [and] the elevation of the prestige of state and military service.» (Nashi 2007a)

Nashi is thus part of a hegemonic project aimed at strengthening the patriotic values of Russia's youth in particular. The federal program for patriotic education calls for a «conservation and development of [Russia's] glorious military and labor traditions» (Rossiiskaia Gazeta 2001).[38]

Another key demand of the program is the «un-falsified presentation of history» (ibid.). Again, the central historical event in question is the Great Patriotic War. Even though other aspects of Russia's history are highlighted and the Orthodox Church is mentioned as an important actor in the patriotic education of Russia's youth, most of the 1500 planned measures are related to the war. Veterans' organizations are the main actor in organizing an array of museum expeditions, silent vigils next to war memorials, and promotions of patriotic clubs (Orlova 2002: 101ff.). This fostering of historical pride is meant to contribute to a stronger sense of duty to the fatherland among Russia's youth (Lipkovich 2005: 93). The «Our Victory» event served the same rationale.

---

38 This formula is reminiscent of the «All Soviet hikes to the places of military, patriotic, and labor glory» that were important components of Brezhnev-era programs of patriotic education. In 1975, 30 million young people participated in these hikes (Kämpfer 1994: 336f.).

The promotion of a more patriotic narrative about the Great Patriotic War is a hegemonic response to the perceived dislocations that resulted from critical discussions in the 1980s and 1990s about the Soviet role in the war.

The most discussed example of how this answer played out was the banning of Igor' Dolutskii's critical history textbook from Russian schools in 2003.[39] The Ministry of Education decided to remove the book from Russian schools. Putin justified the removal through the need to introduce a more «factual» approach to the teaching of history:

> «I think we can be glad that we have left behind the single-party and single ideological interpretation of our country's history. This is of course a major achievement, but I think you will agree that we should not go to the other extreme. Modern textbooks, especially textbooks for schools and institutes of higher education should not become a platform for a new political and ideological struggle. These textbooks should really present historical facts; they should inspire, especially among young people, a feeling of pride for their own history, and for their country.» (Putin 2003)

In order to introduce a less «political and ideological» textbook, the Ministry of Education organized a competition won by Nikita Zagladin, a professor at the Institute of the World Economy and International Relations of the Russian Academy of Sciences. His book, *Istoriia Otechestva. XX Vek*, devotes more attention to Soviet achievements. Put briefly, «the emphasis on modernization places the Russian state, not the problematic of democratization, at the center of the historical stage» (Sherlock 2007: 176).

History is thus used as a tool for consolidating Russian political identity and the Russian state. At the same time, Putin's claim that the teaching of «historical facts» is the same as inspiring patriotic pride in young people naturalizes and depoliticizes a highly political narrative. An «objective» narrative that stresses the achievements of the Russian state in modernizing the country is presented as a reaction against «political» moves to belittle these achievements.[40] Like securitization, this presentation of history fulfills the role of re-

---

39 Scholars have discussed this incident at length and often very controversially. A thorough and balanced discussion of the «Dolutskii Affair» can be found in Thomas Sherlock's book on historical narratives (Sherlock 2007: 168-185).
40 This «balanced» or «objective» approach is often a euphemism for highlighting

moving it from the realm of «normal» discussion and defining it as an issue that only «responsible» specialists are qualified to discuss.

Some authors even claim that Russia's enemies use history as a weapon. Oleg Rozhnov writes that Western NGOs had coproduced and co-financed «certain modern teaching materials» in order to convey a negative image of their country's history to Russian youth: «[They even] obfuscate, who won World War II» (Rozhnov 2005: 30). Il'inskii believes that these teaching materials' portrayal of Russian history as «dirty and vulgar» is part of the same «information war» that caused the Orange Revolution (Il'inskii 2005: 35).

Vasilii Iakemenko himself drew this direct connection between the threat against memory and Nashi's foundation. According to him, the latter is a grassroots reaction against historical revisionism:

> «On the eve of the 60th anniversary of Russia's victory in the Great Patriotic War, a number of regional youth organizations put forward initiatives for the foundation of a political movement 'Idushchie Vmeste', and I personally support this healthy reaction to the growing popularity of the political seducer Limonov [the leader of the NBP] and his fascist preemies (*nedonoshennye fashisty*) in pseudointellectual teenage circles. Under the Hitler flag, waved by the National-Bolsheviks, Khakamada and her 'Committee 2008', the 'Iabloko' youth and totally immoral people assemble. The fact that those responsible for the scourge of the 20th century, in which 27 million Russians, Tatars, Belarusians and Jews perished, can show themselves openly, is personally offensive to us. We are putting an end to this unnatural union of oligarchs and anti-Semites, Nazis and liberals. In order to do this, we are founding a new project – 'Nashi'.» (*quoted in*: Balmasov 2006: 20)

More will be said below about the «unnatural union» Iakemenko mentions. For now, it is noteworthy that the defense of war memory is the main justification for the foundation of Nashi. The post-1990s – and ultimately also the post-Orange Revolution – consolidation of Russia then depends in no small degree on the production of what Vera Tolz calls a «usable past» (Tolz 2004: 171): the war narrative articulates not only Russia's defense-capabilities

---

positive aspects and remaining silent on negative ones. Work on the new unified history textbook for schools shows that this tendency is alive and well: citing difficulties in determining the exact extent of stalinist repression, the historians in charge are planning to omit numbers on victims altogether. On the other hand, they highlight the positive effects of Stalinist social reforms. (Samarina 2013)

against domestic and foreign enemies, but also the vision of a modern and strong country.

The Manifesto

Nashi's manifesto, first published in April 2005, continues to be the movement's most important programmatic document. It articulates Nashi's view of Russia's history and contemporary position in the world, its most important goals and the challenges to be overcome in reaching this goal. The manifesto's style is simple, and it is uses the colloquial *ty* (informal version of «you») to address its youthful audience.

On its surface, Nashi's worldview is agonistic and positive. Today's globalizing world is one of international competition, and the spread of democratic values has also anchored this kind of competition in the domestic politics of most countries, writes the organization. Nashi thus sees constant development and modernization as preconditions for competitiveness (Nashi 2005a).

By defeating the National Socialists in World War II, Russia is seen to have created a world order that prevented a new «global hegemony of one country – whether this be fascist Germany or the USA» and a new world war. In this way, every country in the world has the right to choose its own path of development (ibid.). Furthermore, the Soviet Union and its ideals of social justice are proven to be intellectually influential and to have contributed to decolonization movements.

Communist leaders nevertheless never understood «the role of individual liberty in social development», and had led the USSR into a «blind alley» (*tupik*) (ibid.). At the end of the twentieth century, however, «Russia, on its own, renounced communism and voluntarily left the territories it had controlled. This decision created the foundations for the contemporary world order as we know it.» (ibid.) This came at a high cost: economic collapse, rising inequality, and ethnic conflict have plagued Russia, but Nashi justifies these sacrifices as necessary for promoting individual liberty and modernization (ibid.).

In this first part of the manifesto, Nashi develops a narrative that places the Soviet Union and Russia at the center of historical development: current world order was decisively shaped by the country's actions during and after both World War II and the Soviet collapse. Here, the Soviet Union and Russia are used interchangeably. However, Nashi distinguishes the Soviet Union from communism: while contemporary Russia has left *communism* behind, Nashi continues to use the Soviet *state* as Russia's main point of reference. Andrei, the Nashi-commissar, states this very explicitly in the interview: «Russia is the historical successor of the USSR, on the national, cultural (…) and territorial level».

A strong state is crucial for claiming the position Nashi believes Russia objectively deserves in the contemporary world order. International competition is «hard and sometimes cruel. The weak have to accept the rules of the game of the strong, get stuck in their wake and are culturally assimilated» (ibid.). This is what the liberal forces that governed the country in the 1990s and who oppose Putin today do not understand, argues Nashi: they sacrificed the nation's independence for the sake of individual liberty. Communists and «fascists», on the other hand, sacrificed individual rights for state power:

«Individual liberty and national sovereignty are two sides of the same coin. This is why for us a strong and independent Russian state is as much a condition for freedom as democracy and a market economy. Russia is and will be a sovereign democracy.» (ibid.)

In order to be able to compete and safeguard its national identity, Russia needs to be «open but strong». Only in this way can it avoid lagging behind economically and being taken over by stronger competitors. The new generation of leaders – the commissars Nashi wants to train – must ensure that Russia becomes this country. In the words of Andrei: «[e]ach commissar has to be a patriot, a leader and a specialist».[41]

Nashi's commissars are to become the cadres needed to modernize Russia and to ensure opportunities for all of its citizens. Opportunities are key to Nashi's vision of a «just» society, in which «a young and talented person from even the most distant village gets the chance to receive an education from the best university of the country». Nashi's motto can thereby be realized: «[f]rom passivity – to activity. From copying – to creativity. From imitation – to

---

41   This phrase appears almost verbatim in Nashi's manifesto. During my interviews, the extent to which commissars use sections from this manifesto to describe their own attitude was very striking. This seems to indicate that Nashi's ideological indoctrination of its activists was quite effective.

showing initiative.» These domestic changes create the conditions for Russia's global leadership:

> «We do not understand Russia's leadership as its military-political dominance over other countries and peoples, but as Russia's influence in the world, based on the attractiveness of Russian culture, the Russian way of life and its political and social system. To be a leader means to strive constantly for the new and to create the conditions for the success of others.» (Nashi 2005a)

Russian envisioned leadership is thus based on «soft» rather than «hard» power. Many of the basic notions related to Russia's position in the world correspond almost verbatim to Surkov's Sovereign Democracy, most clearly outlined in his two articles «Suverenitet – Eto Politicheskii Sinonim Konkurento-Sposobnost'» (*Sovereignty is a Synonym for Competitiveness*) and «Natsionalizatsiia Budushchego».[42]

The similarities are so striking that Surkov may well have coauthored the document. Like Nashi, Surkov emphasizes the Soviet Union's important role in the postwar global order and the influence of its values and its modernization project (Surkov 2006a: 47). He holds the Soviet Union's «ineffective elite» and closed society responsible for its collapse and emphasizes the high price Russia paid for its «return to the right path» in 1991 (ibid.: 48). He highlights the importance of human capital for the country's modernization (Surkov 2006b: 5) and insists on the importance of Russia being strong and open in order to participate in global decision-making (Surkov 2006a: 60).

The ideology of Sovereign Democracy sees the strengthening of the state as a precondition for both the economic and democratic development of society. In the 1990s, according to both Surkov and Nashi, Russia lost the ability to make sovereign decisions, thereby «distorting» democracy and rendering it meaningless (ibid: 50).

Putin's stabilization of Russia, in Surkov's formulation, has enabled the country to begin «real» democratic development, a precondition for global leader-

---

42   Much has been written about Sovereign Democracy in recent years. Viacheslav Morozov calls it the «ideological horizon» of contemporary Russian politics (Morozov 2008: 152). The most important collected volumes in Russian on the subject are: Garadzha, N. Ed. 2006. *Suverenitet. Sbornik*. Moskva: Evropa; Poliakov, L.V. Ed. 2007. *PRO Suverennuiu Demokratiiu*. Moskva: Evropa; Various authors. 2006. *Suverennaia Demokratiia: Ot Idei k Doktrine*. Moskva: Evropa. On Sovereign Democracy, see also: Hudson 2009.

ship (ibid.: 62): «[t]he need for democracy is obvious. Only a society that is based on the competition and cooperation of free people can be effective and competitive» (ibid.: 58). This kind of a strong and open country is ready for global competition: «Sovereignty is openness, it means going out into the world, participating in an open fight. I would say that sovereignty is the political synonym of competitiveness» (ibid.: 60).

Surkov and Nashi thus present a vision of Russia's political identity that combines notions of individual self-realization, strong statehood and modernization. The concept unites signifiers from discourses that promote a «Western» developmental model for Russia with those that embrace more conservative/patriotic nodal points (See: Casula 2011: 171ff.). In this way, a seemingly coherent vision of values is articulated in order to consolidate and mobilize a new, «nationally oriented» elite (Okara 2007: 10).

Education is also central to the realization of Nashi's goals. The organization started collaborating with the State University of Management in Moscow, where commissars have take courses in government, relations with civil society organizations, and in other similar fields (Nashi 2005f). Marina, the other commissar I interviewed, describes the content of these «master classes» as follows: «communication, leadership, dialogue, technologies of social communication and manipulation». «Manipulation» she clarifies, relates mostly to working with crowds: «how to assemble them, how to disperse them, how to redirect their attention». Though educational programs are designed to provide commissars with both the street fighting techniques to prevent an Orange Revolution and the management skills to modernize Russia, Marina's response suggests that the emphasis lies on the former.

This illuminates one of the central dilemmas of Sovereign Democracy: given the potential incompatibility between the dual goals of strengthening the state and democratic rights, which takes precedence? Morozov identifies the strengthening of the state as the dominant theme in Russian politics, defining strength as «the ability of the state to control all significant domestic and transnational processes in and involving Russia» (Morozov 2008: 174). Political analyst Andrei Okara notes that Sovereign Democracy envisions a collectivist notion of «the people», «ruling out the rise of democratic procedures to the level of institutions» (Okara 2007: 19). Within this interpretation, individual rights are subordinate to collective well-being.

Nashi's manifesto calls on people to «stop talking about defending human rights» and dismisses liberal criticism of Putin as an ideological weapon and an expression of Western double standards on democracy (Nashi 2005a). In this sense, it takes up similar Soviet criticisms from the 1970s. The statement, however, also reveals Nashi's deep disdain for a set of legally binding human rights, suggesting that human rights are a matter of political opportunity and pragmatic considerations.

Andrei freely admits this: «Nashi has never set itself the task of creating a list of civil rights for each citizen». For Nashi, individual self-realization is achieved through putting one's efforts at the service of Russia, thereby helping to promote its modernization and attainment of great power status (see the discussion of patriotic songs in chapter 4). For Surkov and Nashi, a democratic order could be an effective way to achieve this goal, but it is not necessarily a value in and of itself.

The same applies to civil society, the establishment of which, after sovereignty and modernization, represents Nashi's third goal:

> «The goals of our movement can only be reached if the modernization initiatives from 'above' can rely on support from 'below'. Today's Russian society suffers from despondency, dependence, apathy and an inability for self-organization.» (Nashi 2005a)

Through debates, demonstrations and collaboration with state and civil society organizations, Nashi hopes to revive Russian society, particularly focusing on fighting against corruption and violence within the military (*dedovshchina*). Yet the scope of civil society's actions remains limited: Surkov defines civil society exclusively as a partner for the state in the task of modernization (Surkov 2006a: 64). Nashi perceives its role very similarly

Surkov and Nashi recognize as legitimate only political actors who support officially declared goals for the development of Russian society. Independent actors in civil society are often framed as threatening the consolidation of Russia's political system. Okara correctly notes that one Sovereign Democracy's key goals is to «[p]rovide ideological and operative grounds for narrowing the scope of public politics» (Okara 2007: 11).

Putin remarks in a 2008 speech on Russia's development until the year 2020:
> «Irresponsible demagogy and attempts to divide society and use foreign help or intervention in domestic political struggles are not only immoral but also illegal. They belittle our people's dignity and undermine our democratic state. (…) No matter what their differences, all of the different public forces in the country should act in accordance with one simple but essential principle: Do nothing to damage the interests of Russia and its citizens and act only for Russia's good, act in its national interests and in the interest of all its people's prosperity and security.» (Putin 2008b)

The passage shows that the field of political actors in Russia's Sovereign Democracy remains limited to those who act «responsibly» – that is, in accordance with Russia's national interests. The state is still threatened from external forces and their domestic allies. The societal field of Russian politics is hence still «criss-crossed by antagonisms» (Laclau and Mouffe 2001: 135), which contradicts the agonistic worldview that Sovereign Democracy purports on the surface.

Foreign Enemies

According to Nashi, enemies still threaten to undermine the progress made under Putin toward a strong and modern Russia, intending to weaken the country. In Nashi's worldview, Russia has to defend itself in a warlike situation. The myth of the Great Patriotic War in a figurative sense is used to illustrate this situation. Above, we have seen that Nashi's foundation was presented as a measure against Russian neo-fascists. This same discursive equivalence between «fascists» and Russia's modern enemies is applied to describe foreign threats:

> «Russia is the central military-strategic space of the Eurasian continent. Those who want to dominate Eurasia and the entire world must control Russia. For this reason Napoleon and Hitler dreamt of asserting their control over Russia. Today the USA on the one, and international terrorism on the other hand, strive for control of Eurasia. Their eye is on Russia. It is the task of our generation to safeguard the sovereignty of our country, just like our grandfathers did 60 years ago.» (Nashi 2005a)

Russia is simultaneously fighting two foreign enemies, both of whom threaten its national unity and sovereignty. The issue of terrorism is closely connected to Chechnya. In official discourse, the de-facto independence of Chechnya in the 1990s is presented as a great threat to the Russian state. In Surkov's words, Russia's «shameful capitulation at Khasaviurt» brought the country to «the brink of losing its sovereignty» (Surkov 2006a 52). Only Putin's decisive actions reversed this situation:

> «[T]he question was to be or not to be. Russia (...) answered 'To be!' And it answered by making a choice – Vladimir Vladimirovich Putin was elected president, and he himself took care of normalizing the country.» (ibid. 53)

The threat of terrorism was used to justify various centralizing measures in domestic politics – such as strengthening the power vertical, the abolition of governors' elections and the reigning in of «oligarchs'» political influence. According to Bacon and his co-authors, terrorism served as a justification for wide-ranging political measures in various areas, which constitutes a clear securitizing operation (Bacon et al. 2006 49). During the Putin presidency, the fight against terrorism became a veritable «building block» of political identity and a central factor for Putin's popularity (Baev 2005 334ff.). In spite of Putin's «normalization», however, the threat of terrorism remained intact in 2005, as the bombings in Moscow and the tragedy in Beslan had showed. Like in many Western countries, the war against terror has created a political situation that justifies «securitizing» measures against an elusive enemy.

In Nashi's discourse, this vague sense of threat is amplified by the presence of a second powerful enemy – the United States. Russian-American relations reached a high point after the terrorist attacks in the USA on 11 September 2001, with Russia joining the alliance against terrorism and Putin and George W. Bush celebrating their close personal friendship publicly. In the following years, though, the relationship between the two countries became strained.

One cause of this deterioration was the long-standing conflict over what Russia considers its sphere of influence. The US (and its European allies) had ignored Russian opposition against NATO's eastward extension and the bombing of Serbia in 1999. US and European support for Color Revolutions in Georgia and Ukraine further aggravated Russian fears of being passed over and «contained» by other great powers. That the Russian government considers the reconsolidation of the country's position in the post-Soviet space – the «near abroad» – a precondition of its reemergence as a great power contributed to rising tensions with the United States.

Furthermore, the US-led invasion of Afghanistan led to the deployment of American troops in Central Asia. Russia had initially consented to this deployment – under the condition that it would be temporary. However, the US pursued an increasingly unilateral policy under Bush and used its presence to strengthen American influence in Central Asia by securing energy resources and providing military aid to allies (Kanet and Homarac 2007: 184). The containment of Russian influence in Central Asia remained an explicit goal of US policy (ibid.: 181).

Nashi and Surkov articulate the threat emanating from the United States on two interconnected levels: ideological and geopolitical. The «double standard» of democracy promotion refers to the fact that Nashi believes the US only insists on democratic standards when it is geopolitically convenient. At anti-US protests, Nashi produced posters that showed pictures of US soldiers abusing Afghani and Iraqi prisoners, thereby highlighting the contradictions of democracy promotion by way of military invasion in the Middle East.

Nashi commissar Andrei is convinced that Americans try to «propagate the American Dream everywhere, everywhere, everywhere!» The influence of American culture is perceived as a threat to Russia's traditions and its national security. Russian official discourse sees the spread of US cultural influence as a tool in a geopolitical struggle. For Surkov, it amounts to an attempt at establishing an American «global dictatorship» (Surkov 2006b).

Andrei believes it is Nashi's task to fight the US influence in the world:

> «[Russia] has the right (…) to fight for a leading position in the modern world. I am a proponent of a multipolar world. I do not think it is right if one country can dictate its conditions to the rest of the world. Under these circumstance, I see the USA as Russia's opponent (*protivnik*).»

Andrei does not exclude that this antagonism could lead to a war with Russia, and declares his willingness to «take the weapon and defend my native land».

This antagonistic perception of the United States in Nashi's discourse reflects widespread anti-Americanism in Russia's political establishment. At the same time, it contrasts the agonistic vision of global competition outlined above. Official discourse demands that Russia form a counterweight to American power on the global stage. Surkov insists that Russia wants a «just globalization» with a level playing field (Surkov 2006b). However, Russia's inability to compete on the world stage is presented as the result of «unfair» practices by its (American) opponents:[43] Surkov portrays Russia as willing to play by the rules of international competition. However, says official discourse, the Americans use unfair means – broken promises and double standards in the promotion of democracy – to keep Russia down. In this way, Russia's problems on the international stage are externalized and attributed to its constitutive outside.

The discussion of Russia's foreign enemies according to Nashi illustrates the nodal point of strengthening the Russian state against antagonists. At the same time, it reveals a marked sense of weakness and vulnerability on the global stage that can once more be linked to the 1990s. Russia's position in the «club» of great powers continues to be tenuous. This is due in part to its continued economic inferiority to international actors like the EU or the United States (Oldberg 2007: 22).

Other writers, however, attribute Russia's insecurity on the international stage to its hesitation to integrate economically and politically with other powers, instigated by fears of losing sovereignty in the process. Russia's position as an agonist in global politics is then often subverted by «a highly securitized vision of the Russian state» (Makarychev 2008: 68). Martin Müller sees the constant subversion of Russia's great power ambitions by domestic and international forces as one of the defining features of official discourse under Putin:

> «The discursive construction of a strong Russia, however, is bound up with fears of a weak Russia – a Russia that fails to realise its ambitious plans to live up to its great-power potential, that is perceived to be marginalised, or is even excluded from world politics.» (Müller 2009b: 329)

This fear of Russia's inadequacy is furthermore – in Nashi's discourse – combined with a radical portrayal of the country's perceived enemies: they are presented as equivalent to the fascists of 60 years ago. On one hand, this combination releases mobilizing potential. On the other hand, however, the

---

43 Nashi states that collaboration with Western countries is an important precondition for Russia's modernization (Nashi 2005a). Furthermore, both Surkov and Nashi commissar Andrei underline that Russia is a European civilization with European values (Surkov 2005). Nashi's position is thus less anti-Western than anti-American.

need to take extreme measures against a deadly enemy in order to securitize the nation can lead to simplistic worldviews and contains considerable potential for (at least rhetorical) violence. A strong figure of a «fascist» enemy that discursively undermines Nashi's demand for unity, modernity and strength remains the structural precondition for articulating its hegemonic political identity. In the next section, we will see how this potential plays out on the domestic scene.

Domestic Enemies

The domestic component of the «unnatural» union of enemies that Nashi's manifesto identifies consists of «liberals, fascists, Westerners and ultranationalists» (Nashi 2005a). The economic liberals around Boris Yeltsin are held responsible for the chaotic 1990s, called the «times of trouble» (*smuta*), an allusion to the political instability in the early 17th century (ibid.). Surkov draws similar conclusions: «[w]e really believe that it would be dangerous and detrimental to our country if the 'Liberals' took power» (Surkov 2005: 13). The «Liberals» are discursively connected with international foundations and NGOs responsible for weakening Russians' patriotism and trying to bring about a «Birch Revolution» in Russia.

The political leaders of the 1990s are further presented as weak and unpatriotic. In Nashi's discourse, the signifier «defeatist» (*porazhentsy*) is crucial: the defeatists came to power in the 1980s (with Gorbachev). They had «lost their belief in the future, gave up national ambitions and a feeling of historical responsibility» (Nashi 2005a). They allowed the Russian state to be corrupted by «oligarchical capitalism», had personally profited from these processes and lived «like parasites» off of the Soviet heritage (ibid.)

These defeatists' policies led to the weakening of the Russian state and Russia's global influence. It brought about general insecurity for Russian citizens, the dissolution of common values and «our defeat in the realm of modernization» (ibid.). The new generation should not support this regime of «oligarchical capitalism», but instead «liquidate it, because this regime is unfair, unfree and lacks solidarity». Nashi has to replace the generation of defeatists that is still partially in power.

However, revolutionary rhetoric is immediately toned down. Nashi emphasizes that this is «a revolution in content, not in form» (ibid.). This limitation is crucial: while Nashi fights against defeatists, it acts to strengthen the state, not to weaken it. Nashi therefore supports Putin: he was «the first to declare Russia's pretension to leadership in the world of the 21st century» and «the first to really challenge the regime of oligarchical capitalism». Only Putin can guarantee Russia's modernization. And his modernizing efforts will only be saved from being «choked» by his domestic and foreign enemies if Russia's youth supports him.

While the «Liberals», according to Nashi, threaten to gridlock Putin's project, the «fascists» reject it in its entirety. Nashi addresses a large problem in Russia indeed: it is estimated that there are 50'000-70'000 skinheads in Russia, the largest population in the world (Laruelle 2009: 63). The first decade of the new millennium saw large-scale racial violence. An attack of 300 skinheads on shops and kiosks mostly run by Caucasian merchants in October of 2001 at Tsarytsino metro station in Moscow left 4 dead and nearly 100 wounded. The 2006 riots in the Karelian town of Kondopoga involved 2'000 people. The number of racist attacks increased drastically through the end of the decade: In 2004, they left 270 people injured and 47 dead. In 2008, these numbers reached 486 and 109, respectively. Since then, there has since been a slight decrease (Kozhevnikova 2010). The ethnically motivated destruction of a market in Southern Moscow by ethnic Russians in October 2013 shows nonetheless that right-wing groups continue to enjoy considerable popularity in the capital and in other parts of Russia.[44]

In principle, most Russians disapprove of racist attacks and are in favor of severe punishment for «fascists» (Strelkova 2006: 236). However, Laruelle has shown that the issue is more complicated. She quotes a survey from 2003, according to which 81 percent of the population disapproves of «nationalism». At the same time, 53% spoke out in favor of «maintaining the purity of the race» (Leonova 2003). Laruelle explains this contradiction by differences in terminology: disdain for «fascism» has a long tradition in Russia going back to World War II and further. The term «patriot», however, has moved

---

[44] The issue of illegal immigrants also played an important role in the Moscow mayoral election of September 2013.

to the center of contemporary Russian political discourse. Political actions are legitimate as long as they are «patriotic». Often, the same racist and xenophobic ideas are met with support or disdain depending on their discursive framing by the media and the authorities (Laruelle 2009: 38).

The fight against neo-Nazism and racist ideas is further complicated by the racism of the police who lack the dedication to investigate and prosecute racist acts and often look the other way. Even though Article 282 of the criminal code provides the means to prosecute racist acts, only a small number of persons have been tried, less than 100 cases in 2006 for example. The vast majority of racist attacks are attributed to «hooliganism» (ibid.: 70).

The issue of xenophobia is moreover tied to migrants from the Caucasus and specifically from Chechnya. Local populations have regarded this migration into the cities of European Russia in the 1960s and 1970s with great suspicion – particularly in economically depressed areas. Lev Gudkov and Boris Dubin described the relationship between the «core population» (*korennoe naselenie*) and Caucasians as one of antagonism and distrust (Gudkov and Dubin 2005: 16). As a result, many Russians – and the vast majority of the media – have perceived skinhead attacks on Caucasian merchants in Kondopoga as a kind of «self-defense» of ethnic Russians (Laruelle 2009: 37) against an ill-defined «other». Xenophobia, racism, and fear of terrorism form an explosive mix in popular perceptions.

Official discourse has not been immune to these tendencies. Putin called for support for the «core population» after the unrest in Kondopoga. Vasjunin states that Putin's slogans following the incident were coopted from the (now illegal) Neo-Nazi «Movement Against Illegal Immigration» (Vasjunin 2007).[45] Nashi strictly opposes «fascist» organizations in its manifesto:

> «In the worst case, the country will face a split (*raskol*) along ethnic and religious lines, and civil war. Fascist organizations in Russia are working actively toward the realization of the latter scenario. Here, they are the allies of the Russian liberals.» (Nashi 2005a)

---

[45] This movement – in Russian, «Dvizhenie Protiv Nelegal'noi Immigratsii» – brought together various neo-fascist movements after its founding in July 2002 and was the largest radical rightwing movement in Russia, with 5'000 members in 30 regions. It ran on a platform of enforcing law and order and defending Russians against «the Chechenization» of their country (DPNI 2006). Its leader, Aleksandr Belov, is the former head of the fascist *Pamiat'*-movement.

Nashi draws a chain of equivalence between «liberals» and «fascists», seeing them both as interested in destroying Russia. The fight against fascism is once again a «fight for the unity (*tselostnost'*) and sovereignty of Russia» (ibid.). Nashi claims that Russia is held together by a shared culture and identity through the shared «super-ethos», that of the *Rossiianin*:[46]

> «The word *Rossiianin* [describes] the inhabitant of a territorially defined, historically grown society. (...) *Rossiianin* is a super-ethos. (...) And I claim that the majority of nationalities currently living in Russia see themselves as a part [of this ethos]. The bases for this understanding are a shared history, culture and tradition. And of course the Russian language.»

Russia, then, draws its unity from a shared «rossiiskii» identity. Attempts to define Russia along ethnic lines, Surkov notes, would lead the country back to early Muscovite times (Surkov 2006b). If Russia wants to consolidate its statehood and become a leader on the international stage, today's youth has to fight for an inclusive definition of «Russian» (Nashi 2005a). Again, the commemoration of the Great Patriotic War is used to further this aim: According to Andrei, the fact that «people from all 120 Russian nationalities» fought for their native land provides the most important historical foundation for this «Russianness». In this way, Nashi articulates a central aspect of official Soviet and post-Soviet interpretations of the war: it was won because of the united efforts of a multinational Soviet Union, under the leadership of the ethnic Russians (Kudriashov 2007: 131).

In many ways, then, the promotion of «rossiiskii» patriotism represents an official strategy of defining the meaning of the signifier «patriotism» by incorporating nationalist rhetoric into a broader, ethnically inclusive and state-centered discourse. Nashi, for example, has placed great emphasis on the fact that it opened an office in the Chechen capital of Grozny right after its 2005 founding. Ramsan Kadyrov, the Chechen president, has been a regular guest at Nashi's summer camp at Lake Seliger (see chapter 4). Nashi actively declares it is not against Chechens loyal to the Russian state. In Nashi's discourse, cooperation between Kadyrov's (notoriously violent) security forc-

---

46 Russians distinguish between «russkii» and «rossiiskii». The first describes an ethnic definition of Russianness, derived from the historical Rus', the pre-modern entity that gave rise to modern Russia, and the second a civic definition.

es and the Russian military has been the key to the «normalization» in Chechnya.

Another example of how Nashi implements this strategy of cooptation is the «Russian March». This march has been taking place on Unity Day, celebrated on 4 November and intended to replace Revolution Day (7 November) as a patriotic holiday. After 2005, it was quickly coopted by rightwing extremist groups, who regularly staged large marches in Moscow and St. Petersburg (Simonov 2009). In recent years, the police have begun to arrest participants. While Nashi had little to say about right wing radicals marching in earlier years (Leonova 2006: 117), it began to coopt Unity Day in 2009. For a few years, Nashi regularly brought together 20'000 and more youth for a large demonstration and a celebration of Russia's historical achievements – ranging from the defeat of the Poles in 1612 to Olympic gold medal winners (Nashi 2010). Nashi thus managed to reframe the «nationalist» into a «patriotic» holiday and thus reintegrate it into the political mainstream. At the same time, this mainstream has become increasingly nationalist.

Unusual Fascists

In Nashi's fight against «fascism», the cooptation of neo-Nazis is not the central aspect. First and foremost, «fascist» is the term that Nashi attaches to its enemies and to the enemies of Putin's stabilization project. In order to illustrate this, we turn our attention back to May 2005. On 11 May, even before the «Our Victory» event, Vasilii Iakemenko and Federal Commissar Aleksandr Gorodetskii, together with Georgii Zemtsov, a veteran of the Great Patriotic War, presented the brochure «Unusual Fascism» (*neobyknovennyi fashizm*) as part of the program for patriotic education discussed above (see also appendix I).

Iakemenko declared that 33'000 copies of the 12-page brochure would be distributed in most middle and high schools across Russia at a later stage (Zarubin 2005). The brochure's main message states that Russia was facing a new kind of fascism on the eve of the 60th anniversary of Victory Day – «unusual fascism»:

«Yes, and how can there be fascism in the country that smashed the backbone of Hitler's units? Only an unusual [fascism], brought about by carefully cultivated all-powerful political intrigues and emigrants.» (Nashi 2005b)
When Nashi presented the brochure, the presence of the World War II veteran Zemtsov was meant to lend moral credence to its accusations. Zemtsov declared that the «enemy» was well organized and used «propaganda, hypnosis, and the newest scientific and technical achievements» to achieve its goals (Kashin 2005b).[47]
Nashi's plans to distribute the brochure were soon revealed to be a pipe dream. Minister of Education Andrei Fursenko declared he had never seen the brochure. The Head of the Education Department in Moscow, Liubov' Kezina, stated that she knew nothing about plans to introduce the brochure to Russian schools. She also criticized the indiscriminate labeling of opponents as «fascists»: «Khakamada or Rogozin may not be real patriots, but even president Putin said that there should be an opposition in the country.» (*quoted in*: Kashin 2005b) The brochure quickly disappeared from Nashi's website. The reason for this roundabout description of the «unusual fascists» lies in Nashi's «unusual» definition of fascism. It essentially counts anyone as a fascist who is part of the opposition. This includes members of Committee 2008, with Irina Khakamada singled out specifically as the «most mentally undone» (*raskruchennyi*) among the liberals. It also encompasses the party Iabloko, the youth organization of the SPS, and Il'ia Iashin, the leader of Oborona.

Furthermore, the «fugitive oligarch» and former Yukos shareholder Leonid Nevzlin is declared part of the conspiracy. The brochure also identifies this kind of «fascism» in some Baltic states, where «Nazism raises its head» (see chapter 3). The main target of the brochure, however, is the National-Bolshevik Party (NBP). According to the publication's logic, the other groups are simply fascist by virtue of their association with the NBP.
This organization has used radical symbols to get attention in Russia on a regular basis. Within the party, members address Limonov as «vozhd» (*Füh-*

---

[47] Zemtsov's ideas are reminiscent of the «sufficiently general theory of governance», a brand of patriotism based largely on conspiracy theories, enemies and the power of collective hypnosis. Serguei Oushakine describes this theory as one brand of patriotism that emerged as a reaction to the loss of power and reliable societal structures in the 1990s. (Oushakine 2009: esp. 67-78)

rer), and the NBP's flag is inspired by the National Socialist flag but replaces the swastika with a hammer and sickle. The NBP ideology is equally eclectic, uniting «imperial nationalism and extremely socialist tendencies in the economy». The NBP considers this combination «paradoxical, like reality itself» (NBP 2004a).

More than half of the brochure is dedicated to NBP's symbolism. Nashi uses a mixture of NBP posters and sensationalist stories about the National-Bolsheviks to illustrate the danger they pose. A first thread focuses on NBP founder and leader Eduard Limonov's «seduction» of Russia's youth. Nashi quotes passages from his book *It's Me, Eddy* that feature allusions to homosexuality. Underneath, it says: «[a]nd our 'liberals' call such an author 'great'! (...) Parents! Save your children from the political seducer of underage children – E. Limonov!» (ibid.)

Nashi then shows various NBP-posters that imitate National Socialist propaganda materials from the 1930s and 1940s. Continuing the «young victims» line of argument, Nashi claims that the NBP regularly produces postcards of naked teenagers in front of «fascist symbols» to raise money. Nashi warns that the NBP is a «totalitarian cult»: «[t]he main attributes of a totalitarian cult are the deification of leaders and the use of special methods for the 'zombification' (*zombirovanie*) of its members.» (ibid.)[48] Nashi does not further elaborate what these methods are, however.

Under the heading «The Fascist Limonov – the only candidate?», Nashi finally describes how some political «speculators» – Rogozin's Rodina and the Communist party – have begun to support these «fascist»: «These facts, together with terrorist acts, 'colored' bandit-like coup d'états, and dirty intrigues (...), are all links in one and the same chain, one and the same campaign against Russia.» (ibid.) In the end, the chain of equivalence includes all opponents of Putin, the personification of a non-fascist Russia.

NBP goals intersect with those of the liberal opposition only insofar as both oppose the Putin regime and demand a more competitive political system (Schwirtz 2007: 78). NBP criticism of the Kremlin is often harsh. It depicts the

---

48 Pro-Kremlin political scientist Pavel Danilin argues that the NBP turns its members into «zombies» as well. His reasoning is that the party has no ideology except for its opposition to Putin and is only interested in «partying» (*tusovat'*) (Danilin 2006: 174).

Putin-regime as a new «Kremlin-oligarchy», agitates against government corruption and demands that the money of oligarchs and officials be distributed among «the majority of the population» (NBP 2004b). Unlike other neo-fascist organizations, the NBP has no history of racially motivated attacks.

However, it has consistently opposed the Putin administration, often by illegal means and «direct action»: on 2 August 2004, seven activists had occupied the health ministry in protest against the monetization reforms, and on 14 December 2004, 39 activists stormed the building of the Presidential Administration (Yasmann 2005). These were only two of dozens of radical actions. Those members of the NBP who participated in the occupations were arrested and received long prison sentences in penal colonies. The organization not only attained a large membership – more than 10'000 by 2003 – but also had considerable appeal among a wide variety of non-conformist youth on both the left and right side of the political spectrum (see: Bowden 2008). Even Pavel Danilin admits that the NBP was the only potential mass movement in 2005 (Danilin 2006: 212).

Nashi's vilification of the NBP and the legal steps taken against the National Bolsheviks had thus less to do with the latter's «fascist» ideas than with its opposition to Putin. Laruelle writes:

> «As practice quickly confirmed, the law against extremism and the new version of Article 282 are rarely used against skinheads or extra-parliamentary parties, but instead are instrumentalized by the authorities to fight against movements that trouble them. In the political field, the principal targets are the National Bolshevik Party.» (Laruelle 2009: 69)

By focusing on the NBP's scandalous rhetoric and symbolism, Nashi manages to present the party as a dangerous «other» that has no place in the legitimate political realm. Judging from the brochure «Unusual Fascism», the NBP is a fascist, pedophiliac and totalitarian cult. In the logic of securitization, the fight against this kind of an enemy legitimizes even violent means.

Nashi's fight against the NBP and other opposition figures may indeed have gone beyond the legal realm. Iakemenko boasted in the past that he had recruited soccer fans for Nashi to use in case of revolutionary situations in Russia:

«If I had to resolve a situation like the one on the Maidan, (...) I would do it very simply: I would get in touch with my colleagues from the fan movement 'Spartak',[49] they would bring about 5'000 of their supporters, armed with the blue plastic chairs they use to fight in the stadium (...). We would bring them to Kiev, (...) and with these chairs they would drive those 100'000 that came to the Maidan into the Dnepr (...).» (Moskovskii Komsomolets 2005) [50]

Even though no Nashi involvement has been proven, there have been numerous violent incidents that journalists and researchers connected to the movement: On 29 August 2005, a group of unknown perpetrators attacked a meeting of the NBP and leftist organizations with baseball bats and other weapons. The police arrested the perpetrators, but they were quickly released (Loskutova 2008: 262). Nashi has denied these allegations and claims that the NBP itself staged the attack. That the attackers were released immediately and without charges nonetheless points to official intervention. In another incident, a young man who purportedly wore a Nashi t-shirt under his sweatshirt, hit opposition leader Garry Kasparov over the head with a chessboard (Romanov 2005).

The fact that a wide public in Russia and abroad considers it plausible that Nashi was behind these attacks points to a serious image problem for the organization. It continues to be seen as prone to violence, which overshadows its self-image as a future pillar of the Russian state.[51]

Nashi's strict discursive separation between *us* and *them*, between friends and enemies, is not conducive to agonistic political competition. The fact that official discourse and Nashi claim they are defending the Russian state against deadly threats does little to facilitate peaceful political processes. Moreover, the use of war memory as a discursive template for understanding the contemporary political struggle in Russia further exacerbated it. The «fas-

---

49 Fan groups of the Moscow soccer club «Spartak Moscow» are notorious for their propensity to violence. The connection between Iakemenko and these groups and their reputed involvement in Nashi has done much to discredit the organization in the eyes of the media.

50 Because of the closeness between Iakemenko and these soccer fans, some authors argue that Nashi welcomed neo-Nazis in its ranks in 2005 in order to fight against the opposition in the streets (Tkachuk 2008).

51 A recent documentary about Nashi called *Putin's Kiss* shows that the violent elements within Nashi also create moral dilemmas for the organization's more progressive commissars, among them the movie's protagonist, former Nashi press secretary Masha Drokova. See: http://putinskissmovie.com/

cists» – in Russian political discourse essentially a synonym for «enemy» (Tumarkin 1994: 222) – cannot be understood as a legitimate opponent but only as a threat to be eliminated. In this sense, the war myth has proven to be a powerful mobilizing tool and a means of claiming moral superiority over opponents in Russia's political struggles in the stormy spring of 2005. At the same time, it contributed to the securitization of political fields and legitimized extraordinary, sometimes violent, measures. Though it remains unclear how much of the abovementioned violence was perpetrated by Nashi activists, the organization discursively created the preconditions for violence.

Nashi after the Orange Revolution

By 2006, the political sphere in Russia was effectively stabilized, or, if you will, securitized. The new law on extremism provided the authorities with the means to limit the actions of critical NGOs. The rebellious Pensioners' Parties and Rodina had been merged to form the «oppositional» *and* pro-Kremlin Just Russia (*Spravedlivaia Rossiia*) Party. Dozens of NBP-activists served long prison-sentences. The demonstrations of liberal youth organizations had been small enough to start with, and police harassment contributed to lowering any potential appeal.

According to its own view, Nashi had fulfilled its task. It had shown that the government was able to keep the upper hand in mobilizing masses of youth in an effective manner and in using the media – particularly state-controlled television – to create effective images of a patriotic, pro-government youth (Hemment 2009: 47). If necessary, Nashi would not hesitate to use soccer fans for «forceful actions» (*silovye aktsii*) against the state's perceived enemies (Tsentr Politicheskoi Informatsii 2005: 11). Andrei thus concludes:

> «In 2007, it was clear that we had fulfilled our most important task, the safeguarding of [Russia's] sovereignty. (…) It became clear that an Orange Revolution was impossible here. To a large extent, this was thanks to Nashi.»

Nashi's real importance is hard to determine. Even the number of its supporters is unclear. Nashi itself claims to have had 300'000 supporters (*storonniki*) active in the organization on the eve of the Duma and presidential elections in 2007/2008 (Atwal 2009: 743). As the event «Our Victory» showed, however, the category of «supporter» is rather vague and may include many who were only partially aware of their involvement with Nashi. Other researchers assume a more conservative estimate of 20'000 commissars and 120'000 supporters (Heller 2008: 2). Since Nashi publishes no reliable statistics about its activities, these numbers are hard to verify.

Another indicator by which to approximate Nashi's influence on the youth sphere is its public recognition in Russia. A survey by the Levada-Center, conducted in August 2005, showed that only ten percent of Russians had heard of Nashi and only two percent shared its goals. Among Russians aged 18-24, these two numbers were slightly higher, at 12% and 4%. Nashi was thus ranked only ninth in terms of name recognition. The best-known youth organizations were skinheads (32%) and the NBP (23%). However, even the young Communists, Iabloko and the SPS ranked ahead of Nashi. Nonetheless, the percentage of Russians between 18 and 24 who shared Nashi's goals, was higher than for any other organization. Half of Russians and even 54% of youth said that they did not share the goals of any of the youth organizations in existence in Russia (Levada-Tsentr 2005).

These low numbers indicate that, in spite of its numerical size and comparative importance, Nashi's influence on broader society was limited. Comparing Nashi's influence to that of the Komsomol, as some have done (Kokorev 2006: 90) therefore seems an exaggeration. Nashi can be compared to the Komsomol only in terms of its equally centralized structure, closeness to the ruling party and patriotic symbolism (Hemment 2009: 44).

A second important question is how successful Nashi has been in its attempts to provide a hegemonic political identity for Russia's youth. Nashi's discourse, which combines the commemoration of the Great Patriotic War with the articulation of a clear enemy and puts the emphasis on a strong and modern state, unites a number of socially significant discursive moments. In this way, Nashi attains a «recognized status in society» (Laruelle 2012b: 76). Ulrich Schmid believes that particularly the use of war memory as a basis for Nashi's ideology is a skillful maneuver:

> «Vor diesem Hintergrund erscheint die Verbindung von Kriegserinnerung und diskursiver Reanimation eines verschwommenen Faschismusbegriffs als geschickte PR-Strategie der *Unsrigen*. Die Jugendorganisation vereinnahmt jene Themen für sich, die ohnehin schon einen zentralen Ort im Bewusstsein der russländischen Bevölkerung einnehmen. Gleichzeitig verleihen die Unsrigen ihren Mitgliedern eine nationale Identität, die hauptsächlich auf der Ne-

gation von 'Feinden' beruht. Dabei wird die komplexe politische Realität radikal auf zwei Pole reduziert: Dem verteufelten 'Faschismus' steht die Lichtgestalt Putin gegenüber, der mutig und entschlossen das Natterngezücht von links und rechts abwehrt.» (Schmid 2006: 14)[52]

Nashi allows young people to inscribe themselves into the official hegemonic project. The emphasis on the role of youth in bringing about the vision of a modern and powerful Russia provides an opportunity for self-realization and participation. In this way, Nashi's discourse does articulate many of the grievances of Russia's youth.

Commissars and supporters were active, put to work in *subbotniki* (voluntary urban cleanup days) and hospitals.[53] For the most part, their social engagement was related to the Great Patriotic War and included the restoration of monuments and care for veterans. To what extent the promise of upward social mobility has materialized for Nashi-activists remains somewhat unclear. A small group – mostly consisting of the highest echelon of federal commissars around Vasilii Iakemenko – has received prestigious jobs working for the state. Many of those who joined Nashi early got employment in local and regional governments. A handful of Nashi commissars have become Edinaia Rossiia deputies in the Duma. The newly founded Agency for Youth Affairs, headed by Iakemenko until June 2012, anchored Nashi's ideas and some activists in official discourse and in the government structures. Furthermore, Laruelle has found that Nashi members have benefited from internships in state-run companies and the government (Laruelle 2012b: 88). Iakemenko furthermore claims that hundreds of innovative projects by Nashi activists received government grants at the summer camp at Lake Seliger (Azar 2012).

---

52 «The connection of war memory and the discursive reanimation of a vague notion of fascism appear to be a good PR-strategy by *Ours* in this context. The youth organization appropriates those topics that already occupy a central position in the consciousness of the Russian population. At the same time, *Ours* endows its members with a national identity that relies heavily on the negation of 'enemies'. The complex political reality is thus radically reduced to two poles: Putin acts as a beacon of hope that opposes devilish 'fascism'. He courageously and resolutely fights the left and right 'offspring of vipers'.»

53 Even Iuliia Malysheva, one of the leaders of Oborona, begrudgingly recognizes the power of Nashi's charitable activities – even if she attributes this power exclusively to Nashi's access to government resources. Malysheva states that when an opposition youth movement «organizes an outreach program at some hospital, Nashi will go to ten hospitals» (Arias-King 2007b: 124). Malysheva sees this kind of «doubling» of actions as a preferred strategy employed by Nashi.

For many, however, the perspective of a durable political or administrative career has remained unrealistic because of the high barriers that exist for entry into this field (Lukov 2006: 85). Nashi commissars, most of whom did not come from the families of the political elite, were far less well positioned for entry into high political positions than members of other youth movements. The youth movement Young Guard *(Molodaia Gvardiia)*,[54] for instance, consists to a significant extent of government officials' sons and daughters.[55]

Neither for Andrei nor for Marina was the promise of upward mobility realized. She has worked as a saleswoman and been temporarily unemployed since her engagement for the movement. Andrei draws an ambivalent conclusion about his involvement in Nashi: «I have lost and gained a lot». Although he does not elaborate what he lost, the gain is clear for him: «I met a huge number of people all over the country and got to know my native land.» The fact that Nashi provides activists with a notion of home and community constitutes its main draw. At the same time, the kind of ideological dedication and time-commitment an organization like Nashi demands comes at a cost.

Paying this price without the concomitant upward mobility creates the potential for frustration. Nashi effectively channels this potential unrest by deflecting it onto various «enemies». The strict discursive separation between «ours» and «them» creates a worldview in which enemies are omnipresent (Borusiak 2005: 20). The template of the Great Patriotic War only encourages

---

[54] The Young Guard is the official youth organization of Edinaia Rossiia. Like Nashi, it was founded after the Orange Revolution and is named after a prominent Soviet youth organization that had carried out sabotage acts against the Nazis during World War II. That the governing party named its youth organization after World War II-partisans attests to the war's central position in official Russian discourse.

[55] Since the December 2011 elections, Surkov's prominent position in the government has been somewhat diminished. He was removed from his influential post in the Presidential Administration and put in charge of innovation. At the beginning of Putin's third term, Surkov served as Prime Minister Medvedev's Chief of Staff but had to resign after he openly criticized Putin. Nashi's fate appears to be quite closely linked to his. Izvestiia reported that Nashi would be disbanded in summer of 2012, a claim that turned out to be premature. Reports of its disbanding in February of 2013 appear more believeable. Izvestiia reporter Evgenii Ershov argues that Molodaia Gvardiia, patronized by Surkov's successor Viacheslav Volodin, will become the main actor in official Russian youth politics (Ershov 2012). How Surkov's reinstatement in the Presidential Administration in September 2013 will affect this equation is as of yet unclear.

such an antagonistic view of the world, as it evokes, even in its figurative use, a warlike image of societal and international relations.

Russian defeats on the international stage, failure to modernize the country, domestic political tensions and corruption, are all presented as the results of enemy activity that subverts Putin's und Nashi's honest efforts. This forestalls self-criticism, which does not contribute to constructive debate in Russia's political sphere.

Nashi's revolutionary rhetoric suggests that some of Russia's problems are grounded in the shortcomings of state institutions: *porazhentsy*-bureaucrats need to be replaced if Russia is to become great again. Such formulations initially caused unrest among officials in Putin's government. The former Chairman of the Federation Council, for instance, Sergei Mironov, called Nashi activists uncontrollable «political wolves».

Initially, it seemed like officials indeed did need to fear Nashi. In March 2005, the movement successfully initiated the dismissal of a senior police officer who had refused to investigate an attack on Nashi's regional offices in Kaluga (Horvath 2011: 16). However, events like this have remained isolated. For the most part, Nashi's hierarchical structure and loyalty to Putin have kept serious criticism of the government in check at the same time that government support has sustained the organization. Danilin wrote in 2006: «[i]f the Presidential Administration controls the further development of the movement as tightly [as it has so far], then the movement has a political perspective.» (Danilin 2006: 205)

The question is only: What kind of political perspective? If the goal is to keep youth controlled as a potential source of instability, then Nashi has done very well. However, if the goal is to engage a significant number of Russia's youth in the construction of a modern and internationally attractive country, the prospects seem bleaker. We have seen that over half of young Russians do not share the goals of any movement. Andrei confirms the importance of overcoming this indifference:

«We want to get people to be active, so they do not only live for their own benefit. And we want to do this all over the country. (...) And now, let me tell you what I think personally. Maybe Nashi will have me thrown in prison for this (*laughs*): I like people who have convictions that are different from mine better than those who do not care about anything. But there are very few of them [people with convictions] in this country.»

Marina similarly states that for her, the main problem is the great indifference among Russian youth.

Unfortunately, the Russian government and Nashi have proactively attempted to identify politically legitimate topics and the groups entitled to a place in the public sphere. Those who do not play by these rules are ignored and sometimes persecuted. If Nashi vilifies and intimidates the few politically active young Russians who oppose the movement's views, it ultimately promotes political indifference instead of engagement.

Nashi's rigid ideological framework and its hierarchical structures mean that the organization can provide only very limited opportunities for meaningful activism and self-realization for young Russians. Omel'chenko demands that official Russian politics treat youth as a subject instead of an object in order to mobilize it in a meaningful way (Omel'chenko 2006: 16). This means giving young people room to articulate their interests and encouraging them to organize in independent associations that can present their grievances through public procedures (Gavrilov 2006: 90). Because of official fears of instability, these avenues have, however, remained largely closed in Putin's securitized youth sphere, often producing either frustration or indifference. If Nashi's purpose was to mobilize youth as a dynamic actor in Russia's political and economic life – to counteract the threat of economic stagnation that Surkov articulates – its success has remained limited at best. In fact, in 2013, considerably fewer illusions about a reinvigorated and innovative Russian economy that is independent of natural resources remain than in 2005.

IV Remember! Nashi and the Bronze Soldier

Nashi credited itself with the deflection of an immediate revolutionary threat for Russia. This does not mean that the organization considered the «post-revolutionary» situation in the country stable. Rather, the domestic – and particularly foreign – enemies discussed in the preceding chapter continued to loom large in official discourse. A sense of threat and antagonism competed with a more agonistic worldview in Nashi's discourse.

Moreover, Russia's relations with many of the post-communist states continued to be strained. A number of political conflicts erupted in 2006 and 2007, in which historical grievances exacerbated geopolitical issues. Russian-Polish relations were difficult as a result of disagreements over oil supplies, Poland's support for the Orange Revolution and the Russian refusal to transfer documents about the Katyn massacre. Russian-German plans to circumvent Polish territory with a new oil pipeline prompted Polish Defense Minister Radek Sikorski to draw analogies to the Molotov-Ribbentrop Pact (Voice of America 2006).[56] Relations between Russia and Latvia, on the other hand, warmed in 2007, when they signed a border treaty on 27 March. The treaty, however, had been drafted ten years earlier. It was only signed in 2007 because of disagreements over whether Latvia joined the USSR voluntarily or by force (Sheeter 2007).

These examples illustrate that the Soviet legacy – and particularly the legacy of World War II – continues to influence the economic and political relations in the former Soviet Union and Eastern Europe. Eastern European and Baltic states have joined the EU and NATO and have tried to distance themselves from Russia. Nonetheless, interdependencies with Russia persist, contributing to often tense and unstable relations.

In most of these conflicts, Nashiplayed a marginal role. In April and May 2007, however, the movement made international headlines during the Rus-

---

56 On energy issues in Eastern Europe, consult the 2009 *Osteuropa* special issue *Blick in die Röhre: Europas Energiepolitik auf dem Prüfstand*, 59, 2.

sian-Estonian conflict over the so-called «Bronze Soldier». Nashi's actions escalated the conflict from a domestic issue to an international diplomatic crisis. The experience of the war lies at the center of not only Russia's but also Estonia's political identity (cf. Brüggemann 2008: 139). This chapter's analysis of Nashi's discourse and actions during the conflict will investigate how the war has served as a template that has framed the organization's view of the conflict. This chapter shows that the official Russian war narrative struggles to accommodate competing interpretations by other formerly Soviet nations. The conflict over the interpretation of history triggered the diplomatic crisis between Russia and the European Union.

I follow Heiko Pääbo's notion of the «securitization of memory» to analyze the conflict over the Bronze Soldier (Pääbo 2008: 7). The late historian Tony Judt called the conflicting war memories in Russia and Eastern Europe in the 1990s a «positive archipelago of vulnerable historical territories» and observed a veritable memory war between different national historical narratives (Judt 2002: 172).[57] In the conflict over the Bronze Soldier, both sides linked the defense of their historical narrative with that of national security. The Bronze Soldier came to embody the referent objects of Russia's political identity and was perceived as a threat to Estonian national security.

History, National Identity and Ethnic Tension

Russian-Estonian relations have been troubled by divergent interpretations of World War II and the plight of ethnic Russians in Estonia, all of which are intertwined, contentious points that shaped the conflict over the Bronze Soldier. The re-appropriation of its history has been at the core of Estonia's nation building process since the late 1980s. Newly founded civic organizations demanded that the Soviet Union acknowledge the existence of the secret protocol of the Molotov-Ribbentrop Pact. The first anti-Soviet mass protests during *glasnost'* demanded recognition of the protocol's immorality. Until 1989, So-

---

57 On «memory wars», see the special issue of the journal *Osteuropa: Geschichtspolitik und Gegenerinnerung. Krieg, Gewalt und Trauma im Osten Europas* (6/2008) und the issue *Pamiat' i Zabvenie: Bitva za proshloe* of the journal *Otechestvennye Zapiski* (5/2008).

viet historiography insisted that the Baltic states had joined the USSR voluntarily in 1940.[58]

The struggle over the interpretation of the secret protocol is linked to World War II more broadly. The Soviet Union and Germany divided up Eastern Europe on 24 August 1939. The Germans ceded the Baltic nations to the Soviet Union. In the following year, the USSR annexed them. In 1939, the Estonian government was forced to agree to the stationing of tens of thousands of Soviet troops on its territory (Sarv and Varju 2005: 8f.). Less than a year later, in June 1940, Estonia «voluntarily» joined the USSR, with 100'000 Soviet troops waiting at its borders. During the war, Estonia was under German and Soviet rule. At the time of the German occupation of Estonia in August 1941, the latter had already lost 100'000 people through deportation, forced recruitment into the Red Army, imprisonment, emigration and execution. At least 4'000 Estonians had been shot by the Soviets (Rahi-Tamm 2005: 27f.). Under the new German rulers, the Estonians collaborated in the deportation and killing of Jews. Of the 5'000 Estonian Jews, most had fled to the Soviet Union before the German invasion. None of the 1'000 who remained survived. It was Estonians, not Germans, who did most of the killing (Maripuu 2004: 410). The occupants also persecuted real and perceived Soviet sympathizers ruthlessly. The Estonian State Commission on Examination of the Policies of Repression estimates that the Germans executed 8'000 Estonians.

A wave of terror followed the Soviet re-conquest of Estonia in 1944. Over 20'000 Estonians were deported to Siberia (Sarv and Varju 2005: 20). After the war, Estonians who had fought in the German Army or against the Red Army as part of resistance movements were subjected to political repression. Between 1944 and 1953, 25'000 to 30'000 persons were sent to prisons and labor camps,[59] of which 11'000 never returned (Rahi-Tamm 2005: 31f.).

---

58   The Congress of People's Deputies of the Soviet Union publicly admitted the existence of the secret protocol of the Molotov-Ribbentrop Pact for the first time in 1989. Before, Soviet propaganda had dismissed it as Western propaganda. The Congress condemned the signing of the secret protocol and admitted that it had violated «the sovereignty and independence of a number of (...) countries» (S"ezd Narodnykh Deputatov SSSR 1989).

59   Many of them were so-called «Forest Brothers». This guerilla organization resisted Soviet rule until 1953. Its fighters numbered between 16'000 and 30'000. 8'000 of them were killed in military confrontations with the Red Army.

A significant ethnic Russian minority in Estonia, however, has no personal memory of the war in Estonia. In the postwar era, the Soviet government promoted the migration of more than 500'000 ethnic Russian workers to the Baltic republics.[60] The vast majority of them only learned the official Soviet narrative of the war, particularly during the Brezhnev era. «Soviet power (...) banned all reference to uncomfortable or conflictual moments save those which retroactively anticipated its own arrival and enforced a new 'fraternity' upon the eastern half of Europe.» (Judt 2002: 172) In this narrative, all resistance against the Soviet system was labeled as «fascist».

Ethnic Russians enjoyed a privileged position in Estonia. Soviet authorities provided immigrants with higher pay and special housing. Furthermore, they usually worked in all-Union enterprises where the working language was Russian, and their children went to Russian-language schools. In essence, these policies created two separate communities in Estonia, with a privileged minority and a more disadvantaged majority (ibid.: 14f.).

Independence led to a drastic reversal in status between the ethnic groups. The rejection of the Soviet experience was a crucial act of identity construction in Estonia (Scheide 2008: 127). This manifested itself in policies aimed at ousting the Russian «colonizers». Estonian politicians hoped that the migrants and their descendants would return to the Russian Federation by their own initiative. When they did not, the authorities began to take discriminatory political measures against the Russian minority.[61]

At the same time, the two ethnicities remain largely self-segregated. The Russians are concentrated in the eastern part of the country and in Tallinn. There are no Russian language television channels in Estonia, which means that the minority rarely takes part in Estonian culture and politics. Its image of Estonia is shaped by the Russian mass media. Furthermore, the new millennium has seen a reassertion of ethnic and cultural identities as a result of

---

60 Between 1944 and 1991, the percentage of Estonians in the country dropped from 97.3 to 61.5 (Vetik and Helemae 2010: 14).
61 The Estonian Law on Citizenship, first passed in 1991 and amended in 1995, recognizes as Estonians only those born in the country before 1940 and after 1991 (see Thompson 1998: 111ff.). Those who wanted citizenship had to apply for naturalization, pass strict Estonian language requirements and take a pledge of allegiance. Only about forty percent of the ethnic Russians in Estonia are citizens today. A quarter are still of «undefined citizenship» (stateless). The rest have applied for Russian passports (Pääbo 2008: 9).

globalization. This tendency has solidified identity divisions between ethnic Russians and Estonians (ibid.: 150f.).[62]

The fact that the ethnic Russian minority has close ties to the Russian Federation adds an international dimension to the interethnic tensions in Estonia. Even though the Russian Federation unconditionally recognized the independence of the Baltic states in 1991, the status of the Russian minority remains a frequent source of international conflict. In recent years, the two countries' interpretations of the past have become equally contentious. Both have insisted increasingly forcefully on their nationalist narratives. This disagreement has escalated into physical conflicts over war monuments.

In 2002, a group installed a monument in the Estonian town of Pärnu, dedicated to the Estonians «who died for their native land and a free Europe in the second war of liberation 1940-1945». The helmet of the soldier on the monument carried SS-insignia, undermining the seemingly inclusive message.[63] After protests from Europe, the monument was disassembled.

However, two years later it was re-erected in the town of Lihula. This time, the SS-insignia were removed, and the inscription read «To the Estonian men who fought in 1940-1945 against Bolshevism and for the restoration of Estonian independence».[64] The soldier, however, still wore a German uniform,

---

62   Because of their lack of language skills, many ethnic Russians in Estonia also struggle in the labor market. Nonetheless, ethnic Russians profited from the economic growth in Estonia. Various authors see a rapprochement of ethnic Russians and Estonians in the second half of the 1990s on the basis of shared, mostly materialistic, values (Vihalemm 2008: 91; Ehala 2009: 151). Ehala further shows that the number of ethnic Russians who learned Estonian «satisfactorily» rose from 43 percent in 1993 to 67 percent in 1999 (Ehala 2009: 149).

63   Many Estonians fought in the Wehrmacht in so-called «Ostbataillons». Estonians also made up two SS-divisions. Their total number in German military service is estimated at 20'000 (Sarv and Varju 2005: 18). The Germans applied techniques of forced recruitment. The extent to which Estonians joined the German Army voluntarily is thus subject to debate. Latvians were not indicted for war crimes at Nuremberg because they had been forcefully recruited (Scheide 2008: 121).

64   In February of 1944, former Prime Minister Jüri Uluots founded the «National Committee of the Republic of Estonia». This secret organization fought for Estonia's independence and against the advancing Red Army with German support. Estonian resistance forced the Red Army's temporary retreat, and often, Estonians were on both sides of the battle lines. When the Germans began their retreat from the Baltic states in September 1944, Estonian resistance crumbled. Nonetheless, an independent Estonian state was declared on 18 September and lasted for five days. When the Red Army reached Tallinn on 22 September, it toppled the Estonian government under Jüri Uluots and reestablished a Soviet republic.

with the Cross of Liberty on the collar. Moreover, the nationalist and governor of Lihula parish, Tiit Madison, stated at the unveiling: «This monument is for people who had to choose between two evils, and they chose the less evil one» (BBC 2004). He thus explicitly stated that the Soviet regime had been worse than the National Socialist regime.

The embarrassment for the young EU member state was so great that Prime Minister Juhan Parts' government decided to remove the monument. When the police carried out the order, clashes ensued with demonstrators who wanted to make sure the statue stayed in place (Münch 2008: 24).

After September 2004, debates about the commemoration of the war in Estonia became increasingly heated. Extreme positions on both sides started to dominate the debate in the media (Ehala 2009: 153). The controversy began to affect relations between Estonia and Russia. Facing political protests at home, Estonian president Arnold Rüüte decided to decline the invitation to the festivities for the 60th anniversary of victory in Moscow in 2005.

Vladimir Putin contributed to the animosity. In an interview with the French newspaper *Le Figaro*, he rejected Baltic states' demands for financial compensation in 2004 and for an apology from Russia. He maintained that the Supreme Soviet's condemnation of the Molotov-Ribbentrop Pact in 1989 was enough for Russia to fulfill its historical responsibility. The Baltic states, he added, were incapable of putting the issue to rest:

«[T]hey continue to demand some kind of 'contrition' (*pokaianie*) from Russia. I believe that it is their goal to garner attention. In this way, they try to justify their governments' (...) discriminating policies against significant parts of their own, Russian-language populations and to block out their shameful past as [Nazi] collaborators.» (Rossiiskaia Gazeta 2005: 3)

Putin thus presents Baltic grievances as illegitimate and merely aimed at distracting from their own historical and contemporary wrongdoings. Russian and Estonian official discourses on the war were monologues at loggerheads already in 2005. This rhetorical belligerence set the stage for the conflict over the Bronze Soldier.

The Bronze Soldier

The fact that the spark of the «memory war» (Pääbo 2008: 7) was ignited over the Bronze Soldier is not surprising. The monument, a statue of a Soviet soldier erected in downtown Tallinn after the war, was the most important memorial of the Great Patriotic War in Estonia. It had been a subject of contention since the end of the war: on 8 May 1946, a group of schoolchildren blew up the older monument that had stood on Tallinn's Tõnismägi Square after victory. «Alesha», as the Bronze Soldier is sometimes affectionately called, was unveiled on 22 September 1947, the anniversary of the Red Army's conquest of Tallinn.

Following French historian Pierre Nora, the Bronze Soldier can be seen as a realm of memory: a place of symbolic excess existing on a material as well as a symbolic level that is full of multilayered, at times conflicting meaning (Nora 1990: 33). It marked downtown Tallinn as Soviet and provided the location for the commemoration of the Soviet war narrative (Scheide 2008: 126). The date of its unveiling, and the date of the attacks against the monument – 8 May is the day on which the end of World War II is celebrated in the West – were both highly symbolic.

Since 1991, the Bronze Soldier's significance has only become more complex. Ehala identifies at least four levels of meaning: First, it commemorates all the fallen of World War II, which accounts for the fact that it stood in downtown Tallinn for 16 years after independence.[65] Secondly, it stands for the Soviet victory. It is thus a place of emotional attachment for Estonia's ethnic Russian population that implicitly connects it to Russia. Furthermore, the Bronze Soldier is a symbol for the liberation of Estonia from Nazi Germany. Finally, in recent years, Estonian nationalists have come to see the monument as a symbol of Soviet occupation (Ehala 2009: 144f.).

After the removal of the monument in Lihula, Estonian nationalists began to demand that the Bronze Soldier be displaced as well.[66] On 9 May 2005, young Estonians threw red paint at it. The symbolic meanings of the Bronze Soldier clashed physically for the first time on 9 May 2006. A nationalist with an Estonian flag walked into the traditional holiday celebration of ethnic Russians. Estonian police had to remove him to prevent major unrest (Brügge-

---

65 Ehala writes that even in 2007, 67% of the Estonian population either wanted the Bronze Soldier to stay in place or were undecided about what to do with it (Ehala 2009: 44).

66 Already on the 50th anniversary of victory in the Great Patriotic War in 1995, Estonian nationalists called for the removal of the Bronze Soldier, but their demand was not met.

mann 2008: 140). An Estonian television team recorded the incident. It caused great outrage and was politically exploited. Subsequently, the Estonian Reform Party under Andrus Ansip ran an election campaign with the promise to remove the Bronze Soldier from downtown Tallinn within a year (Ehala 2009: 142).

In response to the events of May 2006, a group of ethnic Russians founded the organization Night Watch (*nochnoi dozor*) and held nightly vigils in front of the Bronze Soldier, stating that they would protect it at all costs. Night Watch's view of history is very similar to that of Nashi, and the two organizations supported each other during the protests against the removal of the Bronze Soldier. According to one of its leaders, Dmitrii Linter, Night Watch had almost 200 members in 2009. Its mission consisted in defending the memory of World War II and in the fight against historical revisionists who «belittled» Soviet efforts in the war, he explained:

> «Estonia became a bridgehead (*platsdarm*), where new forms of activities, new forms of influencing mass consciousness, were adopted to reevaluate the course of World War II and to weaken Russia's role in the world community.» (Zavtra 2009)

Further on, Linter clarified that he believed the United States played a significant role in these activities, all of which were part of an «information war» (ibid.). This view of the politics of history is in line with those aspects of official discourse that emphasize the struggle over history's interpretation as a tool in geopolitical competition.

The Estonian Security Police has consistently claimed that Night Watch and its political ally, the marginal ethnic Russian Constitution Party, were financed and controlled by the Russian Foreign Intelligence Service SVR (Estonian Security Police 2008: 8f.). A meeting of the First Secretary of the Russian embassy in Estonia, Vadim Vasil'ev, with representatives of the Constitution Party and Night Watch in April of 2007 led to allegations that they planned the riots of 26-27 April together (Shegedin et al. 2007).

These organizations are not, however, representative of the ethnic Russians in Estonia. The Constitution Party garnered less than one percent of the votes in the 2007 elections. Since 1991, the vast majority of the ethnic Russian vote has gone to the Centre Party of Edgar Savisaar, who signed a cooperation agreement with Edinaia Rossiia (Vihalemm 2008: 77). The Centre

Party nonetheless supported the relocation of the Bronze Soldier under certain conditions and organized a roundtable to find a way of carrying it out that would satisfy all parties. Night Watch strongly criticized this «defeatism» (Zaks 2006).

On the eve of the «Bronze Nights», as the riots on 26-27 April have often been called, relations between Estonia and Russia, and between ethnic Estonians and Russians in the Baltic country were thus caught in a web of unresolved identity issues. Discursively, attempts to securitize the discussion co-existed with efforts to resolve and defuse the situation by «normal» political means. When Andrus Ansip followed through on his election promise to remove the Bronze Soldier, however, lines between the ethnic groups and the two states quickly solidified.

Nashi and the First Protests

Nashi had not systematically cultivated the memory conflict with Estonia before April 2007. Subsequently, however, the movement set up an entire dossier on «Estonian State Fascism» (Nashi 2006). The first entry originated on 16 November 2006, when 40 commissars and supporters protested in front of the Estonian embassy in Moscow against plans to move the Bronze Soldier. The Estonians' actions were compared to those of «grave desecrators» who spray swastikas on tombstones (ibid.).

The next entry is dated 24 January 2007, when Nashi, Molodaia Gvardiia, Young Russia (*Rossiia Molodaia*)[67] and the Locals (*Mestnye*) protested on Manezhnaia Square in Moscow against the «Protection of War Graves Act». Estonian parliament passed this act, which gave the government the legal authority to move war graves, on 10 January 2007.[68] Three hundred Nashi

---

67 *Rossiia Molodaia* is another pro-Kremlin youth group. It was founded in 2005 in order to «prevent any revolution and any coup that leads to the colonization of Russia». Furthermore, the organization wanted to make sure that no one «makes history in our stead» (Rossiia Molodaia 2005). In 2009, Young Russia declared that the danger of a coup was over now that Medvedev had assumed power, and that it would focus on fighting Scientology.

68 The «Protection of War Graves Act» provided the Estonian Ministry of Defense with the authority to move war graves «located in an unsuitable place», particularly in «parks, other green areas and buildings within densely populated areas outside of cemeteries» (Riigikogu 2007). The Bronze Soldier was removed based on this legal code.

commissars dressed up in World War II-era Soviet uniforms and imitated the pose of the Bronze Soldier, whom they referred to as «warrior-liberator» (*voin-osvoboditel'*). In their right hands, they each held a helmet, and they pressed their left hands against their bodies.

In its press release, Nashi declared that these 300 commissars were ready to travel to Estonia and become «living monuments» if the Estonian government removed the Bronze Soldier. Like in 2005, Nashi stressed historical continuity and claimed to fight for the historical memory of the Russian people. In this case, the Nashi activists literally embodied Russian memory as «living memorials». Nashi founder Iakemenko stated:

> «We do not fight for the monument (*pamiatnik*), but for memory (*pamiat'*) (…). They can remove the monument, but what will they do with the 145 million Russians, what will they do with the more than one million Estonians, of which each one (…) is a living monument to those heroes to whom we owe our lives?» (Nashi 2007b)

The signifier «Bronze Soldier» is highly overdetermined in meaning. In Nashi's discourse, it stands not only for the memory of ethnic Russians in Estonia and the Russian people. It becomes the foundation for the very existence of all postwar generations, all of which owe their lives to the victory their predecessors had attained. To underscore this historical continuity, Nashi threatened that if the Estonian government removed one monument, it would get «thousands of living ones», each one a Nashi activist (ibid.).

At 4.30 am on 26 April, Estonian police forces drove up to Tönismägi Square in central Tallinn. Three activists of Night Watch who had been waiting in a car by the square were dragged out and arrested. The police forces set up a tent that covered the Bronze Soldier and large parts of the square. The Estonian government declared that it was beginning archeological work on the square to determine where exactly the remains of the 13 Soviet soldiers buried there since World War II lay. The government's justification for excavating and reburying them was that the soldiers supposedly lay directly underneath a bus depot: Andrus Ansip declared that the graves could easily be «defiled» because of this proximity and guaranteed that the reburial would be executed according to international norms (Shegedin et al. 2007).

At this point, the Estonian government insisted that no decision had been made to move the monument (Zygar' 2007a). Throughout the day, small groups of ethnic Russians and Night Watch activists protested, mostly peacefully. Nine people were arrested after screaming insults. Nonetheless, Ansip declared on 26 April that he expected no major clashes in Tallinn.

On the diplomatic front, however, patience was quickly wearing thin. On 23 April, the Russian Ministry of Foreign Affairs had demanded that Estonia move neither the Bronze Soldier nor the remains of the soldiers. This move, the ministry claimed, would violate «the elementary principles of human morals and humanism» and constituted an attempt to rewrite the history of the war. It dismissed Ansip's reasoning as a ploy.

In response, the Estonian Ministry of Foreign Affairs declared that the Russian protest was full of «deliberate lies and slander». Only Vladimir Zhirinovskii, leader of the Liberal Democratic Party and often a notorious *agent provocateur*, criticized the Russian government's stance:

> «They have the right to disassemble [the monument]. It is a foreign country. It would not be bad if we first focused on what is going on in Russia itself. We ourselves are disassembling monuments.» (*quoted in*: Shegedin et al. 2007)

This was one of very few statements made by Russian politicians that questioned Russia's right to interfere in Estonia's domestic affairs. The Estonians and the European Union would continue to emphasize that the removal of the statue was an issue of domestic, not international, politics throughout the conflict. Zhirinovskii further referenced the recent move of a monument to Soviet pilots from the Great Patriotic War in the Moscow suburb of Khimki to make room for the widening of a highway.[69] Events on the ground, however, soon ended these discreet political discussions.

Bronze Nights

In the evening of the 26th, protests in Tallinn escalated. According to a Night Watch activist interviewed by the Russian newspaper *Kommersant"*, the number of mostly young protesters rose rapidly to about 3'000 (Zygar' et al. 2007a). The BBC estimated approximately 1'000 protesters (BBC 2007a). Among the demonstrators, rumors had circulated that the Bronze Soldier had

---

[69] Even though the local veteran association had asked for this particular move, it was carried out so sloppily that journalists found human bones sticking out of the ground after all human remains had supposedly been cleared. The incident caused great controversy in Russia and was used by representatives of the Estonian state to point out what they considered to be Russian hypocrisy (Kashin 2007).

been moved or destroyed. When they tried to break through the police cordon to gain access to the monument, the police used tear gas, shock grenades, rubber bullets and clubs.

After being driven away from Tönismägi Square, protesters smashed windows at the Justice Ministry, ransacked the offices of Andrus Ansip's Reform Party and looted stores in Tallinn's old town. The police made 300 arrests and temporarily detained 468 persons. Over 40 were injured, and one young ethnic Russian was killed (ibid.). At 3.40 am, the Estonian government decided in an emergency meeting to move the Bronze Soldier to a war cemetery on the outskirts of Tallinn immediately.

The Estonian government, initially overwhelmed by the intensity of protests, cracked down on them, at times with indiscriminate violence. Protesters were crammed into a hangar in the harbor, banned from communicating with lawyers or relatives and apparently beaten. The Estonian courts subsequently acquitted the police of all complaints of wrongdoing and justified its actions by arguing that the riots had endangered national security (Münch 2008: 50f.).

Nashi's reaction to the removal and the crackdown on the protests contained harsh language and serious accusations against Estonia:

> «The Estonian authorities who allow fascists to walk the streets and beat war veterans have today removed the monument to the Soviet soldier from downtown Tallinn and desecrated the fraternal graves (*bratskie mogily*) of the fallen soldiers that were buried there. First they called the fallen 'occupiers'. Then the Prime Minister declared that these were the graves of drunks (*p'ianits*) and marauders. People came to the monument. Some came to defend the monument and the memory of the fallen. Others – to pay their respect. (…) They chased them with gas, dispersed them with water cannons, beat them, cracked their skulls. They murdered one defender of the monument. The fascist authorities of Estonia act like fascists are supposed to: they defile graves, remove monuments, maim and kill people, to whom the memory of the fallen is dear.» (Nashi 2007c)

In this statement, Nashi attributed the signifier «fascist» to the Estonian authorities to emphasize the absolute immorality of their actions. Nashi rejected the Estonian claim that the remains of the Soviet soldiers were moved in accordance with international norms. By referring to past demonstrations of Estonian nationalists and veterans who fought with the German Army or the SS,

Nashi recognized ethnic Russians and the Russian memory of World War II as a whole as victims of Estonian «fascist» aggression and disrespect.

Particularly Andrus Ansip's statement on 24 April enraged Nashi and the wider Russian public. He explained that it was necessary to open the graves by Tönismägi Square to determine the identity of those buried there and that a «total [drinking] binge» had occurred among Soviet soldiers after they liberated Tallinn. As a result, he claimed, soldiers were run over by tanks and might have been buried in the mass graves. Ansip said that those buried might have been executed looters or patients from a nearby hospital (Regnum 2007).

Andrei, the Nashi commissar from St. Petersburg, explains that this statement incensed Nashi activists more than the removal of the monument:

> «For us the relocation was an insult to our state and to all those who fought against fascism. But an ever bigger insult were the words of the Prime Minister, saying that no warriors and fighters against fascism were buried under the monument, but only drunk marauders. And when he said that, he insulted all of the soldiers that had actually fallen in the fight against fascism.»

For Andrei and Nashi, the removal of the monument was an insult to the memory of the Russian soldiers who had died in the war. Interestingly, however, Andrei also equated the attack against the Bronze Soldier with an attack on the Russian state. Nashi turned the protest against the monument's removal and the defense of the official war narrative into an issue concerning Russia's national honor. As we will see below, Nashi would also try to articulate this as a national security concern.

On 27 April, the protests spread to Moscow. Youth organizations, initially headed by the Eurasian Youth Union, began to picket the Estonian embassy. At 2 pm, Nashi took over the protest, joined by Molodaia Gvardiia and the youth organization of the Liberal Democratic Party.

Nashi used the outrage over the monument's removal for mobilization purposes: Nashi stated that it «is obligated to do everything to stop Estonian fascism» and emphasized, «if OUR[70] fathers and grandfathers defeated fascism sixty years ago, we must defeat it today». In order to do so, Nashi called for

---

70   The capitalized OUR once more emphasizes the close connection between the organization's name, which means «ours» and Russia as a whole. Russians are often referred to as «ours» as well. Nashi thus claims to represent all of Russia.

economic and political sanctions against Estonia. Furthermore, the organization demanded that the removal of the Bronze Soldier and the suppression of the riots be brought before the UN Security Council.

To emphasize this request, Nashi called upon «all those who have a conscience, all those who hold dear the memory [of the fallen], who hate fascism, who are not ready to tolerate the humiliation of OUR soldiers, the humiliation of our native land» to assemble before the Estonian embassy in Moscow (Nashi 2007c). Immediately after the riots in Tallinn, the Estonian embassy became the next focal point of the conflict, which had already assumed warlike traits in Nashi's discourse.[71]

Events at the Estonian Embassy

In the late afternoon of 27 April, Nashi declared its intention to picket the Estonian embassy day and night (Nashi 2007d). According to the movement, most of the protesters were clad in uniforms from World War II. Nashi demanded an apology from the Estonian ambassador to Russia, Marina Kaljurand, and the restoration of the Bronze Soldier in downtown Tallinn. If she refused, Nashi would «insist that the Estonian ambassador leave Russia and would be ready to accompany Kaljurand to the airport Sheremetovo.» (ibid.). In the evening, Nashi began to play loud music in front of the embassy, and activists in groups of 30 took shifts, relieving each other periodically. According to Nashi, throughout the protests, up to 1'000 activists were in front of the embassy at any one time (Nashi 2007g).

Already on 27 April, 80 Nashi activists had effectively shut down the Estonian embassy. When Kaljurand tried to leave the premises in her car to head to a television interview with *Russia Today*, the activists blocked the exit, and the ambassador had to return to the embassy. The Russian police and special paramilitary OMON troops did not restrain the Nashi activists (Nashi 2007e).

This surprisingly tolerant attitude of Russian police forces in Moscow indicates at least implicit state support for the protests and contrasted sharply with that of their colleagues elsewhere in Russia. Though the police initially

---

71 The question of whether Nashi activists participated in the riots remains a subject of debate. *Kommersant"* quotes evidence from the Estonian newspaper *Postimees* that Nashi activists arrived at the Meriton Grand Hotel Tallinn immediately before the riots (Shegedin et al. 2007). Nashi denied any involvement.

tolerated the protest of 150 Nashi activists in front of the Estonian consulate in St. Petersburg, it arrested eight Nashi members when they tried to picket the consulate around the clock (Nashi 2007f.). In a similar vein, police in the Ivangorod Raion arrested 11 Nashi activists who tried to block the main throughway between Estonia and Russia, the *Tallinskoe Shosse*. The commissars tried to stop trucks with Estonian license plates as part of an attempted blockade of Estonian goods (Nashi 2007g).

The diplomatic crisis between Russia and Estonia was in full swing by the morning of 28 April. Ene Ergma, Speaker of the Estonian parliament, called the riots a «planned provocation», instigated by those «who want to destroy everything that Boris Nikolaevich Yeltsin founded» – referring to the Russian government (*quoted in*: Zygar' et al. 2007a). On the other side of the debate, Sergei Mironov called for the suspension of diplomatic relations between the two countries. Various Duma members demanded sanctions against Estonia. The Russian Meat Association followed suit and began to boycott Estonian meat. Various supermarket chains cleared Estonian goods from their shelves (ibid.). Zhirinovskii performed an amazing volte-face in one single day. After showing sympathy for Estonian actions the day before, he threatened that if the country did not put the monument back in place, «our landing division from Pskov might move to the Estonian border and lose its way. There, they organize a nightmarish night.» (*quoted in*: ibid.) At around the same time, hackers using Russian government servers organized a large-scale attack on Estonian government servers.[72]

On 29 April, Nashi took a further step to escalate the conflict rhetorically. Supported by Molodaia Gvardiia and Mestnye, Vasilii Iakemenko presented an ultimatum to the Estonian ambassador. Estonia had ignored all protests, moved the monument and murdered a defender of the monument, Nashi wrote. For this reason, the time had come to «transition from words to deeds» and set an ultimatum:

---

72 Estonian government officials, among them also Foreign Minister Urman Paet, claimed that the hacker attacks originated from the computers of the Russian Presidential Administration (Zygar' 2007a). The Estonian government had to subsequently admit that it possessed no proof for these allegations (Ria Novosti 2007). The origins of hacker attacks are notoriously difficult to prove. There have also been claims that Nashi was behind the attacks, as one activist of the movement, Konstantin Goloskov, stated that he had been involved (Yasmann 2007).

> «If the Estonian authorities do not restore the monument of the warrior-liberator to its previous place by 1 May, we will set a date for the dismantling of Estonia's embassy in Moscow. If Estonia found a 'lawful' way of dismantling the monument to the heroes that saved Europe from fascism, we can certainly find a lawful way of disassembling the building of the Estonian embassy and moving it first to the outskirts of Moscow and then of the Russian state.» (Nashi 2007h)

In this ultimatum, Nashi elevated the Bronze Soldier to a symbol of the Russian state equal in significance to an embassy. Nashi used Estonia's «fascism» to justify the demand for a removal of its embassy. Estonia's actions against the Bronze Soldier and against war memory amounted to a warlike situation, in which all means were justified.

Nashi writes:

> «In 1991, Estonia received independence. As it seemed at the time – for the creation of a solid, free and independent state. As it turns out now – for the consolidation of fascism and the rewriting of history, for endless provocations against Russia. (…) History shows – fascists do not understand words, persuasion, appeals to common sense and consciousness. They only understand resolute action. Let us get it across to them. The first step was the blockade of the embassy. The second will be its dismantling. On our land, there is no room for fascists.» (ibid.)

To Nashi, Estonia abused the independence it *received* from Moscow to become a fascist state and a Russian enemy. The Estonians abused the freedom they were granted by a generous Russia. By trying to rewrite history, the Estonians had effectively become fascist and thus the constitutive outside of Nashi's discourse. The expulsion of these fascists was thus the task of Nashi activists, just as the expulsion of the Germans had been the task of Soviet soldiers 60 years previously.

In order to show that Nashi's demands enjoyed popular support, it collected signatures for its ultimatum. Within two days, Nashi declared, it had assembled over 100'000 (Nashi 2007i). Nonetheless, official support for the plan was not forthcoming: Mironov, the Federation Council chairman who had advocated the suspension of diplomatic relations between the two countries, called Nashi's demand «wrong» and unworthy of a great power (Itar-Tass 2007). Putin remained quiet throughout Nashi's picket of the embassy.

On 1 May, Nashi called for a redoubling of Russian efforts. In a passage reminiscent of Nashi's manifesto, the movement identifies Russia's weakness in the 1990s as the underlying reason for the conflict over the Bronze Soldier. Only this weakness had enabled the Estonians to turn Russians into «second-class people» and to remove the monument. The weakness had led to «the death of the Russian boy (*russkii paren'*) Dmitrii Ganin», who had been stabbed on the night of the riots. «If we do not overcome this weakness, if we do not stop humiliating ourselves, monuments will continue to fall time and again, and people will die» (Nashi 2007i). Nashi thus called for a concerted response by citizens, officials and state institutions aimed at dismantling the Estonian embassy, which, according to Nashi's plans, was to begin on 12 June.[73]

Nashi presents this struggle as one of life and death and uses the example of Ganin to underline its acuteness. The circumstances surrounding his death remain unclear. The official Estonian police report maintained that the ethnic Russian Ganin had been one of the rioters, as they found stolen goods in his pockets (Münch 2008: 48). The Russian Duma delegation that visited Estonia immediately after the riots accused the Estonian police of deliberately not calling an ambulance for thirty minutes and thus letting him die. The Estonian authorities did arrest two young ethnic Estonians for the murder on 14 May, but observers remained skeptical of their guilt, as the arrests came right before the EU-Russia-Summit on 18 May (Solov'ev and Shegedin 2007).

Nashi used the mystery surrounding Ganin's death to argue that the Estonian «fascists» had «murdered» Ganin (Nashi 2007j). Nashi organized moments of silence at various protests and meetings in late April and early May. In one of them in front of the Estonian embassy in Moscow on 28 April, Iakemenko mentioned him along with Boris Yeltsin and the cellist Mstislav Rostropovich, as one of the «great people» who had died in the same week. Marina Zade-

---

73 Lassila's interpretation of this ultimatum is somewhat different from mine. He believes that the ultimatum's political style resorted to the Soviet tradition of *steb* (banter), in which official discourse was mocked and led *ad absurdum* by an overly literal identification with it. However, because of the development of events and Nashi's emotional commitment to war memory, it was ultimately forced to stick to this «absurd» demand, inevitably leading to a «symbolic loss» for Nashi (Lassila 2012a: 126, 132).

mit'kova, the leader of Nashi in Voronezh, even presented Ganin's death as a part of «genocide against the Russian people»:

> «We have come here, and we have stood here for three days already. We will not permit a rebirth of fascism, because if we do, the death of 27 million Soviet soldiers was in vain. If one of us leaves from here, this means that we have died.» (ibid.)

This kind of rhetoric served an important mobilizational purpose, as Nashi upheld its blockade for almost a week.

On a discursive level, Russia's weakness in the 1990s dislocates the hegemonic discourse of Russian strength and power. In official Russian discourse, the Baltic states are closely linked to the loss of the Soviet empire and fears of geopolitical weakness. The Russian Federation has never renounced its right to assert influence in the post-Soviet space, or the «near abroad». Andrei Tsygankov writes:

> «The idea of reestablishing and consolidating Russia's exclusive sphere of influence throughout the former Soviet Union without military intervention has supplanted the recognition of the independence and sovereignty of the former Soviet republics.» (Tsygankov 1997: 252)

As we saw in chapter 1, the reassertion of Russia's influence in its «backyard» is one of the cornerstones of Putin's hegemonic project.

If it is true, then, that Russian political identity is closely tied to the state, as I suggest, the Baltic states represent a particular dislocation of this identity. The Baltic states, once an integral part of the USSR, are today independent and pursue a foreign policy aimed at distancing themselves from Russia. The removal of the symbolically overdetermined Bronze Soldier and Russia's powerlessness to restore it come to symbolize Russian weakness in Nashi's discourse. Only the call for decisive countermeasures could compensate for this dislocation.

The International Dimension

The fact that Estonia is a member of the European Union inevitably added an international dimension to the controversy over the Bronze Soldier. Initially, however, the European Union insisted that the conflict was a domestic Estonian issue and refused to get involved. As the tensions and Russian attacks –

from hackers and from Nashi – intensified, however, European politicians were compelled to take action.

Interestingly, Nashi, too, called for an internationalization of the conflict on 27 April: it demanded that the leadership of the European Union condemn Estonia for its actions and that «the question of the defilement of the mass grave and the destruction of the monument, of the beating and murder of its defenders» be put before the UN security council (Nashi 2007c).

The first European intervention was a phone call between German Chancellor Angela Merkel and President Vladimir Putin on 28 April. Her diplomatic request was «moderation on both sides». As the riots in Tallinn had ended by this point, her remarks were undoubtedly directed against Nashi's actions. Merkel's call, in addition to the increased international attention directed at the events in Moscow, led to the arrest of a handful of activists. They had thrown pig feet and a pig's head symbolizing the Estonian Prime Minister Andrus Ansip onto the territory of the embassy. The special paramilitary unit OMON restrained Nashi activists as they tried to prevent ambassador Kaljurand from leaving the embassy in her car a second time. Other activists who had thrown rocks at the windows of the embassy evaded arrest (Savina and Pushkarskaia 2007).

In this phase of the conflict, it was slowly becoming clear that Nashi would not receive official support for its demands. Russian companies did not cut off business relations with Estonia, nor did the Foreign Ministry issue travel bans against representatives of the Estonian state (Nashi 2007c). The latter would have meant the implementation of travel bans against representatives of a EU member state. The political price of such a limitation would have been high for Russia, and the government was not willing to pay it in order to pacify the patriotic fervor in Russia.

The turning point against Nashi came on 2 May. Ambassador Marina Kaljurand was scheduled to hold a press conference on the events surrounding the Bronze Soldier in the editorial building of the Russian weekly *Argumenty i Fakty*. According to Nashi, a group of 250 activists (other sources counted 150) from various pro-Kremlin youth organizations had gathered in front of the building with posters and chants claiming «victory will be ours» and «no to fascism!» Nashi declared it wanted to ask the ambassador six questions. Its activists were denied access to the press conference. In a tension-laden atmosphere, Vasilii Iakemenko told the news agency Interfax:

> «We have entered the building and want to ask the Estonian ambassador our questions. Apparently we are superfluous in our own country. We have handed our questions to journalists and are waiting for the end of the press conference. I ask everyone to remain calm and to leave the territory around the editorial building of *Argumenty i Fakty*. We will wait quietly for the end of the press conference.» (Interfax 2007)

Iakemenko's statement expresses both a frustration over Nashi's futile attempts and the lack of official support («we are superfluous in our own country»). At the same time, there appears to be an implicit concern that he might lose control over the Nashi activists, who were clearly riled up. Iakemenko's worries were not unfounded. The Nashi activists inside of the building did not heed his words. Sixteen of them entered the room in which the press conference was held and rushed to the podium where the ambassador was standing. Nashi later stated that one of its activists merely wanted to hand Kaljurand a bouquet of dandelions (Nashi 2007k).[74] According to *The New York Times*, however, the activists were trying to rush the podium, when bodyguards repelled them with pepper spray (Myers 2007).

Following this incident, Nashi set up another blockade outside of the Estonian embassy. Iakemenko, apparently also carried away by the general frenzy among Nashi activists, declared that his organization had assumed the function of the «law enforcement agencies» (Zygar' et al. 2007b).

When a car carrying a Swedish diplomat arrived at the embassy, Nashi surrounded it, suspecting Kaljurand to be inside. They detained the car for fifteen minutes and broke off one of the side view mirrors. Subsequently, the activists also stopped Kaljurand's car and tore the Estonian flag off of it.

In spite of its militant and violent actions, Nashi presented itself as the victim. In a statement that referred to the pepper spray attack but remained silent about the other events of the day, the movement wrote, «Estonians on the

---

[74] One can only speculate about the symbolic meaning of the dandelion: it is sometimes associated with love and faithfulness. In northern countries, however, where it is not native, it is often considered an invasive species and a weed. It seems probable that Nashi wanted to convey the latter meaning.

territory of the Russian state have begun to use fascist methods against those that protect the memory of their forefathers» (Nashi 2007l).
Nashi was alone in this interpretation of the events. The Russian Ministry of Foreign Affairs declined to comment on the events in Moscow. One of its spokesmen stated drily: «We still believe that the tension and the reaction of civil society in Russia were provoked.» (*quoted in*: Myers 2007) No further official support for Nashi was forthcoming.
Internationally, Nashi's actions were already causing a diplomatic crisis. Its physical attacks on diplomats were widely considered to be unacceptable. Both Estonia and Sweden delivered formal notes of protest condemning the physical attacks against their diplomats. Above and beyond this, «a tornado of statements from Western countries came down on Moscow», wrote *Kommersant"* (Solov'ev 2007b). For the most part, these were protests against Russia's violation of the Vienna Convention, which ensures the protection of diplomats. Estonian President Toomas Hendrik Ilves had accused Russia of violating this convention throughout the picketing of the embassy and called Nashi's actions «psychological terror» (Solov'ev 2007a). The strongest statement came from NATO:

> «NATO is deeply concerned by threats to the physical safety of Estonian diplomatic staff, including the Ambassador, in Moscow, as well as intimidation at the Estonian Embassy. These actions are unacceptable, and must be stopped immediately.» (NATO 2007).

American diplomats also demanded respect for the Vienna Convention. State Department spokesman Tom Casey asked Russia to stop its harsh rhetoric and prevent further escalation of the conflict. Daniel Fried, advisor to Condoleezza Rice, also urged Estonia to show more sensitivity toward the Russian ethnic minority. (*quoted in*: Solov'ev 2007b)
The European Commission showed concern over the «rising tensions around the Estonian embassy»: «we decisively demand that the Russian authorities fulfill their obligations with regards to the Vienna Convention» (*quoted in*: Solov'ev and Zygar' 2007).
On 3 May, Germany, which held the presidency of the European Union in the first semester of 2007, also became active. Foreign Minister Frank-Walter Steinmeier called his colleague Sergei Lavrov, who assured him that the se-

curity and freedom of movement of Estonian diplomats would be guaranteed (Solov'ev 2007b).

The fact that the conflict over the Bronze Soldier occurred only weeks before the EU-Russia Summit on 18 May 2007 gave additional leverage to EU demands. Estonia skillfully used the impending summit to close the ranks of the European Union behind it. Estonian Foreign Minister Urman Paet wanted the European Union to react to Russian behavior «harshly» and presented various anti-Russian measures to the EU that included a possible cancellation of the summit (Solov'ev and Zygar' 2007).

It was under this pressure from Europe that the Russian authorities acted. In the evening of 3 May, Nashi declared it had lifted the blockade around the Estonian embassy. Nonetheless, the organization did not admit defeat. Iakemenko underlined that Nashi had won a partial victory. It had offered Kaljurand the choice of either apologizing or leaving the country. She had chosen the «cowardly» option:

> «Marina Kaljurand left the Russian Federation in a hurry. But the victory is not a full one. Today we lift the blockade of the Estonian embassy. We will not stand here anymore, but this does not mean that we will stop. The actions will continue until the repression against the Russian-speaking population of Estonia stops.» (Nashi 2007m)

Nashi presents the lifting of the blockade as the result of the Estonian ambassador's «flight» from Russia. Kaljurand did indeed leave Russia, officially to go on a vacation that had been postponed because of the crisis.

> «Nonetheless, the departure of the ambassador was most likely a pretext [for Nashi] to fulfill the demands of the international community (...), [which] had demanded an end of the (..) forceful actions around the Estonian embassy»,

wrote *Kommersant"* correspondent Ekaterina Savina (Savina 2007). The rapid lifting of Nashi's blockade as a result of international protests strongly indicates that the previous tacit official support for the picket had been withdrawn.

Nashi's displeasure with the international criticism of its actions and the resulting domestic pressures was revealed in another statement by Iakemenko, in which he said that «the USA and NATO had better mind their own business» (*zaniat'sia svoimi delami*) (Nashi 2007n).

Nashi did not entirely stop its protest against Estonia. It organized various demonstrations with its own activists and schoolchildren, one of which took place in front of the European Union's representation in Moscow. The meeting's goal was a lesson for the EU about democratic values. From Nashi's point of view, the fact that the EU protested against Nashi's actions, while tolerating Estonian discrimination of ethnic Russians, «fascism», and the violence during the riots in Tallinn, was hypocritical (Nashi 2007o). Nashi again presented itself as the defender of «antifascist» memory of World War II and, additionally, of «true» European values.

After 9 May, Nashi made good on its January promise to send «living monuments» to Estonia – uniformed activists who placed themselves on the spot where the Bronze Soldier had stood. These activists were quickly arrested, deported to Russia, and barred from entering Estonia for five years (Nashi 2007p). As it turned out, these Estonian deportations would have consequences for Nashi activists for years to come: when Estonia joined the Schengen treaty, the travel bans began to apply to the entire Schengen Area, which prevented Nashi activists from travelling to Europe (Schwirtz 2008). The end of the picket had clearly weakened Nashi's position domestically and internationally.

Aftermath

The conflict over the Bronze Soldier overshadowed the EU-Russia summit on 18 May. Contrary to the hopes of many, no new bilateral treaty was signed in Samara. Events in Estonia occupied a significant part of the official press conference. Putin repeatedly brought up the death of Dmitrii Ganin to counter accusations of human rights violations in Russia. He termed the fact that Estonian police had not initially helped Ganin «murder by negligence»: «This constitutes a voluntary crime, and we demand that the perpetrators be brought to justice.» Putin, like Nashi, called the death of Ganin a «murder». He also linked the events in Tallinn to the discrimination of the Russian-speaking minority in the Baltic states and called the latter «unacceptable and unworthy of Europe». (*quoted in*: President of Russia 2007)

Putin asked whether there were «any limits to (..) solidarity» within the European Union. Implicitly, he raised the question, how a country like Estonia, which, according to the official Russian position, violated «European values» could be part of a united Europe and receive the support of other EU member states. Nashi had similarly criticized this perceived contradiction.

In response, Barroso reiterated that the Estonian problem concerned the entire European Union, and that it stood behind the small country in solidarity. Furthermore, he absolved the Estonian police of all wrongdoing: «We consider that the Estonian authorities made all the appropriate decisions with respect to the judicial system, and that is important.»

The conflict over the Bronze Soldier aggravated tensions between Russia and particularly the Eastern European EU-members. Nashi's actions, the cyber-attacks and the economic sanctions that Russia imposed against Estonia increased distrust and suspicion. It undermined Russia's desired position as a reliable economic and political partner of the European Union – in spite of the large trade volume between the two regions. The failure to agree on a new bilateral treaty illustrates this fact.

The conflict over the Bronze Soldier's effects on Russia-EU relations were mostly temporary, and even during the aforementioned press conference, all actors kept insisting that the relations were generally good. Nevertheless, the episode illustrates how official Russian portrayal of the country as a «pragmatic, business-like international actor» got «sidetracked by highly sensitive identity-related issues, such as the May 2007 conflict with Estoniaover the World War II memorial» (Makarychev 2008: 62).

Nashi's escalating and finally violent protests in Moscow forced an initially reluctant European Union to step in and defend Estonia against what appeared to be Russian bullying to most outside observers. Russia found itself pictured as a large country that used its economic might and administrative resources to pressure a small neighbor. The protests hurt Russia's image in the world and became an embarrassment for the government.

Russia could not justify official economic or political sanctions without impairing its own credibility as a serious actor on the international stage. According to international law, Russia had no right to interfere in the internal affairs of Estonia. The chances that an international body like the UN Security Council would have followed Russian justifications of such interference were so small that diplomats did not attempt it – in spite of Nashi's demands.

Secondly, Russia's options of actually hurting Estonia economically were quite limited and expensive for Russian businesses. Dmitrii Butrin, business editor at the *Kommersant"* newspaper, pointed out that Russia had essentially two options in adopting sanctions against Estonia. The first one would have been a limitation of fuel deliveries. This step would have had grave international consequences, as two thirds of all Russian fuel exports into the European Union go through Estonian ports. Moreover, it would have hurt Russian businesses as much as Estonian ones.

The second set of measures, which some businesses adopted, was an embargo against Estonian, mostly agricultural imports. However, according to Butrin, the main effects of this measure were lower prices in Estonian supermarkets. Not surprisingly, Butrin concluded that Russia had to choose between sanctions that were either very expensive for its own economy or ineffective. (Butrin 2007). Russia chose the ineffective path and thus an inexpensive way of demonstrating official political activism to angry conservative base.

On a discursive level, Estonia was considerably more successful in presenting a hegemonic discourse about the conflict than Russia. Estonia was able to present itself as the victim of neo-imperial Russian interference in its domestic affairs and managed to marginalize criticism against the violent actions of Tallinn's police. The Estonian Foreign Minister openly criticized Russia's neo-imperialism, when he said that «the return of Estonia into the Russian sphere of influence is impossible» (*quoted in*: Zygar' 2007a). Official Estonian discourse tied Russia's new assertiveness in the post-Soviet space to a discourse of threat and national security. The European Union, the United States and NATO accepted Estonian explanations for the violent police actions during the riots in Tallinn and the subsequent human rights violation as part of the «extraordinary measures» necessary to contain an existential threat to state security. The Estonians thus successfully securitized the conflict over the Bronze Soldier.

The international community almost completely ignored the notion that the discrimination against the ethnic Russian minority in Estonia could have contributed to explaining the violence in Tallinn. Instead, these ethnic Russians were often collectively portrayed as the spearhead of Russia's neo-imperialist ambitions and as stooges of the Russian government. The fact that over 98% of ethnic Russian Estonians had not rioted on the night of 26 and 27 April was ignored (Brüggemann 2008: 133).[75]

Russian reactions left an uncoordinated and contradictory impression. Official Russian discourse presented an opaque melee of historical grievances and traumata as well as geopolitical concerns rarely disentangled outside of Russia. First and foremost, the fact that the conflict concerned the removal of a World War II monument affected one of the nodal points of Russian official discourse. It thus affected national pride and the patriotic emotions of a wide segment of the Russian population. Even Russians who had few sympathies for Putin showed little understanding for the Baltic war narrative and even less for the removal of the Bronze Soldier.

As far as Russia's official political identity is concerned, the template of the Great Patriotic War influences discourses on Russia's current position in the world strongly. The Soviet victory represents a strong state, generational continuity and the unity of the people against state enemies. However, Estonia – once a Soviet republic and thus part of the victorious «Soviet people» – interprets victory diametrically opposed to the Russian narrative. This represents a dislocation of a nodal point of Russia's official political identity.

As we have seen in previous chapters, Nashi's discourse articulates the historical continuity between the geopolitical situation in World War II and the present in a very immediate fashion. In the conflict with Estonia, this equation was employed as well. Nashi directly associated Estonians' support for the Nazis during the war, Estonia's anti-Russian foreign policy in the 1990s, and its suppression of the protests in 2007. All of these moments were subsumed under the common signifier «fascist». By calling Estonia «fascist», Nashi radically «othered» the Baltic state and treated it like an enemy rhetorically and through its protests.

This antagonization of Estonia is linked to fears of weakness and a vague sense of historical threat, which finds resonance beyond Nashi's activists. Estonia had served as a gateway for invasions of the Soviet Union in 1919 and during World War II (Brüggemann 2004: 131ff.). Moreover, Estonia's inde-

---

75 On Estonia and the «Bronze Nights», see also: Rozenfel'd, I. 2009. *Estoniia do i Posle «Bronzovoi Nochi»: Estonskaia Respublika 1991-2009. Levotsentristskii Vzgliad.* Tartu & St. Petersburg: Kripta.

pendence shortly before the collapse of the Soviet Union is discursively tied to the moment of perceived Russian weakness in the 1990s. Estonia's marked pro-Western foreign policy underlined Russia's loss of influence in the post-Soviet space. In 2007, Putin stated at the Munich Security Conference that this loss threatened Russia's security. He criticized NATO's expansion to the Baltic states on 29 March 2004.

> «NATO has put its frontline forces on our borders (...). I think it is obvious that NATO expansion does not have any relation with the modernisation of the Alliance itself or with ensuring security in Europe. On the contrary, it represents a serious provocation that reduces the level of mutual trust. And we have the right to ask: against whom is this expansion intended?» (Putin 2007a)

Putin's speech marked a departure from earlier Russian policies that had accepted NATO expansion and highlighted opportunities for cooperation (Konnander 2005: 114ff.). Instead, NATO expansion had become a matter of national security in official discourse, and the Baltic states another potential bridgehead for an attack against Russia.

In this context, it is not surprising that Nashi took «extraordinary measures» to counter the removal of the Bronze Soldier. It signified an attack against a hegemonic historical narrative and was carried out by a country that official Russian discourse has depicted as a contemporary military threat. The organization's measures, however, failed to be recognized as a viable political option by a wider audience. Its demands received little official support because Russia would have had to pay a price on the international stage that was much too high. Economic and political sanctions were unrealistic, and suggestions such as the removal of the Estonian embassy from Russian territory were outright ridiculous. Nashi's securitization of memory must thus be considered unsuccessful.

The conflict with Estonia reveals the problems inherent in using the historical template of the war as a hegemonic discourse to describe political problems of the present. Nashi's antagonization of «fascist» Estonia stands in clear contradiction to an agonistic view of Europe. Russia's official discourse frames Europe as a partner for Russia and Russia as a European nation. The latter notion is also central to Sovereign Democracy. Surkov calls Russia a «European country» and believes that it should aim for the same civilizational goals that European countries have pursued throughout the modern period: cooperation, material well-being and popular participation in decision making (Surkov 2006a: 44ff.). As we have seen in chapter 2, Nashi shares these goals.

The official war narrative that Nashi defended so vehemently during the conflict with Estonia is also closely tied to a defense of European civilization in Russia's official discourse.

> «The heroic narrative of the Great Patriotic War links Russia with Europe and/or civilization, because it can be told in such a manner that the Soviet Union will appear at the centre of the struggle for genuine European values against a barbarian force (stemming, by the way, from the very heart of Europe).» (Morozov 2008: 159)

Nashi articulated this notion of defending «European values» during the conflict with Estonia. The question is, however, how Estonia could simultaneously signify both «fascism» and «Europe» in Nashi's discourse.

Viacheslav Morozov suggests an interesting resolution for this apparent discursive paradox: the distinction between «real» and «false» Europe. According to this differentiation, the «real» Europe, which stands for humanist and enlightenment values with which Russia identifies itself is different from the «false» Europe – a Europe under American influence (Morozov 2004: 320). In this narrative, an (American) antagonist is using a «false» Europe for the purpose of weakening Russia and thereby keeping it distant from its «natural» partners in Europe.

During the conflict with Estonia, Nashi articulated this distinction in various ways. One such way was the appeal to the European Union to exercise its influence on Estonia and defend «European values». Another was Nashi's verbal attack on NATO and the US. Ironically, Russian attacks against Estonia during the conflict only promoted a stronger role by NATO in Estonia and led to the establishment of the NATO's Cooperative Cyber Defence Centre of Excellence in the country, which has become a strategic priority for the alliance since.

Victory Day 2007 and Beyond

On 8 May, Estonian Prime Minister Andrus Ansip, accompanied by government officials and diplomats from many countries, laid flowers on the Bronze

Soldier, now on the outskirts of Tallinn – in an attempt to «honor the memory of all the fallen», (*quoted in*: Zygar' 2007b). Then, Ansip visited the cemetery Maarjamjagi, where those Estonians who had fought with the Germans lay buried.

The Russian ambassador did not participate in the ceremony. The Estonian government's choice of 8 May instead of 9 May for the celebration represented an attempt to establish the former date firmly as the official Estonian holiday, which was also a statement for a European, rather than (post-)Soviet, interpretation of the war. The Russian ambassador went to the cemetery on 9 May, along with thousands of ethnic Russians, who peacefully laid down flowers on the Bronze Soldier.

The «war of memory» over the Bronze Soldier showed deep incongruities in the Estonian and the official Russian war narratives. The Estonian narrative dislocates its Russian counterpart because it emphasizes those elements that official Russian discourse still struggles to integrate into the heroic war narrative: Stalinist terror and the Molotov-Ribbentrop Pact. Tensions between Russia and Estonia are significantly tied to these conflicting interpretations.

The discourse on the war established in the Brezhnev-era and rearticulated by Putin and Nashi, presents the Red Army as liberators and all those that opposed it as «fascists». Estonians who had fought with the Germans or the «Forest Brothers» were collectively reviled and many of them persecuted. This narrative admits neither the involuntary nature of the Baltic states' incorporation into the USSR nor the existence of an independent Estonian government before the Red Army's 1944 arrival. Historian Carmen Scheide calls this imposition of the official Soviet war narrative a form of «ideological colonization» that went hand in hand with the Sovietization of the economy and society (Scheide 2008: 125).

The suppression of alternative war narratives in the Soviet Union has laid the groundwork for the politicization of history in the post-Soviet space (Hackmann 2003: 90). No effort was made in Soviet discourse to incorporate Baltic resistance and suffering into an inclusive political identity. As a result, these signifiers became the uncontested basis for a counter-hegemonic, independent Estonian identity that constructed the Estonian nation as a victim of Soviet policies. Estonian collaboration in the annihilation of the Jews, ethnic Estonians' participation in the Red Army and their involvement in establishing a postwar Soviet order were excluded from this narrative. Public debate on the past has remained extremely limited in post-Soviet Estonia[76] and historical responsibility is passed on to either the Germans or the Russians (Memorial 2008: 79). As a result of the conflict over the Bronze Soldier, the official Estonian view on history has become even more rigid.

Estonian ethnic Russians' cultural ties remain oriented toward Russia, and most embrace the official Soviet and post-Soviet war myth: «Many of them still seem to perceive themselves as carriers of a particular war memory that corresponds largely with what is the dominant narrative in Russia today.» (Onken 2007: 37) As a result, many of them feel even more alienated from the Estonian government since the conflict over the Bronze Soldier.

On 9 May 2007, there were no new clashes, but the ethnic and cultural divisions between Estonians and Russians had become very apparent. The Bronze Soldier's divergent meanings had, at least for the time being, been neatly separated and attached to different holidays. The creation of a mutually compatible narrative was never more distant than in the aftermath of the conflict.

In Moscow, in the meantime, Nashi had established a gigantic stage and organized a «holiday concert» in the evening, with 15'000 members of various pro-Kremlin youth organizations, all dressed in the Russian tricolor. Nashi celebrated Russia's regained strength and its pride of the Soviet Union's achievements in the Great Patriotic War (Nashi 2007r).

The anger and outrage that drove Nashi's radical actions against Estonia weeks earlier had given way to a highly staged patriotic demonstration. Looking back on the conflict over the Bronze Soldier, Andrei, the Nashi-commissar from St. Petersburg, highlights the unplanned nature of the organization's protests.

> «It was a wave. My comrades and I were outraged by what was happening. It was not just a political reaction, which was without doubt necessary (…). We

---

76   Estonia officially commemorates the Holocaust on 27 January – with little public participation. An International Historical Commission was set up in 1999 to examine the country's past: «Thus, on the level of historical fact-finding much has been done over recent years, but in terms of triggering critical debate among local historians that would support the development of a diverse and pluralist public history culture, this commission has been rather passive.» (Onken 2007: 35)

wanted an answer, an apology, we did not want to allow what was happening to happen!»

There is no doubt that Nashi used this «wave» of outrage for its own purposes. Andrei's statement, Iakemenko's futile calls for moderation in front of the *Argumenty i Fakty* building and the sudden end of the embassy picket on 3 May indicate, however, that the organization had temporarily lost control over its activists' actions in Moscow. Particularly the realization that Nashi's demands would not be met led to frustration and to violence. Andreev's concept of «managed passion» provides a good explanation, since it sees emotional mobilization against an enemy as one of Nashi's basic traits (Andreev 2006: 50). However, particularly in situations of crisis, when emotions run high, these passions can spin out of control. As the diplomatic fallout of Nashi's actions demonstrated, «managed passion» remains a double-edged sword for Nashi and Russia's authorities.

In his speech on Victory Day that year, Putin assumed a somber tone. It mostly resembled his 2005 address (see chapter 1); he emphasized the «enormous moral significance» of victory and mentioned Russia's neighbors in the post-Soviet space in particular. He highlighted that the Soviet people who had won the war had passed on a tradition of «brotherhood» and «solidarity» to later generations: «We will preserve this holy memory and this historic heritage» (Putin 2007b). However, he added a new antagonistic moment to the speech:

> «Those who attempt today to belittle this invaluable experience and defile the monuments to the heroes of this war are insulting their own people and spreading enmity and new distrust between countries and peoples. We have a duty to remember that the causes of any war lie above all in the mistakes and miscalculations of peacetime, and that these causes have their roots in an ideology of confrontation and extremism.» (Putin 2007b)

This obvious stab at Estonia frames opposition to the official narrative in highly antagonistic terms, especially in combination with an «ideology of confrontation and extremism» – a synonym for «fascism». In 2007, then, the official war narrative is presented as threatened by those who try to belittle the Soviet Union's role in World War II.

Leonid Slutskii, the member of the Duma delegation that visited Tallinn, explicitly connected Estonian actions to attempts at «reassessing the events of World War II» (*quoted in*: Kommersant" Vlast' 2007). He articulated a discursive moment also found in Nashi's statements – namely that history is used as a tool to weaken Russian influence in the world. Dmitrii Linter, the leader of Night Watch, along with many Russian pundits and politicians, explicitly identifies the United States as standing behind (Zavtra 2009) this «rewriting of history» (*perepisanie istorii*). As discussed in chapter 1, this discourse interprets disagreements over the interpretation of history as means of geopolitical power struggles.

The memory of the Great Patriotic War became even more of a security issue in official Russian discourse after the conflict over the Bronze Soldier. In May 2009, President Dmitrii Medvedev announced the creation of a «Presidential Commission of the Russian Federation to Counter Attempts to Falsify History to the Detriment of Russia's Interests». This commission, chaired by the head of the Presidential Administration, Sergei Naryshkin, was to supervise the opening of sensitive Russian archives. The commission consists mainly of military officers, members of the secret service and a handful of «patriotic» historians (Afanas'ev 2009b: 5), and its function is explicitly defensive. President Medvedev said in his video blog on Victory Day 2009

«[m]ore and more, we see ourselves confronted with what is today called the falsification of history. Meanwhile, as many of us have noticed, these attempts are becoming ever harsher, more vicious and aggressive.» (Medvedev 2009)

The notion that the «falsification of history» is an immediate threat to Russia's identity has thus become firmly entrenched in official discourse.

Still, one should not overestimate the importance of this rhetoric and the actions taken to «defend» the official war narrative. A cable of the US embassy on this topic, published by Wikileaks, provides a rather instructive interpretation of the Russian government's actions against the «falsification of history». The report states that the government's efforts «to sanitize Soviet history have continued throughout the year» and quotes isolated cases of obstruction of historical research by state institutions. Furthermore, the cable reports that the schoolbooks that promote an official war narrative outnumber more critical ones by a ratio of almost 20 to 1.

At the same time, however, Russia has no institutionalized system of censorship, the US embassy notes: «GOR [government of Russia] leaders have shown that they are willing to adopt nationalistic postures when it buttresses their popular support, but attempts to dictate academic terms thus far appear half-hearted.» (American Embassy 2009) The defense of the highly idealized official war narrative, then, enters official discourse primarily in times of political conflict with other nations. Since a large majority of Russians feel pride in the country's achievement in World War II, the use of the heroic war narrative to further official policy goals is an obvious but also double-edged method for the mobilization of political support.

Russia's leaders rarely discussed the problematic aspects of this idealized war memory publicly. Particularly under Medvedev, however, one could observe a greater willingness to acknowledge the difficult aspects of history on the part of both the president and Putin. In 2010 Putin initiated a kind of *détente* over historical issues with Poland when he visited a commemorative service for the victims of Katyn and bowed before them. The Russian government also handed over NKVD files about the executions to the Poles. Shortly before Victory Day, Medvedev openly spoke about the «mass crimes» that Stalin had committed against the Russian people in an interview on state television.

Such clear condemnations of the dictator by national leaders have been rare. Instead, according to Sherlock, official discourse addresses the troublesome figure of Stalin with a mix of «silence, praise, and criticism – in that order» (Sherlock 2007: 183). The figure of Stalin is difficult to reconcile with the claim of defending democratic and «European» values. Still, Stalin remains popular among many Russians, even among younger ones, particularly in nationalist circles. Andrei told me as we were parting: «At least under Stalin, we knew who we were». While Nashi does not openly glorify Stalin in its publications, it has not condemned him either. The figure of Stalin continues to stand as a discursive signifier for order, security and global power for many, including Nashi. The inclination to condemn him remains very limited beyond intellectual circles, precisely because his name is so closely connected to victory in World War II. This achievement pushes Stalinist crimes into the background.

The muted discussion in Russia on the problematic aspects of the war and its glorification make it increasingly difficult for a young generation of Russians to form their own image of the Great Patriotic War. Most Russian schoolchildren grow up with a «patriotic» version of the war narrative. This has consequences. The organization *Memorial* has gathered material on Stalinism since the early 1990s and hosts annual essay contests in Russian schools. Irina Shcherbakova, the organizer of these contests at Memorial, notes a steady rise in the number of stereotypical patriotic expressions in essays since 2004. However, these phrases often have little connection with the actual events and the tragic stories that are told subsequently (Shcherbakova 2010: 24).

This leads to a general feeling of ignorance. In a survey conducted by Lev Gudkov in 2005, 68 percent of Russians said that they felt they did not know the whole truth about the war, even though they were proud of Soviet achievements (Gudkov 2005: 68). This number is unlikely to have decreased in the meantime, as the commemorations have become even more politicized. Politicization and ignorance go hand in hand, writes Memorial:

«Statt ehrlichem Bemühen, die Geschichte des 20. Jahrhunderts in ihrer ganzen Tragik und Tragweite aufzuarbeiten, statt einer ernsthaften Auseinandersetzung des Landes mit der sowjetischen Vergangenheit erleben wir hier, wie der sowjetische, patriotische Grossmachtsmythos nur leicht verändert wieder aufersteht (...). In diesem Mythos ist weder Platz für Schuld, noch für Verantwortung, noch auch für die Anerkennung der Tragödie. Aus Heroismus und Aufopferung aber erwächst keine staatsbürgerliche Verantwortung. Viele Bürger Russlands sind daher schlicht nicht in der Lage, sich die historische Verantwortung der Sowjetunion gegenüber den heutigen Nachbarländern Russlands und das Ausmass der Katastrophe für Russland selbst bewusst zu machen. Das Land verweigert die Erinnerung.» (Memorial 2008: 81)[77]

---

[77] «Instead of making an honest attempt to process the history of the 20th century, its tragedy and momentousness, instead of a serious confrontation with the country's Soviet past, we are witnessing the reemergence of a barely changed Soviet and patriotic great power myth (...). In this myth there is neither room for guilt, nor for responsibility or the recognition of the tragedy. No civic responsibility grows out of heroism and sacrifice. Many Russian citizens are thus simply not in a position to recognize the Soviet Union's historical responsibility towards Russia's neighbors

In Russia, and in most other Eastern countries, we thus face a paradoxical situation: constant calls to remember the war promote the forgetting of its tragic and difficult aspects. The idealized narrative is cleansed of the «affective radicality» of the war, as Lev Gudkov calls it (Gudkov 2005: 62). It thus prevents a broader societal process of coming to terms with difficult memories and human losses, not all of which were simply «heroic». As we have seen, it is exactly these taboos that provide fertile ground for political conflicts that mix history and current geopolitics, as well as a general feeling of historically founded distrust. In order to eliminate this source of conflicts, Russia and its neighbors must confront all pages of their history.

---

and to understand the extent of the disaster for Russia itself. The country rejects [its own] memory.»

V Seliger: The Foundry of Modernization

Nashi's role in the conflict over the removal of the Bronze Soldier from downtown Tallinn in the spring of 2007 marked the peak of the youth organization's prominence in Russia and the global arena. In the years that followed, Nashi's influence dwindled.
The man moving into position to succeed Vladimir Putin, Dmitrii Medvedev, was considerably more critical towards Nashi, even if he never criticized the organization publicly. Regina Heller believes that this reservation about Nashi has had much to do with the negative international publicity that its actions – particularly the one surrounding the Estonian embassy in Moscow – had created (Heller 2008: 4). Many commentators were convinced that Nashi's end had come in January 2008, when 45 of its 50 regional offices were closed and the number of commissars and supporters decreased dramatically. Nashi's financial means, believed to amount to hundreds of thousands of dollars per month, were cut and fringe benefits for its commissars, such as the free use of cell phones, curtailed (Konovalova 2007).
Nashi found itself in an existential crisis and needed to prove its usefulness anew to an increasingly skeptical government. The goal that had been the impetus for the organization's creation in 2005 – preventing an Orange Revolution – was achieved. Dmitrii Medvedev had won the 2008 elections by a landslide, and Edinaia Rossiia's hold on power was secured. Nashi repositioned itself by avoiding controversial political actions like the siege of the Estonian embassy and by placing more emphasis on its role as an important actor in Russia's economic modernization. This repositioning corresponded to the new president's priorities.

In her in-depth analysis of Nashi's reorganization, Maya Atwal conceptualizes this process as an elaborate strategy. She believes that the Russian government was unwilling or unable to pay the political costs required to close down Nashi but still wanted to maintain a modicum of control over the movement. By strengthening its activities in the economic sphere, the youth organization has widened its appeal among well-educated youth, a partially new constituency. More than before, Nashi tried to distance itself from its potentially violent constituency.

However, these new activists do not necessarily share all of Nashi's values: «In the regions, to where the projects are spreading, the vast majority of participants are new to Nashi, not knowing much about it beyond hearsay» (Atwal 2009: 756). As modernization had been one of Nashi's discursive nodal points from the beginning, this realignment did not necessitate a reinvention of the organization. Instead, it meant that Nashi shifted the emphasis of its actions and directed publicity to its contributions to Russia's modernization.

In this chapter, I will retrace this realignment through a case study of Nashi's most important annual gathering at Lake Seliger. One can consider this summer camp, located halfway between Moscow and St. Petersburg, as the organization's «home» of sorts. It is from this nature preserve, sometimes referred to as the European Baikal, that the river Volga springs out of a system of lakes, rivers and creeks. And it is here that Nashi has held its annual summer camp since the organization's inception in 2005.

Each year the movement's activists gather here. Here, leaders have been able to train thousands of activists, and activists have exchanged ideas and projects. The Seliger camp has thus served as Nashi's most important place for developing a shared sense of purpose and identity. In the camp, activists have found the «embodiment» of the organization's ideas and values.

After 2008, the camp's audience was extended beyond Nashi to include broader segments of Russian youth, and – since 2010 – international participants. A case study of the Seliger camp can thus serve as a window onto how Russia is presented to a Russian and international audience in official discourse. First, this chapter provides an account of the Lake Seliger camp between 2005 and 2010 and the changes during this period. I then offer a participant observation of the International Youth Forum Seliger 2010.

Seliger: The Early Years

The annual summer camps at Lake Seliger have contributed significantly to Nashi's fame and notoriety. Particularly in the first three years of its existence, many analysts and commentators saw the Seliger camp as the place where the Kremlin's spin-doctors indoctrinated youth with patriotic values and trained them to fight an Orange Revolution.

In 2005, 3'000 Nashi-commissars attended over 870 hours of lectures, as well as 400 separate classes, seminars and workshops over two weeks (Buchacek 2006: 37). Among the speakers were notable personalities such as Vladislav Surkov, the political scientists Gleb Pavlovskii and Viacheslav Nikonov, as well as the Duma member Andrei Kokoshin. Estimates placed the cost of the camp at around two million dollars (Eremin 2007).

Back then and today, everyday life at the camp was guided by strict discipline and a strong emphasis on sports, including running, hiking, cycling, rafting and survival training in extreme natural circumstances. The camp spirit is hierarchical and patriotic. Participants are woken at 8 am by the Russian national anthem. They gather in front of a main stage half an hour later and follow Nashi leader Iakemenko on a five-kilometer run. Many representatives of youth movements wave the flags of their organizations and chant slogans during the run. The camp's uniformed security service maintains order and ensures that no alcohol is consumed at any point. The guards also search participants and their luggage at camp entrances. No one is allowed to leave without official permission. Violators of these «dry laws» are evicted from the camp and left on their own at the train station of nearby Ostashkov.[78]

Between 2005 and 2007, participants received extensive training in street fighting and crowd control. At times, controversial personalities conducted these sessions. In 2005, for example, Dmitrii Korchinskii taught a master class entitled «methods of forestalling mass unrest» (Loskutova 2008: 262). Korchinskii is the leader of the radical Ukrainian nationalist organization Bratstvo (*Brotherhood*). In 2006, the FSB and Chechen authorities filed a suit against him for participating in the First Chechen War on the side of the rebels (Grani 2006).

The number of participating commissars at Seliger increased to 5'000 in the following year, and in 2007, Nashi opened the camp to members of the pro-

---

[78] According to the Russian language newspaper of the camp, the *Seliger Times*, one Russian participant from Kaliningrad was evicted from the camp in 2010. He had apparently already been sent off in 2009 and was unable to go home both times, as he lacked the 7'000 Rubles necessary for a train ticket. In 2009 he had apparently managed to sneak back into the camp for food. His fate in 2010 was unknown (Nekhorosheva 2010: 2).

Kremlin organizations Rossiia Molodaia and New People (*Novye Liudi*). These groups lived in separate sections of the tent city that comprises the camp. Judging from the available information, relations between the various groups were largely peaceful.[79]

One big exception occurred in 2007. Nashi conducted a role-play called «Maidan at Seliger» on July 26th, modeled after the events in Kiev. Members of Rossiia Molodaia and Novye Liudi played the roles of protesters, and Nashi commissars were supposed to learn how to disperse the crowd.

What happened next is subject to some dispute: Novye Liudi complained via their website that several members had suffered injuries when 7'000 Nashi activists smashed tents and ripped up flags of the 300 «protesters». Novye Liudi claimed that even though Iakemenko had told his activists to break up the «protest» by «soft means», some of them had gone too far and did not limit themselves to nonviolent means. Novye Liudi demanded an official apology (Novye Liudi 2007).

In response, Iakemenko maintained that the exercise had gone according to the scenario and accused Novye Liudi of overreacting:

> «It is possible that some less attentive people, or emotional girls (*devushki*), took this [exercise] at face value. All people who have been injured should say so, and then we can talk about it substantively. But without these statements, all of this is nothing but an attempt to discredit what we do.» (Nashi 2007q)

Though Iakemenko denied wrongdoing on the part of his organization,[80] Novye Liudi reportedly received an unofficial apology from a Nashi commissar and put the issue to rest (Novye Liudi 2007).

---

79   Still in 2010, the groups were very clearly distinguishable. The large youth organizations and different ethnic groups had their own «neighborhoods». I wrote in my field diary: «[o]ne group that catches my eye this morning is the Chechens. They are burly, slightly intimidating young men that carry the Chechen flag. Some of the flags feature a somber portrait of Ramsan Kadyrov. The Chechens have hung posters with information about their republic in front of their tents to showcase the achievements of their president. (...) I notice that the various youth groups take great pains to cultivate their own 'corporate identity'. Mestnye [The Locals, a pro-Kremlin youth group], for example, have their own tent city. A green poster with information about the organization closes this tent city off to the outside. They all wear identical green t-shirts.»

80   This reaction to criticism is very characteristic for Nashi. The organization almost never admits wrongdoing on its part.

The year 2008 was a caesura for Seliger. Political changes in early 2008 discussed above also affected the camp. Aleksandr Temnitskii, a sociologist at the Higher School of Economics in Moscow, defines the mood at Seliger 2008 as one of «'peaceful' respite» among the participants (Temnitskii 2010: 44). With Medvedev firmly in place as Putin's successor, training youth to fight potential revolutionaries had become less important. Temnitskii surveyed participants in 2008 and found that their values did not differ fundamentally from other Russians of their age. Evident among participants were strong idea-based motivations to participate in the camp (ibid.: 47) and civic-mindedness. Among the older cohort (24-33 years of age), this meant a strong sense of patriotism (ibid.: 52). Compared to 2007, people who came to Seliger had a slightly more individualistic outlook than their average Russian peers (ibid.: 57).

For the camp organizers, 2008 was a difficult year because of power struggles and financial problems. Nashi founder Iakemenko had declared his intention to step down as the head of the movement at Seliger in 2007 and organized an election for a new leader at the camp. However, over 70 percent of the camp participants elected Nikita Borovikov over Marina Zademid'kova, whom Iakemenko had favored as his successor. In reaction, he declared he would stay on until March 2008 and that the election had been mere «role play» (Loskutova 2008: 271).

Already in October 2007, Iakemenko was appointed chairman of the State Committee of the Russian Federation for Youth Affairs. Eight months later, he became the head of the newly created Federal Agency for Youth Affairs in the Ministry for Sports, Tourism and Youth Politics.[81] With Iakemenko out of the picture, Nikita Borovikov remained the leader of Nashi and oversaw the movement's reorganization and repositioning, placing more emphasis on its contribution to Russia's modernization.

---

81 The Federal Agency for Youth Affairs is the only unit of the Russian government that deals exclusively with youth. The agency sees Russia's youth as «the main resource for the country's development in the 21st century». Its tasks are to include youth in the process of Russia's modernization, foster youth initiatives, help young people in difficult social circumstances and foster patriotic education (Federal Agency for Youth Affairs 2011). Iakemenko stepped down from this post in 2012 and has since been involved in various political and economic projects (see also conclusion).

In 2008, the number of attendees at Lake Seliger had dropped from over 10'000 to just half. In 2009, however, Iakemenko reasserted his control over the camp: for the first time, the Federal Agency for Youth Affairs appeared as the official organizer of the camp. The number of participants in the renamed *All-Russian Youth Educational Forum Seliger* – now no longer limited to Nashi-commissars and selected guests – rose to over 40'000 young people from 83 regions (Nashi 2011a). The camp lasted six weeks and was split up into the same number of sessions (*smeny*) on different topics.

The Agency for Youth Affairs designated Seliger as the centerpiece of the Russian *Year of Youth* in 2009 (Newsru 2009). After skipping the event the year before, Prime Minister Putin visited Seliger in 2009 (Nashi 2009b). The camp had also changed its image: no longer explicitly a Nashi camp, it instead marketed itself as an «innovation forum», stressing openness and the modernization of Russia (Samarina and Rodin 2009).

Finally in 2010, Seliger opened itself to international participants. The first week of the camp was called «International Youth Forum Seliger 2010».

Participant Observation at Seliger

The opportunity to attend the camp at Lake Seliger arose in May 2010, about nine months after I had finished writing my MA thesis on Nashi. It provided a unique opportunity for firsthand research as well as a challenge, as it would require a methodological approach that differed from the other chapters. A word on methodology is thus appropriate before I continue my analysis.

In his rich ethnographic discourse analysis of education at the elite Moscow State Institute of International Relations (MGIMO), Martin Müller uses participant observation in order to focus on «the practice component of discourse» (Müller 2009a: 71). Though the ethnographic analysis in this book cannot match Müller's either in terms of the duration spent in the field or its methodological elaboration, it pursues similar goals – to investigate official discourse within an institutionalized setting.

For my analysis of the International Youth Forum Seliger 2010, I kept a field journal to record the daily camp routine, the content of lectures, discussions and activities, conversations with other participants, and personal impressions. The brevity of the fieldwork and the tightly controlled daily routine gave me little time to keep detailed field notes. Participants were kept busy most of the time in organized group activities. My notes do, however, suffice as a «piecemeal and rough» database (Clifford 1990: 51f.). I spent one to two hours writing daily notes on a laptop computer. I describe my research conditions (Hammersley and Atkinson 2007: 15) so as to avoid «the false and misleading presentation of the researcher (and research itself) as inert, detached and neutral» (Fuller 1999: 224).

All participants were assigned to a unit consisting of fifteen to twenty students from Russia and abroad. They were placed under the guidance of a Russian instructor, who, in our case, was not a member of Nashi. Ten of these instructors were subordinate to a «senior instructor» (*starshii instruktor*), who answered to one of the three camp managers. The units that included international participants slept in a separate sector of the camp. Another section hosted entirely Russian groups. Within the international units, a small number of Russians who spoke English acted as guides (called «curators») to facilitate communication.

Participants slept in two-person tents arranged around a fireplace with benches and a table to sit and eat at. Each unit had a storage tent with food and staples, as well as a very rudimentary shower. Each group carried the water for eating and showering to their campsite on foot in large bins and was responsible for cooking its own food. Centrally located composting toilets were cleaned daily and used by all attendees.

Participants had selected one of six themes already in spring: *Russia and Global Politics*, *Civil Society*, *Media*, *Environment and Energy*, *Business and Innovation* and *Art and Design*. They could not change this selection during the camp. I chose the *Civil Society* theme for several reasons. First, I believed it would provide insight into the camp organizers' view of Russia's domestic political situation and their presentation of the country to a broader audience. Secondly, the development of civil society in Russia is one of the stated goals of Nashi, and I was hoping for more details about the movement's ideas on the subject and interesting discussions with other participants. Finally, I expected international participants interested in this theme to be knowledgeable about Russian society. This would have created the potential for exchanges and provided opportunities to create networks.

Having written my thesis on Nashi and knowing the history of the camp, I came to Seliger with the expectation of a strong Nashi presence there. I paid special attention to the organization's involvement. I was surprised to learn that the international guests were kept separate from most Russian participants. Moreover, the organizers concealed Nashi's strong presence in the camp wherever possible. Many Nashi activists slept in a separate section of tents. Unlike those of other groups, however, this section was not labeled separately. I knew that a parallel program was taking place in another section of the camp, but this program was, for the most part, off-limits to international participants.

The vast majority of international participants did not speak Russian and were thus cut off from the information in the camp that was passed down in Russian. In this sense, I was privileged, since my knowledge of Russian figured as a «trading» resource (Hammersley and Atkinson 2007: 69) that provided me with access to additional information. I could hear and read documents and speeches that were not translated and received informal information from our «guides» and other Russian participants.

The question of the overt- or covertness of one's position as a participant observer is another thorny issue (cf. DeWalt and DeWalt 2002: 35). I used a «don't ask, don't tell» policy of sorts: I did not lie if someone asked me what I had written my thesis about and thus told several people that I was conducting a participant observation at the camp. If people did not ask, however, I did not volunteer this information.[82]

International Youth Forum Seliger 2010

Promotion for the International Youth Forum Seliger 2010 started early in the year through a sophisticated website in Russian and English (www.seliger2010.com) and numerous ads in scholarly publications and on university websites.[83]

---

82 Wherever I used personal information, I asked my sources for their permission to include their statements in this chapter and rendered them anonymous when necessary.

83 The domain name seliger2010 no longer belongs to the camp today. It appears that it was sold to a construction company.

The financing came from various sources: Billionaire Mikhail Prokhorov provided the forum with 1.54 million dollars (RIA Novosti 2010). Furthermore, it received at least 5.5 million Rubles (177'000 dollar) from government funds designed to battle the effects of the financial crisis (BBC Russia 2009). In a promotional English language video for the camp, the director of the organizational committee and head of the department of international activities and youth exchanges in the Agency for Youth Affairs, Mikhail Mamonov, explained the forum's purpose:

> «Seliger is a unique international project that seeks to bring together 3'000 young leaders and professionals from all over the world to build a global team. It is your opportunity to meet with prominent politicians, businesspeople, public figures – both from Russia and abroad – and share your views with them. It is a good chance to build a personal across-the-globe network of like-minded individuals that want to make a difference. (...) But of course Seliger is also about fun and adventure on the shore of a beautiful lake that is considered to be in the top ten of Russia's most splendid views list. There will be fashion shows, parties, exhibitions of all sorts – what not. (...) An ideal candidate for the trip is a young leader who likes and is not daunted by challenges and tasks, who wants to learn more about modern Russia, who wants to work with Russia on joint projects.» (Seliger 2010a)

Mamonov's statement positioned the forum as a highly competitive environment for ambitious and open-minded students interested in international networks, hard work and adventure. The apparent goal was to attract qualified foreigners who wanted to learn more about Russian culture and the economic opportunities in the country.[84]

Minister of Sports, Tourism and Youth Politics Vitalii Mutko echoed this emphasis on Russia's modernity and openness. In his speech at Seliger on opening day, he exclaimed that, «Russia is opening its door to all of its friends». He stressed that the «majority of all creative Russians» had gathered at Seliger, ready to develop its talents along with its international coun-

---

84 The camp management told some of the guides in charge of the foreigners that the latter were supposed to be recruited for the prestige project at Skol'kovo – which was supposed to become Russia's «silicon valley». However, as far as I could judge, no recruitment took place at the camp, and none was subsequently mentioned in the Russian media.

terparts.[85] Mikhail Mamonov underlined this message: «Seliger is the true place where we forge talents.»

This claim of assembling the best and the brightest was also apparent in Vladimir Putin's written address to the Russian participants, in which he promised «unforgettable emotions, bright impressions» and «lectures from the best professors from the leading universities in Russia and the world» (Seliger 2010b).[86] All promoters of Seliger highlighted the nodal points of excellence, leadership and community building.

Most foreign participants I spoke to expected a well-organized university summer school of high standing. The educational program, organized in cooperation with the prestigious MGIMO university in Moscow, motivated many participants. In an informal survey I conducted, the Hungarian participant and journalist Krisztian Simon said about his motivation: «We thought it might be a serious summer university, where we might see what academic life looks like in Russia.» His opinion seems representative for many.

However, participants quickly realized that this was no regular university summer school. With or without knowledge of the background of the camp, the patriotic element was apparent to all. The first general assembly surprised international participants by its scale: thousands of mostly Russian young people had assembled in front of the large main stage. They were waving flags of their cities and youth organizations. To the left and to the right of the stage stood two gigantic portraits of Putin and Medvedev, printed on cloth. Behind the stage, it said: «Seliger 2010. Instruments for the development of talent».

The strong Russian patriotic propaganda that has been an essential part of the camps at Seliger since 2005 did not feature either on the website or in the materials sent out to universities abroad. Overall, the Forum appeared to be a mixture of university summer school and Boy Scout teenage summer camp. The two did not always coexist without friction.

---

85   Unless otherwise cited, reports on speeches, activities and lectures at Seliger 2010 are taken from my personal field notes.
86   Putin's address was not translated into English and did not appear on the front page of the English Seliger page. Apparently, the organizers did not think that an endorsement by Vladimir Putin would carry as much weight with international participants as it did with Russian students.

Participants were kept busy throughout the day. They attended obligatory lectures on their topics in the mornings. In the afternoons, participants were able to select from various activities of the *business program*, which included a mixture of sports, lectures and workshops. The evening program was very heterogeneous – including everything from traditional Russian folk celebrations like Ivan Kupala Day, readings from the famous Thaw era poet Evgenii Evtushenko and football games, to discussion sessions and international costume contests. Because of organizational problems, however, many of the original programs and plans were revised repeatedly.

In general, the organizers created high expectations among participants and provided them with a diverse program. However, before the camp had even begun, those interested in attending were confronted with a maze of bureaucratic obstacles. The organizational problems would persist throughout the camp and undermine the organizers' claim that it could compete in the highest (or even the mid-level) echelons of summer schools.

Difficult Beginnings

What the Seliger organizers offered the participants was certainly attractive at first glance: International students only had to pay for their flights, many of which were subsidized by the government, and could spend a week in a beautiful location with their peers. The organizers would provide visas, transport from Moscow and St. Petersburg to Seliger, and free room and board at the camp for everyone. Russian participants had to pay a fee of approximately 50 dollars.

International participants had to apply for the session of their choice with an essay. Those who were accepted received a confirmation letter in early June, about four weeks before the camp began on 2 July 2010. As the Russian visa process can seem daunting to those with little experience with it, future participants had concerns and asked organizers for details.

In response, the organizers sent out a group email on 8 June with the title «GUYS – JUST FOR ALL OF YOU TO CALM DOWN A TAD» [sic]. They guaranteed that everyone would receive their visa by mid-June at the latest. They told participants not to go to the embassy to ask about the status of their visas but instead wait for their names to appear on a list the organizers would upload on their website. The participants could then pick up their visa. Mid-June passed, however, without any news. Some names appeared online. Mine was not among them. A week before the camp started, I decided to write an email to the organizers but did not receive a reply. On 26 June, finally, Mikhail Mamonov addressed the participants. He opened with the encouraging words (again, all in capital letters) that, in spite of some difficulties, «we are here – just a few days from the most exciting adventure of this summer and hopefully – of your life.»

However, the news was not good for all participants. With regard to the visas, Mamonov suddenly absolved the organizers of all responsibility:

> «You tried your best to get a Russian visa, which was an uphill battle with bureaucracy and all sorts of formalities. We celebrate those who made it and sincerely apologise to those who did not. In our defence we must say that we did everything possible and impossible for you – however, it is as good as it got.»

For many participants, this meant that they had booked their flights and were now left with a useless ticket, an unexpected predicament after the high expectations the organizers had raised. I decided to pay for an expensive express visa.[87]

Officially, Mikhail Mamonov claimed that 800 foreigners from 89 countries participated in the camp. He downplayed visa problems and argued that only 30 potential participants had had to cancel (Bratersky 2010). These official numbers are almost certainly inaccurate. During the camp, he admitted to Krisztian Simon that only 700 foreigners were at Seliger. This number corresponds to a count that I made: adding up all the names of those who were cleared for a visa led me to a number of 703 participants.[88] This means that either more people canceled than officially admitted, or that international interest in the camp was very small. Both official and unofficial counts of inter-

---

[87] Many others did not have this option. According to a *New York Times* article about the visa problems, most American participants had to cancel (Taranova 2010). Numerous angry and anxious posts on the camp's Facebook-site indicate that participants from other countries had to cancel their trip as well.

[88] Many of them came from developing countries. The largest delegations were from India (74 participants), Nigeria (64), Egypt (63) and China (50).

national participants are much lower than the 1'000 participants the organizers had expected before the camp.

Seliger representatives met those international participants that made it to Russia in Moscow and St. Petersburg and transferred them to the camp. Some participants who arrived at the airport could not find the representatives. A participant from Slovakia said that he waited 16 hours for a bus, in spite of promises that at least two buses would leave daily. Tunde Cserpes, a female student from Hungary, told a similar story:

> «We waited for our bus to take us to Seliger for 8 hours. We were supposed to leave at 2 pm but finally managed to leave around 10 pm. Moreover, it was very hard to find the organizers who were supposed to meet us at a predefined spot (...), because it was a huge place and they were sitting far away from the station under some tree, using the 'Seliger' signs to sit on.»

I personally waited 6 hours for the bus to leave. Participants would have been more understanding of the complications if the organizers had been more realistic in their promises. Furthermore, they stated that the drive to Lake Seliger would only take four hours. Because of the bad road conditions in Russia, however, it took almost ten.[89]

Once we arrived at the camp at around 2 in the morning, our tents were not yet ready. Over a hundred participants spent the rest of the night in a large tent swarming with mosquitoes. The next morning, we were moved to our campsite and received our passes. Participants also received food. At noon, the first general assembly took place.

The Songs of Seliger

As mentioned above, these assemblies were the centerpieces of official camp culture, as they brought together everyone present at the camp twice a day. Participants were entertained with a mélange of speeches, animation and music. Young animators asked whether «Europe», «Asia» or «Africa» was «in the house» to solicit cheers and applause. The camp managers, first and foremost Mikhail Mamonov, addressed the participants to let them know

---

89 As a matter of fact, it was a wonderful, if choppy, ride through the beautiful Russian countryside. The improvised sightseeing included a break at a rest stop, where elderly Russian ladies in wooden shacks sold homemade pastries and cooked tea in Samovars. However, because most participants were not prepared for this kind of adventure, many had a hard time enjoying it.

about rules, activities and other important information. Before, during and after the assemblies, rousing, patriotic Russian pop music was playing, aimed at creating an excited, emotional atmosphere. The goal of this kind of entertainment at Seliger was, to quote Ulrich Schmid, the provision of ready-made emotions, with an emphasis on group experience, rather than political ideology (Schmid 2006: 9f.). Lassila also refers to the central function of emotions as a stimulant for Nashi's brand of patriotism (2012b: 176)

Music served as one of the most important tools camp organizers used to create this atmosphere. All participants awoke to the Russian national anthem at 8 am, which was followed by Russian children's songs. Shortly before 8.30, the organizers would turn up the volume and start playing a small selection of patriotic pop songs that would be repeated at various points throughout the day. They combined a patriotic message and easily digestible pop with mass appeal. One song, «Davai Rossiia!» («Go, Russia!»), first emerged from the talent show «Star Factory» (*Fabrika Zvezd'*) on Russia's First Channel in 2004 (Pervyi Kanal 2011a). «Star Factory» is the Russian equivalent of «American Idol» or «Deutschland sucht den Superstar», albeit with a stronger element of overt patriotism. «Davai Rossiia!» became the unofficial anthem for various Russian sports teams. It only played for one morning at Seliger 2010. International participants asked the camp organizers to delete it from the repertoire because they found its message too blatant and banal: «Go, Russia! Go! Go! (...) Goal! Goal! Goal! We will win the championship!»

Other songs were no less patriotic but had slightly more sophisticated lyrics. As a result, most international camp participants could not understand them. Furthermore, these songs were slightly less aggressive in their musical style. All of them evoked the image of a new generation doing its part to serve its country. Often, the nodal points of modernization and national unity structured the songs, which contained no antagonistic moments.

Three pieces were written expressly for the camp in earlier years: «Vse my liubim Seliger» (*We all love Seliger*) and «Kto so mnoi na Seliger» (*Who is at Seliger with me?*). «Kto, esli ne my» (*Who, if not us*) is often referred to as the Seliger anthem. Two other songs were aimed directly at «youth» and evoked a vague feeling of generational communality: «Rossiia – Vpered!»

(*Forward Russia!*) talked about youth's role in modernizing Russia; «My pokolenie – my Rossiia» (*We are the generation – we are Russia*) was the official anthem of the Russian *Year of Youth* in 2009. This song opens with a rousing guitar riff in the style of a hard rock song. A male voice begins to sing:

«We didn't make a revolution[90]
Yes, we know, it's complicated
We change our lives for the better
We are Russia, we can do it
We remember our forefathers
No use to think of us as others
We are proud of our history
Russia's youth is Russia's strength»[91]

The song articulates a vision of youth that is active but non-revolutionary, youth that works towards changes within the existing system without trying to change its basic parameters; the youth presented in the song is «Russia's strength». Furthermore, it is a youth that takes pride in Russia's history and continues the country's traditions. The nodal points of historical continuity and work for the state are familiar from Nashi's manifesto. This is not surprising if one considers that the *Year of Youth* was Iakemenko's first prestige project as head of the Federal Agency for Youth Affairs. Nashi's vision of patriotic Russian youth identity had arrived in Russian political mainstream.

In the chorus, female voices fall in with the male voice:

«We youth are no gray mass, youth is a creative power
We kids (*rebiata*) are living people, youth sounds beautiful
Youth, don't sound off, Youth, don't be passive
Youth, that is us and you, youth, that is Russia
We are the generation, we are the generation
We are the country's generation, we are Russia!»[92]

---

[90] Note the contrast to Nashi's revolutionary program in its manifesto. This song provides further confirmation that Nashi toned down its revolutionary rhetoric after its foundation and particularly after the «Bronze Nights».

[91] All English lyrics are my translation and thus only do partial justice to the original version: Мы не сделали революции/Да, мы знаем, что это сложно/Мы изменим нашу жизнь к лучшему/Мы Россия, мы это сможем/Не забыли мы подвиг прадедов/зря нас считают другими/Мы гордимся нашей историей/Россия сильна молодыми.

[92] Молодёжь, мы не серая масса/Молодёжь, это творчества сила/Молодёжь, мы ребята из жизни/Молодёжь звучит красиво/Молодёжь не труби ОТБОЙ/ Моло-

In the lyrics of the chorus, young Russians are depicted as a creative and active force. By framing this as «us» and as «us and you», listeners are addressed directly and called into action. At the end of the chorus, «we» are even equated to Russia.

Other songs played at Seliger, like Mark Tishman's saccharine «Rossiia – Vpered!» (*Forward Russia!*), contained a similar message.[93] The song begins with the words «life prepares many new stories for us», and the first lines talk about young people grappling with fate. The first verse ends with: «There were heroes and examples before us. Now, we have caught up with them». The song goes into a polyphonic chorus, with female voices singing:

«Be strong, be bold!
We can follow a hundred paths
But among them, there is only one for us
Always forward, and we will win!»[94]

The music crescendos, and the second, climactic part of the chorus begins:

«We are opening our wings, we are finding strength
Forward, Russia!
And only the wind is at our backs
For this we thank the heavens
Forward, Russia!
Russia, forward!»[95]

This song projects an image of youth that embarks on a life full of opportunities. The second part of the chorus links the success of Russian youth to that of the country: if young Russians move forward, so does Russia. Like in «My Pokolenie – My Rossiia», the new generation is presented as the future of Russia and its fate is equated with that of the country.

дёжь не будь пассивной/Молодёжь, это мы с тобой/Молодёжь, это Россия/Мы поколение/Мы поколение /Страны поколение/Мы Россия!

93 Tishman is another product of the talent show «Star Factory». After his successful debut hit *I Will Be Your Angel* in 2007, Tishman wrote *Forward Russia* in February of 2008 as the hymn for the youth talent show «Sokrovishche Natsii» (*National Treasure*), which he hosted in 2009 (Pervyi Kanal 2011b). He also performed *Forward Russia* at the concert *I Choose Russia*, which took place in downtown Moscow on 2 March 2008 after the successful election of Dmitry Medvedev (Tishman 2011).

94 Ты сильным будь, ты будь смелей/Пройти сумеем сто путей/Но, среди них наш путь один/Всегда вперёд, мы победим!

95 Мы раскрываем крылья, мы обретаем силы/Вперёд, Россия!/И только ветер нам в спину, за это небу спасибо/Вперёд, Россия!/Россия, вперёд!

«Kto, esli ne my» (*Who, if not us*) reiterates that Russia's future really depends on «us»: «We are on the way to a great discovery», says the first verse, «to a strong, free and rich Russia». In order to make this vision a reality, the singer reassures the listeners, «free and ambitious» people are needed: «Russia's tomorrow depends on us».

«Who, if not us?» asks the chorus, and lists a number of «our» goals and qualities: scientific thinking, the strength of a generation, the unity of a team, and the breakthrough of the century. The chorus closes: «Who, if not us, free Russia». This new generation is capable of many things:

«We don't lose our calm in the midst of the elements

We are realizing the projects of a great country

We remember the history of our Russia

And we are the ones who make history (…)

It won't be easy for us, that's logical

Our success is the country's success.[96]

The new generation presented here has almost Promethean features, heroically resists the elements, builds a great nation and makes history. Once more, though, its activities serve the interest of the country. After this verse and the chorus, a rap intermezzo by the group KMS changes the mood, if not the content:

«It's a different time, a different generation

Moving forward with new ideas and without doubts

It is time to be leaders, not followers

Time to make our own new history, together we're united (…)

We can dream, lead the economy, steer a ship

And there are many of us.»[97]

Like in the previous songs, the projected image of Russian youth links its fate to that of the country and presents youth as the driving force towards a modern Russia. In this song, however, the nodal point of modernization is articulated more clearly than in previous pieces. The well-being of the country is

---

96   Мы штиля не ждем в эпицентре стихии/Мы строим проекты великой страны/Мы помним историю нашей России/И эту историю делаем мы/(…)/Легко нам не будет, и это логично/Успех наш зовется успехом страны.

97   Пришло другое время, другое поколенье/С новыми идеями вперед и без сомненья/Время быть лидерами, а не ведомыми/Время создавать свою новую историю/Вместе мы едины/(…)/Мы можем мечтать, управлять экономикой/Водить корабли, и нас много таких.

depicted as dependent on leadership, scientific thinking and teamwork. Furthermore, the song underlines the importance of a free and strong Russia, which links it more explicitly to the emphasis on strengthening the state in official discourse, discussed in earlier chapters.

«Kto Esli ne My» is often depicted as the second hymn of the *Year of Youth* in 2009 and the anthem of the Lake Seliger camp. The song is another product of the talent show «Star Factory»: the band «Chelsea», a participant of the television show in 2007, wrote the song (Pervyi Kanal 2011c).

The two songs that were written expressly for the Seliger camp both have strong hip-hop and rap influences. «Kto so mnoi na Seliger» (*Who is at Seliger with me?*) also features elements of reggae. The song is less patriotic than those presented before. Instead, it exudes a kind of feel-good vibe with escapist elements. It starts by introducing the camp, referring specifically to the 2007 session, when it was written. Its entire first verse aims to get the listener, addressed directly in the familiar *ty*, active and involved: «Hey, call your friends, come study here, prestigious and fun. Together we realize projects. If you are ready, do your bit!»[98] To do this «bit» can mean many different things, the addressee learns from the song: participation in civic and social debates, running 5 kilometers or just taking pictures. «We are ready to change the course of events. Who are you? A participant? Or just a regular spectator?» The song evokes the same active youth that wants to take charge and presents the camp as the place that offers the opportunity to get involved *and* to have fun. The political content is only of secondary importance.

«Who's with me at Seliger? Studies, parties, 2007
Who's with me at Seliger? Free from the city, free from problems
Who's with me at Seliger? Here, there are no forbidden topics!
Who's with me at Seliger? Ours! There's room for everyone!»[99]

The chorus highlights the carefree attitude of the camp. Only the reference to «Ours» (Nashi) in the last line hints at its organizers, yet the expression is ambiguous enough to simply describe the friendly and like-minded people.

---

[98] Эй, зови друзей, учиться здесь/престижно и веселей/вместе двигаем проекты/Если ты готов/То внеси свою лепту.

[99] Кто со мной на Селигер? Учеба, тусовки, 2007/Кто со мной на Селигер? Свободен от города, свободен от проблем/Кто со мной на Селигер? Здесь нету запретных тем!/Кто со мной на Селигер? Наши! Здесь место хватит всем!

The second piece of music about Seliger, «Vse my liubim Seliger» (*We all love Seliger*), also a hip-hop song, starts out by describing the camp's natural beauty, the opportunity to ride bikes and kayaks, and the chance to make friends: «5'000 people, and all are friends», the verse says. The chorus adds: «My house, my friends, we all love Seliger».
The second part of the song, however, is more explicitly political.
    «The door to the foundry of modernization is open
    Russia forward, our destiny will be sensational
    Improve our system every day
    Seliger 2008 is part of the plan 2020.»[100]

The lyrics describe Seliger as a «foundry of modernization» (*kuznitsa modernizatsii*), producing young people who are innovative and motivated to serve their country. Their efforts are not directed purely at self-improvement, but at the improvement of the political system. Furthermore, the mention of the «Plan 2020» refers to Putin's programmatic speech in front of the State Council in 2008, in which he laid out his plans for the development of Russia through 2020 (Putin 2008b). In the speech, he emphasized technological innovation and his goal to turn Russia into a global technological leader (ibid.: 7). As a result, «modernization» became a nodal point in official Russian discourse.

All the songs analyzed above call upon Russia's youth to become active and to direct their attention in such a way as to benefit their country. More or less explicitly, the goal toward which Russia's youth is supposed to work is modernization. In those songs that mention Seliger explicitly, the camp is presented as the embodiment of this youthful spirit and the place where young people can realize their goals.

The songs convey official ideas about the desired societal role of youth in Russia to the audience. As argued earlier, Nashi's task is essentially the same. These songs affect the audience primarily through the emotional effect of the music. The political messages featured in them are ever present, but they are conveyed in a depoliticized form. Many of these songs form part of official popular culture because of their distribution through television talent

---

100   Открыта дверь в кузницу кадров модернизации/Россия вперёд, наш удел сенсации/(...)/Делать лучше каждый день наша система/Селигер 2008, часть плана 2020.

shows and large concerts. Teenagers do not necessarily perceive them to be political propaganda. In this way, the songs form part of what Martin Müller, in reference to Michael Billig, has termed «banal patriotism»: «the political is incorporated into the realm of the everyday». As a result, discursive demands appear natural and «normal» (Müller 2009a: v). This combination of emotion, popular culture and simple patriotism explains much of the appeal of official youth culture in Russia.

Leisure and Discipline

The demand to work together tirelessly toward personal and societal improvement was evident not only in the songs but also in the tight schedule of the camp. At Seliger, there was very little time for individual activity. Participants were strongly encouraged to spend leisure time with their group in structured activities.

All activities on offer – kayaking, boating, climbing, bicycling and excursions to a nearby monastery – were only available to officially registered units. Their instructors had to sign up for the activity and take responsibility for the group's safety and good conduct. They also needed to make sure that the group arrived at the obligatory activities (lectures, general assemblies, business program) on time. Instructors were penalized if their unit misbehaved.

The camp was also under a strict curfew. At midnight, all participants had to be in their tents. The uniformed security service patrolled the camp to make sure that no one violated this rule. Even participants who held whispered conversations in their tents after 12.30 in the morning were reprimanded.

Some members of our group sat around the campfire one night until 1 am, in spite of admonitions by the security staff. The guards got angry with the participants but did not force them into their tents. However, the next day we learned that this violation had been reported to the camp management, and that our instructor had received a wage cut as a result.

Discipline was a central camp value, sometimes with unfortunate consequences. On the second night, Mikhail Mamonov invited soccer fans to watch World Cup games on the large screen near the main stage. The game Ghana against Uruguay attracted an audience of approximately fifty participants.

However, at exactly midnight, the screen was turned off suddenly and without explanation, and guards demanded that everyone return to their tents quickly. The next morning, Mamonov responded to the incident, stating that turning off the screen so abruptly had been a mistake. He also commented on the strict rules. I wrote in my field diary:

> «Apparently we are not the only group that feels patronized. He [Mamonov] says: 'These rules are needed to maintain discipline. I hope you understand.' This may be so; considering that this is a camp full of adults, and not teenagers, however, the limitations are quite crass. We learn for example that our instructor gets her wages cut if she does not completely assemble her group at the agreed upon time. Moreover, everyone who is not with their group during mealtimes or is found in their tent during the mandatory activities gets a hole in their camp badge.»

These holes functioned according to a «three strikes, and you are out» system. As it turned out, the system was not enforced very tightly with the international students. None of them were sent home. Nonetheless, they experienced the disciplining function of these rules on an everyday basis. The fact that the instructors, in our case a very nice and committed 19 year-old student, received pay deductions because of the internationals' undisciplined behavior gave the disciplining system a particularly perfidious character.

On the third day, the organizers decided to try to enforce general discipline more resolutely than before. It had been a very hot afternoon, and many participants preferred the beach to organized leisure activities. During the general assembly in the evening, Mamonov shamed and threatened them. I wrote in my field notes:

> «Mamonov says: 'I asked the guards to be very gentle with you. But please don't overstep the boundaries.' Since boundaries were overstepped, says Mamonov, the guards would take more forceful actions against 'bad guys'. After he finishes talking, a short film starts playing on the big screen next to the stage. There are no words, and sad music is playing. The animated Seliger-mascot, a smiling face, is making a sad face. Images of people lounging on the beach are shown, and underneath it says 'NASHA lektsiia' [our lesson].»

The next day, the guards pulled anyone who tried to swim out of the water.
The international participants I surveyed experienced these rules as unnec-

essarily strict. The two students from Hungary felt oppressed by them: Tunde Cserpes called the camp «a small remake of the socialist world» and said that the friends she had convinced to come along were shouting at her angrily the first night: «What did you do? You brought us to a communist camp!?!» Krisztian Simon explained that he felt like he was

> «closed in a camp without the option to leave (it was really far from all the summer universities I visited before, I really missed going out for a beer and discussing the topic of the lectures at the end of the day – which is normal in any liberal summer university, instead I felt like I was in a high school or elementary school camp: infantilized and forced under the authority of an almighty teacher.»

These statements reflect a basic misunderstanding between organizers and participants. Since the former had marketed the camp as a summer school for university students, international participants did not expect the strict disciplinary structures that have been an essential part of the Seliger camp since its inception. In fact, some Russian participants of prior years even told me that the discipline had previously been stricter.

The organizers hosted the youth camp at Seliger under a fundamental assumption, derived from official Russian youth policies, that people younger than 30 are a vulnerable resource that must be protected and guided (see chapter 1). Moreover, the camp's hierarchical and tightly organized structures were very much in the tradition of Soviet children and youth camps.[101] Many foreign students in their twenties, on the other hand, do not consider themselves to be youth and are accustomed to more freedom in summer schools.

The only excursion our group undertook outside of the guarded campground led us to the monastery of Nilova Pustyn'. In order to get to this idyllic and moderately touristy spot, we had to receive official permission from the camp management to get past the camp gates. Whether we would get this permission was initially unclear.

> «After lunch we get permission from the camp management to visit the nearby monastery after all. We start walking and pass the camp of the security forces. It is guarded separately and located behind a tall fence. The guards – I can see a few dozen – are sitting around a long table eating lunch. We con-

---

101 This is a point that Giorgio Comai, another participant observer at the International Youth Forum Seliger 2010 highlights as well (Comai 2012).

tinue on. At the exit, two grim guards men our permission. They will search our bags when we return. It feels liberating to be outside of the camp.»

Once the group passed the security gates and was on its own, the mood became relaxed. The participants enjoyed the view of Lake Seliger and the cultural experience of walking around an old Russian monastery. We learned little about the monastery that we visited. At the beginning of World War II, I learned later, it had served as a camp for 7'000 Polish prisoners of war who were subsequently executed at Katyn (Snyder 2010: 119ff.).

In general, it was surprising that Russian history, and the history of World War II, which occupies such a central position in Nashi's ideology, was almost completely absent from the international forum. There was only an eternal flame in the camp where members of Nashi took turns as honorary guards. A replica partisan bunker was constructed next to the flame to commemorate the strong partisan activity in the region. The bunker was closed for most of the international session.

This does not mean that the memory of the Great Patriotic War has become less important in official programs aimed at the patriotic education of young Russians. In 2010, the Federal Agency for Youth Affairs founded the project «Our Shared Victory» (*Nasha Obshchaia Pobeda*), which aims to create a video archive of veterans' memories (Nasha Obshchaia Pobeda 2010). The bunker at Seliger, as well as various art installations with a World War II theme in the camp, played a more prominent role during the later Seliger sessions, after the international participants had left.

It seems apparent that the management of the camp did not consider this historical aspect to be of interest for the international participants and thus understated it during the international session. Whereas victory in World War II plays an important role in conveying a modern and strong Russia to Russian youth, organizers of the Seliger camp most likely considered this connection to be less plausible in an international context.

Lectures

Official discourse was also omnipresent in the lectures. Each group was supposed to attend six mandatory lectures during their week at Seliger. Our group missed two of them, the first due to organizational difficulties on the first day, the last because it was cancelled without explanation. The lectures I attended broadly concerned democracy and civil society. I will discuss three of them in detail.

The first presenter was Richard Lachmann, a sociologist at the University at Albany. His lecture was titled «Balancing the Oligarchy: The Power of Civil Society» and focused on the power of large corporations in the United States. According to Lachmann, these corporations are much more powerful today than they were in the past because the processes of globalization have removed many of their traditional restraints – unions, national borders and markets. His pessimistic conclusion was that civil society in the contemporary United States is largely powerless. I wrote in my field diary:

> «The questions that follow are interesting. One Russian participant asks, how professor Lachmann estimates the power of the international oligarchy [sic], which rules the world and uses the United States for its purposes. Another Russian participant speaks of the 'information war', in which American mass media manipulate the population. He asks if Lachmann considers it possible that the US would begin a large-scale war against Russia to justify its military expenditures. The question of whether there exists an oligarchy in Russia does not come up.»

Strikingly, he did not mention Russia at all, leaving his analysis oddly out of context, particularly since all the other lectures did mention Russia – albeit in a largely uncritical fashion. This lecture focused exclusively on the abysmal state of civil society in the United States. This assessment received additional legitimacy through the fact that the one who judged the United States was an American professor.[102]

The questions illustrated the discursive tenets that government leaders and Nashi had emphasized during the Orange Revolution: the global population is manipulated by a state-guided «information war», and that the American government harbors hostility and even bellicose feelings towards Russia.

The United States also featured prominently in the second lecture about «Freedom and Democracy» by Tatiana Alekseeva, professor and the head of the Department of Political Theory at the MGIMO in Moscow. In what was the

---

102   It is not my intention here to claim that Lachmann's analysis of American civil society and the power of oligarchies in the US is groundless. What I did find striking and propagandistic is the fact that this presentation was held in a youth camp sponsored by the Russian government.

most thought-provoking of all lectures I heard at Seliger, she attempted to decenter Western notions of democracy and discussed the difficulties of establishing a democracy in Russia.

Alekseeva explained that the main Soviet heritage that needed to be overcome in Russia was the atomization of society and the lack of trust that exists in formerly totalitarian societies. Anybody attempting to build a democracy in Russia had to overcome both popular distrust of political institutions and the huge differences in development between centers and provinces, she stated. Nevertheless, «we will never have a Western democracy» because the Western model was not universal, she maintained. Alekseeva criticized former president George W. Bush for attempting to export an American model of democracy without taking into account historical, cultural and regional differences.

According to Alekseeva, democracy is simply «a continuous limitation of violence from above,» all its other aspects differ from country to country. In order to establish a democratic system in Russia, she argued, this process needed to happen gradually. In her assessment, Putin and Medvedev had taken important steps toward democratization, and she explicitly cited the electoral reforms of 2005, the creation of new parties such as Spravedlivaia Rossiia and Medvedev's anti-corruption campaign.

Alekseeva's talk identifies some of the specific obstacles on Russia's path to democracy. She also correctly warns against an uncritical transfer of Western models to Russia. Her views on the issue reflect the views of Russia's mainstream political scientists, which are also shared by Surkov and feature prominently in Sovereign Democracy (Surkov 2006b: 2; Surkov 2006a: 75). At the same time, Alekseeva presented a specifically pro-government position by arguing that the controversial strengthening of the power vertical through election reforms in 2005 was a step towards democratization, an argument that many political scientists disagree with. By presenting Putin and Medvedev as guarantors of Russia's democratic development, she uncritically repeated government views. She ignored any negative influences of the Putin regime on Russia's democratic development.

Ivan Timofeev, lecturer at the MGIMO, also attempted to decenter Western notions of democracy and civil society. He singled out the American non-governmental organization Freedom House for particular criticism and presented a new model with which to measure democracy, developed at MGIMO. He reprimanded the organization's placement of Russia in the lowest category of «not free» (Freedom House 2010).

Timofeev considered Russia's ranking as «not free» in the Freedom House *Freedom in the World* report to be misleading and wrong. Timofeev's model, on the other hand, not only takes the institutional components of democracy into account but also highlights the strength of state institutions, internal and external threats to the state, and the quality of life. Through this assessment, Russia ranked in the middle – 98th among 192 surveyed countries.

Timofeev's focus on statehood corresponds to the prominence of state-centered perceptions of Russia in the political science mainstream. With his criticism of Freedom House, Timofeev contributes to a large body of international scholarship on the subject.[103]

Taken together, these lectures correspond to what Laclau terms «a systematic decentering of the West» (Laclau 1996: 34). Lachmann's presentation illustrated the weakness of American civil society. The other two lectures attempted to demonstrate that Russian democracy was comparable, but not equal to, that in the West. To the extent that such a decentering fosters dialogue and a rethinking of Western paradigms, it is convincing. However, a problematization of the Russian system was entirely absent, and international participants were discouraged from critical involvement with Russian politics and society. No critical discussion ensued after the lectures, and the organizers made no efforts to foster such a discussion. Instead, the lectures were held in a classic, formal presentation format, like in a high school. The Seliger camp differed significantly from other summer schools, at which critical questions to the lecturer form an integral part of the teaching program.

Of the participants I surveyed, no one could remember the content of a single lecture. Tunde Cserpes called it simply «dull», while a man from Eastern Eu-

---

103 Political scientist Diego Giannone similarly believes Freedom House's methodology and personnel to be motivated by a pro-American, neoliberal bias (Giannone 2010: 73ff.). Freedom House has always denied such allegations. In Russia, Freedom House's decision in 2007 to downgrade Russia to «not free» in 2007 caused outrage among officials (Alexandrova 2007).

rope, who otherwise liked the camp, referred to it as «not satisfactory at all!» Many participants felt that their input was neither desired nor required. This attitude contrasted sharply with reactions to the other half of the morning program – the «sharing».

Sharing Sessions

«Sharing», in the course of the week, came to signify a rather open format of exchange among participants, which very much contrasted the formal lectures. On the first day, the camp management tried to organize «sharing» activities, but the lack of organization quickly frustrated international participants. My diary reads:

> «Our 'curator' explains to me (…) that the person who was supposed to organize this session never showed up, so they threw something together this morning. We are all playing 'activity', a game quite similar to 'taboo', in which one has to get one's group to guess a word through gestures and explanations. The situation is quite complicated because the Russian group that is mixed with the international group hardly speaks English, and the foreigners don't understand Russian. Soon, the majority simply starts speaking Russian. The other foreigners in my group think this is nothing but a waste of time.»

For the next few days, «sharing» activities were less formally controlled, but organizers made another effort only on the penultimate day. All units had to participate in discussions about civil society in small groups that rotated between tables. The results, organizers promised, would be transcribed, put online in English, and serve as a basis for further international discussion.

The discussions provided a venue for a meaningful if difficult exchange between Russians and international participants.

> «At our table we are discussing educational measures that could strengthen civil society in the next 15 years. One half of the table speaks Russian, the other half English. A Russian colleague and I are translating a lot. The opinions are quite varied: a Russian participant thinks that one should teach the bible more frequently at universities to strengthen humanitarian values. He claims that violence and crime at schools have risen since the bible is not taught any more. Some 'internationals' on the other hand highlight religious freedom and doubt whether the situation is really as simple as he thinks. They suggest more room for NGOs in curricula and more financial support by the state.

During the second discussion about migration, the standpoints are equally diverse. One Russian participant says that migration weakens the culture of migrants *and* societies, and that many people are uprooted as a result. He says that some forces in the world are very interested in this happening. He says: 'I am a conspiracy theorist, and I am not ashamed to say it'. Others argue against him that identities are not fixed but change over time. No one denies that migration creates certain problems. We all agree, however, that it can't just be abolished.»

These debates gave international participants a chance to discuss issues with their Russian colleagues at length. Differing worldviews became apparent and were articulated, which created a space for creative friction. Unfortunately, this discussion proved to be a one-time-event. They were never put online and thus did not continue. Had the organizers fostered this open exchange between international and Russian participants more actively, the debates may have had a more lasting effect.

The organizers' lessened zeal to control the sharing between participants created room for self-organized discussion. These exchanges were rather improvised, but they contributed more effectively to creating international contacts and to furthering our knowledge of other countries than the official events had done. Our group included participants from Russia, Hungary, Slovakia, Switzerland, India, Pakistan, Thailand and Indonesia. Each of us provided others with basic information about the political systems of our countries and the role of civil society. This exchange inevitably remained superficial but provided the basis for further discussion throughout the week.

In the days that followed, these sharing sessions increasingly became a forum for articulating opinions and criticism about the camp. In reaction to the many organizational problems and especially to our instructor's pay cut, we decided to write a letter to the camp management. This was in part in response to Mamonov's suggestion that we should not hesitate to contact him with suggestions for improvements.

During the session, we gathered the points that group members wanted to have included in the letter. I collected them and put them down in writing. I then submitted the draft of the letter to the rest of the group for criticism and approval.[104] In the first part, we thanked the organizers for making this event possible and for enabling students from all over the world to meet one another. All the people to whom I spoke experienced this aspect very positively. Russian participants in particular were extremely welcoming to international participants, expressed curiosity about life outside of Russia and even apologized for the organizers of the camp.

In the second part of the letter, we mentioned concrete points that we thought could be improved in the future. The first two points of criticism had to do with insubstantial organization and poor communication. Many scheduled activities were cancelled without prior information. One of the most interesting proposed projects from our point of view was the creation of an English-language camp newspaper. Nobody attempted to carry it out, although it would have provided a great opportunity for Russians and international students to collaborate by reporting on the camp.

Another important criticism concerned discipline: as discussed above, many found the strict rules oppressive. We additionally criticized that rules were often maintained even when unfeasible due to organizational difficulties. For example, when we wanted to go climbing, we were told we could only do so within a strictly defined time frame. When we registered and lined up at the appointed time, however, the manager of the climbing park sent us away because he was about to go on break. They only let us in after we had waited for two hours. Our final paragraph concluded as follows:

> «We hope that the organizers will not interpret this letter as an attack against them, but rather as a constructive piece of criticism. We feel very welcome here and know that everybody has worked very, very hard to host us. The staff is extraordinarily helpful and does their best to deal with our grievances. We thus hope sincerely that some of the problems this year will not keep the organizers from making this event happen again.»

---

104 The role I played in this situation of course runs counter to the aim of minimizing one's impact on the data as a participant observer (Harrington 2002: 54). However, as Harrington points out, some interventions by the researcher can create new insights into the field of study and thus create new knowledge. In the case of this study, our letter a) provided an opportunity for my group to articulate and communicate their opinions of the camp, and b) showed how the camp management reacted to criticism.

We were curious whether and how Mikhail Mamonov would react to the letter. Unfortunately, there was no direct response at all. Instead, organizers mentioned at the general assembly that there had been a lot of criticism of the camp management. Il'ia Kostunov, a Nashi commissar and the head of the Seliger Forum, admitted that they had received many critical letters. In Russian, he added, «we hope that we will receive some letters in the next few days in which participants tell us their true opinion about the Forum.» This puzzling statement was not translated into English, and it remains unclear what he precisely meant. However, it appears that Kostunov considered criticism of the camp to be disingenuous.

It became increasingly obvious throughout the week that organizers were frustrated about criticism and took it personally. Particularly Mamonov looked increasingly tired from micromanaging the most diverse aspects of the camp: after every general assembly, a crowd of guides and participants would stop him behind stage to discuss numerous issues and grievances.

On 5 July, *The New York Times* published a critical article about Seliger under the title «Bureaucracy Stymies Pro-Kremlin Youth Retreat» (Taranova 2010). According to eyewitnesses, Mikhail Mamonov was furious about this report and subsequently refused to make any statements to journalists. He also cancelled an interview with Krisztian Simon on short notice. It appears he was no longer able to make statements without approval from above. The camp management's reaction to criticism parallels Nashi's conduct: instead of admitting the validity of criticism, critics are denounced, and little changes.

The World Outside

Despite their negative reactions to criticism, organizers did expect critical questions from participants and prepared for them. The Russian guides repeatedly mentioned a document that had circulated among them with instructions on how to respond to critical questions. I found a copy of this document that had been left on a table.

The document, entitled «Some Inconvenient Questions about the Russian Authorities» (*Neskol'ko Neudobnykh Voprosov Rossiiskoi Vlasti*, see appendix II), is revealing because it shows the camp management's perception of and reaction to foreign and domestic criticism. The document is essentially an instruction manual. There are 21 questions and 21 answers. The answers are between half a page and two pages long.

Questions cover a wide variety of social, political, economic and demographic concerns in Russia. The varied content and style of the document suggests that various authors were at work. Some passages contain sophisticated explanations with graphs and statistics; others are marked by a rude and dismissive style. A number of email exchanges between Nashi and other activists that was leaked recently shows that the brochure indeed went through various drafts by various authors (slivmail.com/ rakinbah/message/25690).

Answers to questions about economic policy are particularly sophisticated. Question six, for example, asks, «Why is the Stabilization Fund kept in American dollars?» Presumably, this would be a question that could be expected from the Russian nationalist camp. The answer explains that the Russian Central Bank has the third highest currency reserves in the world. These are kept mostly in dollars and euro. «In principle, this is how all normal states act.» The authors go on to argue that, yes, the United States profits from the fact that most states have their currency reserves invested in dollars. However, this is «America's fee (*plata*) for the 'service' of guaranteeing the functioning of the international currency system. (…) [There is no] other system (…), and we cannot establish it on our own.» The response continues, noting that dollars and euros are always available on international markets. «Our country can take its money back at any moment». The answer shows a marked economic pragmatism and reflects Nashi's new emphasis on economic topics.

Question 19 claims that the wealth created under Putin (*putinskoe blagopoluchie*) has only been the result of high oil prices. It accuses the government of using this wealth inadequately and without achieving the modernization of the Russian economy. The response opens with a brief jab at the opposition, which, according to the author(s), wants to lead Russia back into the 1990s. The reply further explains that the government has made sure that the country has received the highest possible return for its oil on world markets. In this way, Putin established Russia as «a partner with equal rights» on the international stage. This statement corresponds to the «great power pragmatism» discussed in earlier chapters (Sakwa 2008: 378).

The authors of the brochure do admit that Russia's economy has a problem. They explain that more developed countries achieve a higher multiplier effect for every dollar provided by the Central Bank. In Russia, this effect is 1:3, compared to 1:6 in the United States. In order to increase this multiplier effect, the authors write, Russia needs to raise investors' confidence into Russian markets and its bureaucracy and defend private property.

In the geopolitical sphere, the rhetoric is less self-critical and pragmatic. One questions asks: «Why are we fighting with our brothers (*bratskii narod*) in Belarus? Was it worth it to begin a 'gas war' (…) against them?» In the answer, blame for the worsening bilateral relations is placed on Belarussian president Aleksandr Lukashenko. According to the brochure, Russia has subsidized the Belarusian economy since the collapse of the USSR, enabling the small nation's economic success.

> «With the goal of persuading Russia to make concessions regarding gas prices, Lukashenko more than once declared his readiness to turn away from Russia and begin a cooperation with the West and China. In response, Russia suggested that [Belarus] could buy gas and oil at the world market price (…), which caused Lukashenko to release a wave of anti-Russian propaganda and reactivate nationalist forces that had been weakened in the past. Belarus has so far not recognized the independence of South Ossetia and Abkhazia (…).»

This passage departs from official Russian justifications for the conflict with Belarus: Gazprom's leadership and Dmitrii Medvedev had maintained in June 2010 that the reduction of gas deliveries to Belarus was entirely due to Belarus' unpaid debt. Lukashenko's closer ties to other power blocks and his refusal to recognize South Ossetia and Abkhazia have always circulated as unofficial explanations (The Telegraph 2010). This unofficial rationale of Russia's foreign policy mixes geopolitical motives (Belarus turns away from Russia) and market arguments (as a result, it pays world market prices), a combination very much reminiscent of similar conflicts with Ukraine.

In order to illustrate the extent to which Lukashenko set on an antagonistic course with Russia, the brochure adds that the «disgraced oligarch» (*opal'nyi oligarkh*) and «enemy of Russia» Boris Berezovskii was an advisor to Lukashenko. Hence, the authors go on to argue, «[our] quarrel is with the agent provocateur and hysteric A. Lukashenko – and not with the Belarusian people, toward whom we continue to feel the warmest feelings.» Lukashenko's actions are thus presented as irrational and possibly guided by the machinations of an enemy of Russia.

Other answers to «inconvenient questions» include veritable conspiracy theories. One question presumes that the Russian Armed Forces are not battle-ready and receives this answer: «The myth of the low battle-readiness of the Russian army was already propagated intensely by the West and the Russian 'fifth column' during the collapse of the USSR.» In fact, according to the response, army reforms and the increase in defense spending would put the Armed Forces in a position to react to all future threats. These include China's increased military capabilities, the United States as global hegemon and the extension of NATO to Russia's borders.

According to the brochure «Some Inconvenient Questions about the Russian Authorities», the West threatens Russia in more subtle ways as well. The question, «Isn't it unfair that Russia can command its resources independently, especially oil and gas?» receives the following answer:

> «These kinds of arguments are used by Russia's opponents to prepare public opinion to accept the idea of Russia's dismemberment and its transformation into the West's appendage for natural resources (*syrevoi pridatok*). (...) Is it fair that Russia, and only Russia, can command its natural resources? Certainly! Our ancestors paid with lots of blood and great pains for this wealth, they developed territories that were hardly suitable for life for centuries and defended them in numerous wars.«

This is one of the very few places in the literature from and about the Seliger camp in which history is used to justify geopolitical positions. The authors equate Russia's century-old historical struggles to extend its statehood over its current territory with a duty to pursue this struggle against contemporary threats emanating from the West. This answer corresponds to the arguments found in Nashi's manifesto and in the writings of conservative political scientists in Russia (see chapter 2).

The authors justify the arrest and prison sentence for Mikhail Khodorkovsky with similar arguments. They answer the question, «Why did they jail M. Khodorkovsky? He had the audacity to stand up against the authorities and found himself in prison...» by highlighting Russian sovereignty. The brochure calls talks between Khodorkovsky and Exxon Mobil in the autumn of 2003 a danger to «Russia's strategic security». At the time, Khodorkovsky had been about to close a deal that would have secured the American oil company a minority share in the Russian oil giant Yukos (Myers and Arvedlund 2003).

Citing Yukos' importance as a contributor to the state budget and as an employer, the authors argue that its sale to an American company would have given foreign investors control over ten percent of Russia's state budget. As a result, the government had to safeguard Russia's sovereignty. The authors of the brochure omit that no negotiations over a controlling share of Yukos for Exxon Mobil ever took place (Johnston and Trefgarne 2003). Nor does the brochure mention that Khodorkovsky had provoked Putin's anger by confronting him publicly about government corruption and by supporting the opposition. Instead, the topic is presented as related exclusively to the security and sovereignty of the Russian state.[105]

The harshest pages of the brochure, however, are reserved for Russia's opposition. «Why does OMON disperse the 'Dissenters March' (*Marsh Nesoglasnykh*) of the opposition (...)?», asks an imagined (presumably Western) critic of Russia. The authors answer with an imaginary scenario. A person with legitimate grievances such as low pay – for example «the chairman of a union» – would go to the Moscow city administration and receive a permit to demonstrate on Triumph Square in Moscow.

> «It is the 31st of May.[106] You and your comrades meet to protest. You arrive at Triumph Square, but there (...) are hooded young people who throw rocks at policemen, at windows and at everything that moves; someone runs past with a poster that reads 'we support Khodorkovsky'; and some half-witted granny (*kakaia-to poloumnaia babka*) 'bawls' across the square 'Retire Putin'! No, this is not the filming of the movie 'Open House at our Insane Asylum' – this is the 'Dissenters March'.»

Through this description, the reader is led to believe that none of the demands of the opposition – also termed a «mob of hooligans» – carries any legitimacy. Still, the authors maintain, the OMON-troops of the Ministry of the

---

105 At the time of this writing, Khodorkovsky was just released from prison as part of an amnesty. What role, if any, he will play in Russian politics in the future remains to be seen.
106 The 31st of various months is the day that the «Dissenters Marches» are traditionally held. The number 31 is used in reference to article 31 of the Russian constitution, which guarantees freedom of assembly.

Interior do not disperse the protest because of the illegitimacy of demands, but because it is illegal. «In all developed countries, and also in Russia», one needs a permit for a public protest. The fact that the «Dissenters Marches» have applied repeatedly for permits but have been denied is not mentioned.[107]

More striking than the content of the answer is its style: it is rather crude and disparages the opposition. This disrespect is even more pronounced in the answer to question five. The question, presumably originating from a potential critical Russian camp participant, concerns the government's prestige project for a «Russian Silicon Valley» at Skol'kovo:

> «Why is it necessary to waste money on Skol'kovo – this awkward (*neukliuzhii*) analogy to the American Silicon Valley? In order to create the semblance of innovative activity, or to siphon off money from the budget?»

The answer opens with the declaration that «anything the authorities do – it will always be criticized» by the opposition. According to the brochure, the opposition previously criticized authorities for neglecting the modernization of the country. Now that the government has created the project of Skol'kovo, thereby setting «a course towards the modernization of the Russian economy», the opposition calls this a waste of money and claims Russia does not need modernization, the answer reads.

However, the authors claim, Skol'kovo is a very necessary project and an improvement over the «scientific cities» (*naukogrady*) of the Soviet past. «In Skol'kovo, the plan is not just to build a scientific city, but an innovation center for the most diverse fields.» Such a center, the answer continues, would not only generate revenue but also become the «training center for a new generation» of scientists, engineers, economists and innovators. The authors also quote the involvement of businessmen like Viktor Vekselberg and the winner

---

107 One example: the «Dissenters» applied for a permit to conduct a march from Pushkin Square to Theater Square on 14 April 2007. They were denied because, according to the Moscow city administration, the pro-Kremlin youth group Molodaia Gvardiia was planning a demonstration in the same location on that exact date. When a *Kommersant"* reporter asked Molodaia Gvardiia press secretary Vadim Zharko in early April about the planned demonstration, he could provide no details and would not comment (Savina and Sukhonina 2007). It is very likely that this «planned demonstration» was a pretense to deny the opposition a permit. Nashi in 2005 also occupied public places to forestall possible opposition protests.

of the Nobel Prize in physics, Zhores Alferov, as proof for the seriousness and feasibility of the project.[108]

Skol'kovo has had a very promising beginning, the authors argue. They quote Vekselberg as saying that Russia needs many such centers of innovation. They then continue:

> «Yes, and Russia's potential for similar initiatives is just limitless. Those who are against modernization, however, can enlist themselves among the inveterate collaborators (*kollaboratsionisty*), take 100 Rubles 'prize money' from Kasianov, go and 'protest' against the 'cursed authorities' (*prokliataia vlast'*) and will deserve it when they get [beaten with] a rubber club one by one for their regular illegal political meetings on Triumph Square – the 'dissenters' already know this algorithm of activity well!»

Those who doubt Skol'kovo are presented as opponents of Russia's modernization. Protesters are depicted as paid puppets of opposition politician Mikhail Kasianov. By calling them «collaborators», the authors even insinuate that the protesters work for Russia's enemies: the term is usually employed to describe those who work with occupants, often in connection with National Socialists. If one connects this depiction to other claims of official discourse – namely that the United States wants to keep Russia weak – and to the fact that the liberal opposition in Russia is consistently portrayed as guided by the American government, it becomes clear with whom the opposition «collaborates». The equation of the «hegemonic» United States to the National Socialists is already familiar from the discussion about Nashi's manifesto in chapter 2. The content of the criticism is delegitimized through this analogy, which rhetorically justifies the use of indiscriminate police violence.

A Happy Ending?

The international participants learned nothing of these conflicts between government and opposition in Russia. The fact that the vast majority of international students knew no details about Russia's political system was a very surprising discovery for me personally. Their interest in learning more about Russian politics and society was very limited to begin with, and organizers

---

108 For an overview over current discussions about the Russian government's modernization project, see the December 2011 edition of the *Russian Analytical Digest*. Available at: http://www.isn.ethz.ch/isn/Digital-Library/Publications/Detail/?ots591=0c54e3b3-1e9c-be1e-2c24-a6a8c7060233&lng=en&id=135123.

made sure they only conveyed an official, idealized image. The International Youth Forum Seliger 2010, in spite of its organizational flaws, skillfully combined patriotic celebrations with vague internationalist modernization rhetoric and an apolitical feel-good atmosphere. Complexities and contradictions were ignored.

The closing ceremony of the forum illustrates this approach. The positive aspects were highlighted, and problems were dismissed and belittled. The moderator opened the celebration with the words: «This camp is increasingly like a ship, which we steer through storms and quiet seas together. But what would it be without a captain? So give a hand for our Mikhail Mamonov!» The «captain» stepped on stage, applauded by thousands of participants. He spoke vaguely about «some people's hysteria» surrounding organizational issues and then went on to praise the «high-class academics» participants had enjoyed and the «common language» they had developed.

After Mamonov's appearance, a film showed foreign participants saying exclusively positive things about the camp, such as, «This has been a really great time!» and «I will be back next year!», while soft, melodic music was playing in the background. An Algerian student handed an Algerian flag to Mamonov, signed by all the participants from his country. A British student praised Seliger in Russian. Then, a group of Egyptians handed Mamonov a crystal from their country and praised him. The emotional climax of the celebration, however, was an international couple: he was Russian, she was Indian. They met at Seliger, she said with tears in her eyes, «and it was love at first sight».

Immediately after the closing ceremony, the majority of international participants had to hurry to their tents to pack up. President Medvedev's visit, scheduled for the following day, had created the «hysteria» that Mamonov referred to. Even though the organizers promised multiple buses to Moscow and St. Petersburg on both days, rumors circulated that there would be no buses on the day of the president's visit. Because of their prior experiences with poor organization, no participants wanted to risk missing their flight home. The communication before Medvedev's visit was generally chaotic and disorganized. In our group, one of the Russian «curators» asked us if we wanted to meet the president. Only hours later, we were told that the authorities had made a separate list of approved visitors, a fact that Mikhail Mamonov confirmed personally.

Krisztian Simon experienced how haphazardly this selection was made. A security official sought him out based on his badge number and told Simon to wait with him. Simon was then taken to a field in front of a tent along with nine other international participants.

Mamonov and a number of unidentified men asked them whether they wanted to meet the president and ask him a «spontaneous» question. These questions, however, were prewritten. Simon recalled: «most of them related to Skol'kovo and the possible contribution foreigners can make to it.» As the officials had prepared only five questions, they chose the most enthusiastic. Simon was not among them. According to him, the organizers selected participants from India, China, Latin America and Western Europe. Simon also noted that the heavy rains during the president's visit had apparently led to the cancellation of the planned discussion session with international participants.

During his visit, the president spoke of youth's central role in the modernization of Russia, albeit within a controlled framework. «There should be continuity, but there should also be changes and new approaches. The fact that representatives from 89 countries came is great, it's wonderful», said Medvedev (*quoted in:* Maksimovich 2010). In the main part of his visit, the president inspected innovative projects at Seliger. He underlined the central significance of modernization for Russia's future.

The president's visit and the closing ceremony illustrate the importance organizers placed on the immaculate staging of main camp events. Images of the happy and unified masses at Seliger made headlines on Russia's state television channels. They showed viewers that the government had invited participants from all over the world in an effort to modernize the country and build international collaboration. The communication of camp organizers was indeed very consistent in this regard.

The lectures consistently placed Russia in an international context. It may not be a perfect democracy, they admitted, but it is on the way to becoming more modern and democratic – to becoming a normal country, in other words. All speakers agreed that the Russian government was the guarantor of this process. Criticism was reserved for the double standards of the West and the United States in particular.

At the same time, organizers carefully avoided controversial symbols and statements. The almost omnipresent Russian patriotism in the camp was presented in a modern and non-chauvinist way. The most blatantly patriotic song, «Davai Rossiia», was removed at the behest of participants. Other songs' messages were less easily understood but equally patriotic.

Nashi's presence in the camp was almost invisible to foreign participants, even though the movement controlled significant sectors of the camp management and provided numerous participants. The organizers of the International Youth Forum Seliger 2010 ensured that international students received little information about Nashi. Its name was not mentioned a single time in publications, assemblies or lectures. Participants only found out more about it if they asked Russian peers directly. Few were interested.

In de-emphasizing Nashi's importance at Seliger, organizers attempted to broaden the camp's appeal beyond the political, activist youth and to attract a broader Russian and international audience. Nashi's «home», then, has become part of the Russian political mainstream. The organization itself may have lost much of its influence, but it continues to penetrate Russian politics and culture. Exactly because Nashi reproduced official discourse very closely, «its» ideas continue to be articulated by other actors. The songs discussed above further show that this influence reaches deeply into Russia's commercial popular culture.

Patriotic rhetoric has become a constitutive part of official youth culture just as much as it penetrates Russian culture more broadly. «Banal patriotism» conveys a vague feeling of national pride and community among youth in a form that is seemingly apolitical. However, the shared goals are so vague and at times unrealistic that one must wonder to what extent young people receive the mobilizing message inherent in this patriotic pop culture and act accordingly. In other words, it appears doubtful that this patriotism can really be considered to be a hegemonic discourse in the sense that it describes a new and convincing worldview. Instead, one suspects that its glossy messages do not reach much below the surface.

The surveys I conducted and a review of the forum's Facebook-page suggest that many participants enjoyed their time at Seliger. Most of them, however, were disappointed with the academic program and the organization of the camp. The organizers' original goal of building a «global team» and «a personal across-the-globe network of like-minded individuals that want to make a difference» (Seliger 2010a) appears unrealistic and unrealized.

Judging from the fact that the most lasting Seliger memories of the majority of participants were related to the fun they had and the feeling of togetherness they experienced, the camp was not especially successful in conveying this political message. To conclude from this that Seliger has become an apolitical camp, as some have done (Martinez 2010), would nevertheless be misleading. Since state institutions started sponsoring Seliger officially in 2009, the camp has become a prestige project that showcases Russia's efforts at modernization, which was crucial for the political legitimacy of the Russian «tandem» regime and continues to play an important role during Putin's third term. In assemblies, lectures and leisure activities, political propaganda is still present at the camp. Furthermore, it actively excludes all political views that do not fit into official discourse, which in and of itself represents a political operation.

Tensions inherent in Nashi's ideology nonetheless plague Seliger. The brochure «Some Inconvenient Questions about the Russian Authorities» shows how some nodal points of official discourse – economic modernization and the strengthening of the state against its enemies – are often at odds with each other. As long as critics of projects like Skol'kovo are vilified and presented as foreign agents, the creative energy that the forum at Seliger is supposed to release within Russia will remain limited. Organizers at no point encouraged open discussions, consistently ignored criticism and undermined projects that could have fostered exchange. This contradiction also reflects broader inconsistencies in official discourse between a securitized vision of Russia's international relations and a more open, collaborative view. The latter vision would require a willingness to accept criticism and react to it in a constructive fashion, rather than interpreting it as a threat. This ability is lacking too often at Seliger and in many sectors of the Russian political system.

The contradictions revealed in this case study of Seliger should nonetheless make one wary of perceiving official discourse as monolithic. Instead, they reflect conflicts within camp management. Mamonov unofficially told «curators» before the camp that they should not follow the answers in the brochure because «no one would believe you anyway». This indicates that some members of the management were more intent on controlling the flow of information to participants than others. The heterogeneous style of the brochure also points to different authors.

Mamonov, for his part, made his career in the Foreign Ministry. Unlike Iakemenko and his current successor at the top of the Agency for Youth Affairs, Sergei Belokonev, Mamonov did not rise through Nashi's ranks and has different priorities. Belokonev and other leaders of official youth policy therefore must perform a balancing act between various groups and interests. Nonetheless, the influence of «internationalists» like Mamonov at the Seliger camp remains generally subordinated to that of the Agency for Youth Affairs and its former Nashi-cadres.

The fourth week of the Seliger camp in 2010 in particular demonstrated that the agonistic worldview propagated during the international session had not taken root everywhere in the camp. Members of the Nashi-division Steel (Stal') caused a scandal when they set up an installation titled «We do not like you here» (zdes' vam ne rady). Cardboard heads depicting various domestic Russian and international figures, including the head of the Moscow Helsinki-group Liudmila Alekseeva, former head of the US State Department Condoleezza Rice and Georgian president Mikhail Saakashvili, were set up on stakes. Stal' then put hats from Nazi uniforms on top of their heads (Kozenko 2010). This was the same chain of equivalence that we found in Nashi's 2005 brochure about «unusual fascism» and during the siege of the Estonian embassy in Moscow: Russia's enemies are fascists. The statement stands in stark contradiction to the image of a cosmopolitan Russia that the organizers of Seliger wanted to convey during the international forum.

Nonetheless, the International Youth Forum is alive and well. It was held again in 2011, 2012 and 2013, and another edition is planned for 2014. It appears that the camp management got its organizational problems under control after 2010. Starting in 2011, organizers relied more on «ambassadors» from various countries to take care of the administrative matters involving recruitment and visas.

Camp organizers, first and foremost Sergei Belokonev, recently claimed that they have been successful in convincing sponsors and international partners to support recent editions of the Seliger camp. This was not always the case: over 100 sponsors quit their engagement in Seliger in 2012, not least because of Stal's actions in 2010. As a result, state expenditures for the camp rose from 200 million Rubles in 2011 to 280 (8.5 million dollars) in 2012 (Newsru 2012). In 2013, according to Belokonev, the government paid for less than half of the camp's annual costs of 500 million Rubles (15.2 million dollars). The comparison to the camp's 2005 costs of two million dollars shows, how much more elaborate and expensive Seliger has become.

In spite of all this turbulence, it is evident that Seliger as a whole continues to enjoy high priority in the Russian government and with Vladimir Putin personally. Not only did he visit the camp in 2011, 2012 and 2013, he has also actively lobbied for additional funds. In September 2013, Putin ordered his government to work out plans that would allow for using the campground year-round. Moreover, the government harbors (still vague) plans for organizing a version of the International Youth Forum Seliger in Strasbourg and Seattle – under the name «Interseliger». Belokonev's explanation: «[t]his way we can influence other countries. Or not even influence but collaborate with young people from all over the world without forgetting about [our] national interests.» (RBK 2013) He thus envisions Seliger as an instrument of soft power with which to export Russian values.

At the same time, Belokonev emphasized in the press conference, Seliger remains the most important place to defend Russian youth against «forces across the Atlantic». The statement is telling because the central notion of threat continues to undermine the credibility of Seliger's organizers' assurances that their main goal is international cooperation. Cooperation requires the readiness to give up a certain amount of control, something that the highly hierarchical «defense» of youth against external threats factually excludes. The former Nashi-cadres in charge of developing Russia's youth policy on the international stage appear incapable of escaping their securitized worldview, along with much of the political leadership in Putin's post-Medvedev term as president. At the same time, the nodal point of modernization and economic cooperation with the West quite apparently remains a discursive necessity, to legitimize official activity in Russia's public sphere in times of decreasing growth rates and to secure funds for projects in the youth sphere. If there is no willingness, however, to address the contradictions between security and openness, Seliger will most likely remain another expensive but ultimately inefficient tool of soft power.

VI Conclusions

This book has analyzed Nashi's ideas, opening a window onto official Russian discourse in the sphere of youth politics. The volume discussed Nashi's early actions after its 2005 founding, its role in the conflict over the Bronze Soldier with Estonia in 2007, and the «International Youth Forum Seliger 2010». These «focal points» in Nashi's history were placed in the context of Russia's current political system.

Since Nashi is a government-sponsored project, its worldview must be understood in connection with official discourse. At the same time, the two are neither equivalent nor monolithic constructs. The various demands in these discourses do not coexist without tension. Furthermore, throughout Nashi's history, the relative importance of individual demands shifted depending on the political context.

Nashi was founded as a vehicle for counteracting perceived political instability in 2005. Its mass actions were meant to demonstrate to the opposition that pro-government forces controlled the streets of Moscow and other large cities. Nashi was to provide an ideological basis with which young Russians could identify. The «Democratic Anti-Fascist Youth Movement» promoted self-realization, pride in Russia's historical achievements and the image of a society united against its enemies. Nashi activists were presented as the latest link in a chain of great generations that spared no efforts to create a modern and powerful Russia with a respected global position.

As we have seen, these discursive demands parallel those of official discourse and its central representative, Vladimir Putin. Against the background of the dislocations of Soviet collapse, political turmoil and Russia's enduring weakness in the 1990s, Putin presented himself as a consolidator, a man who could bridge the gaps between political camps and unite the country.

Nashi framed its own role in similar terms. Activists were to assist Putin in the task of stabilization and strengthen the Russian state against domestic and foreign enemies. Nashi's three main goals – the prevention of an «Orange

Revolution» in Russia, the country's modernization and the establishment of a civil society – echoed official rhetoric.

The analysis of Nashi's discourse showed that all three goals are articulated within a state-centered worldview. According to Nashi, a modern economy contributes to Russia's sovereignty; even civil society acts as a state collaborator in resolving the country's problems. Nashi's understanding of these crucial terms corresponds to that of Vladislav Surkov, a key promoter of the organization and the «architect» of Sovereign Democracy.

Nashi also employed symbolic politics very actively. Throughout its history, an idealized narrative of the Great Patriotic War formed a nodal point of the movement's discourse. Its first large demonstration, called «our victory», celebrated the link between veterans and Russia's contemporary youth, as represented by the movement. In this way, Nashi discursively appropriated a war memory still revered by the vast majority of Russians. It followed a pattern of cultivating the commemoration of World War II to mobilize political support for the government.

The idealized war narrative has served as a discursive template on which to project Russia's contemporary challenges and ambitions. Equally consistent with the war narrative is the perception of enemies that continue to bar Russia from becoming a great power. As in 1945, proclaims Nashi, contemporary Russia needs to defeat the «fascists» in order to ensure its own security and power.

This historical analogy is not unproblematic. First of all, Nashi has coined the awkward term «unusual fascists» to subsume Russian liberals, American democracy promoters, hostile heads of state in post-Soviet space and fugitive oligarchs under a single heading. Secondly, the historic parallels suggest a warlike worldview. This worldview inaccurately describes the complicated and interconnected contemporary world order, making it a poor guide for a great power's foreign policy.

This became most apparent during the conflict over the Bronze Soldier with Estonia. Nashi interpreted the removal of the war memorial from downtown Tallinn as a «fascist» attack against official Russian war memory. The movement retaliated by picketing and attacking Estonia's diplomatic representation in Moscow. The Russian government initially tolerated Nashi's actions but moved to end them under strong international pressure. Russia's international image suffered as a result. Estonia, on the other hand, received support from the European Union, NATO and the United States.

The fact that Nashi had caused a diplomatic crisis attests to its strength in 2007. However, this crisis also had serious consequences for the organization, as its funding was cut shortly after the tumultuous events in Moscow. Nashi's political influence in Russia waned, and what was left of its image as a cadre-training unit for Russia's future elite was shattered. Nashi realigned its discursive priorities, de-emphasizing its actions against enemies and highlighting its auxiliary role in Russia's economic modernization. Nashi opened up its summer camp at Lake Seliger to other Russian participants and, in 2010, to an international audience. After 2009, questions of economic modernization and the promotion of innovation took center stage at the camp at the expense of training activists to fight «fascists».

The ease with which Nashi shifted the relative weight of its discursive nodal points illustrates the organization's versatility. Like official government discourse, Nashi articulates demands from various political camps. Its discourse contains the same market liberalism and «national-patriotic» rhetoric that lay at the heart of Putin's success as a politician and his image as a figure of national unification.

This discourse appears to be quite attractive to young Russians who do not want to go back to the isolation of the Soviet Union but harbor strong patriotic feelings and believe in a strong state as a result of their traumatic experiences in the 1990s. Nashi addressed youth with simple language and an offer for identification that draws clear friend-foe distinctions and radically reduces the complexity of political questions. Nashi combines the clear articulation of what it means to belong to «us», to be «ours» (Nashi), with well-organized and staged rituals that reinforce this sense of belonging. The matching t-shirts at Nashi's demonstrations, the bullet casings each participant received on Victory Day, the patriotic pop music and the fireside romanticism of Lake Seliger all add a sense of emotional attachment to the political rhetoric.

This emotional attachment is perhaps more important to members of Nashi than their commitment to the organization's values. Andrei, the Nashi-commissar I interviewed from St. Petersburg, said that the movement gave him an idea of his homeland. Marina, a commissar in Moscow, highlighted the friends she had made in the movement. Moreover, the Nashi-networks have enabled a number of activists to find employment in regional administrations and government agencies.

Even the international participants who attended the International Youth Forum Seliger 2010 looked back fondly when I surveyed them. Negative memories related to the camp's disciplinary nature and poor organization paled in comparison with the well-organized group experience. Nashi has always highlighted this sense of camaraderie in its publications. In an annotated version of its manifesto, Nashi explains what it means to be a member.

> «The movement NASHI will not only actively move its members through all levels of the social ladder (*sotsial'naia lestnitsa*) so that they can replace the generation of defeatists, but it will also actively defend OURs (sic) against the blows of our opponents. We are a united team (*splochennaia komanda*), we will go hand in hand, we display our solidarity not in an abstract manner, but by helping each member of our movement.» (Nashi 2012a)

This emphasis on defending members – and Russia – against enemies played a central role in Nashi's self-conception. In many ways, it is the precondition for the movement's successful provision of a sense of shared identity among its activists. According to the discourse theorists Ernesto Laclau and Chantal Mouffe, the demarcation against a constitutive outside is the precondition of any identity. The question is, however, whether this constitutive outside is perceived as agonistic or antagonistic. The former is an opponent that one fights within the framework of certain rules, while the latter is an enemy that needs to be annihilated.

Nashi's conception of its opponents as «fascists» suggests very strongly that it tends towards an antagonistic worldview, as do its actions against the Russian opposition and the Estonian embassy. Its recent emphasis on Russia's economic modernization and global competitiveness, however, point to an agonistic worldview. The combination of different fundamental visions in Nashi's discourse has therefore been both the organization's strength and weakness. It provides Nashi with impressive versatility when it comes to adapting to new political situations, but it also contributes to a widespread notion that the movement is at best opportunistic and at worst unpredictable and potentially dangerous.

Nashi gave its perceived enemies reason to fear the movement time and again. Attacks against oppositional forces and diplomats showed that the emotions and the simplified worldview by which Nashi mobilized its supporters carried considerable potential for escalation. At the same time, this channeling of aggression towards outside enemies is part and parcel of the logic of the «managed passion» (Andreev 2006: 94) that Nashi operates with.

While this managed passion may be a useful tool to mobilize and unify youth in times of perceived crisis, it served Nashi less well after 2008, when the threat of an «Orange Revolution» became less and less likely and thus less credible as a political rallying cry. Nashi reacted with a strategy of diversification: it created six associated projects – often in collaboration with the Federal Agency for Youth Affairs – that promoted ecology, physical fitness or the fight against the sale of expired foodstuff. Other projects had a more explicit patriotic focus, including a project called «Your Movie about the War» (*tvoi fil'm o voine*).[109] Nashi attracted some activists with grant opportunities for business and scientific projects and aimed to present a business-like, innovative image.

Nonetheless, the «tough actions» that some of Nashi's activists engaged in did not cease. Especially the Stal' (*Steel*) project continued to prove attractive to troubled youth who needed to channel what Vasilii Iakemenko called their «internal aggression» (Azar 2012) in supposedly productive ways – against the enemies of Russia. «[T]he basic idea of the project 'Stal'' was a call to action – active, effective and tough – when Russia needs it» (Nashi 2012b). Stal' made headlines during Seliger 2010 with its controversial depiction of Russia's «fascist» enemies and inherited Nashi's function of channeling discontent in a «patriotic» fashion.

The different moments in Nashi's discourse thus led to serious contradictions. Headlines like those during Seliger 2010 served to discredit Nashi's advertised new role as a champion of Russia's modernization, not only in the eyes of its critics and an international audience, but also among Russia's political elite. The fact that Nashi never controlled its radical activists repeatedly and negatively affected its image and political standing. After its reorganization in

---

109 In this project, young Russians interview veterans and record their war memories. Nashi claims that 50'000 youth contributed over 10'000 films (Azar 2012).

2008, Nashi was caught in a downward spiral of decreasing political importance, curtailed funding and its waning power to mobilize the masses.

Rumors of its imminent demise were heard for a number of years. Surprisingly, they often proved to be premature. Since 2007, Nashi repeatedly tried to rebrand itself but never regained its strength. Its demise was related in no small part to power struggles within the movement but also among its political backers in the Presidential Administration: Vladislav Surkov, considered to be Nashi's main sponsor in Putin's entourage, lost his position as first First Deputy of the head of the Presidential Administration, which meant that political interest and funding for Nashi waned.

Instead, Viacheslav Volodin, Surkov's successor, built up Molodaia Gvardiia, Edinaia Rossiia's official youth organization, as the main actor in Russian youth politics. Molodaia Gvardiia, which recruits many of its members from the children of the elite, has served as a more reliable source for government cadres while only rarely making headlines with controversial activities. Today, it is present in all Russian regions.

Nashi's other key figure, Vasilii Iakemenko, is also out of the picture. He was always a necessity and a liability for Nashi: the organization would never have achieved what it did without his energy and political connections. At the same time, it is impossible to separate Nashi from the person of Iakemenko and his authoritarian leadership style. Moreover, he repeatedly caused much-publicized scandals.

His association with violent soccer fans did much to discredit Nashi's moderate image.[110] In 2011, media outlets uncovered his involvement with the company «Akbars» in the 1990s, which is accused of murder and banditry.[111]

---

110 Even though nothing could be proven because the authorities lacked the will for an investigation, journalists have accused these groups of standing behind the beating of Nashi-critic Oleg Kashin. Unknown assailants beat Kashin savagely in November 2010. He was rushed to the hospital with a skull fracture and multiple broken bones. Iakemenko mocked Kashin in his blog while the journalist was in a coma, calling him a «zombie», among other things (Iakemenko 2010). Kashin accused Iakemenko personally of standing behind the attacks, and Iakemenko unsuccessfully sued him for libel (Galperin and Chernykh 2011).

111 Journalists found official documents that identify Iakemenko as a co-founder of «Akbars». His press secretary stated that someone had used Iakemenko's identity after his passport had been stolen (Newsru 2011). In a recent interview, Iakemenko admitted his involvement with the company. He clarified, however, that he had merely once sold a car to «Akbars» without knowing the buyers' identities (Azar

He also appears to have had an affair with a minor at Lake Seliger in 2009 (Zubov 2010). Most recently, journalist Oleg Kashin alleged that Iakemenko is receiving a salary of 500'000 dollars from Sperbank, which the state-owned bank promptly denied (Alekseevskikh 2013). Iakemenko repeatedly denied these allegations, however unconvincingly.

Despite unsuccessful attempts at creating a new political party, Iakemenko appears to still exercise some power over youth policy through the Agency for Youth Affairs, which he headed until 2012. The agency's new head, Sergei Belokonev, is a former Nashi commissar who defines himself as Iakemenko's «successor» (*preemnik*). According to media reports, Iakemenko actively lobbied for Belokonev. Former Nashi activists staff the top echelons of the agency and the camp at Seliger remains its top priority.[112]

Belokonev is no less controversial than Iakemenko. He made headlines with opaque allocations of agency funds to friendly companies and the statement that NKVD-head Lavrentii Beriia had been «one of the most effective managers of our country» (Regions.ru 2013). Rather than Belokonev's abilities as a manager, however, his loyalty to the former leader appears to have been his main qualification for the job. Whether the agency can reach its high goals – the development of civil society and patriotic education among Russia's youth, the successful export of Russian youth camps and their ideology to the West – under this kind of leadership is doubtful.

Nashi itself, however, has ceased to exist. In February 2013, the newspaper Izvestiia reported that the organization's commissars agreed to the dissolution in a conversation with Volodin. A new organization called the All-Russian Youth Society (*Vserossiiskoe Soobshchestvo Molodezhi*) was meant to take over some of the movement's projects (Sivkova 2013). Nothing has been heard of this society since then, however, and the Nashi-website's last entries

---

2012). The members of «Akbars» were sentenced to a total of over 400 years in prison.

112 In 2010, half of the agency's annual budget, about 200 million Rubles (6.1 million dollars), went to Nashi and its associated projects. Between 2007 and 2010, Nashi received 467 million Rubles (14.2 million dollars) in government money, much more than any other youth organization in Russia (Shleinov 2010). Since 2010, the agency's budget has increased considerably. In a 2012 interview, Iakemenko maintained that the current Nashi leadership made its own decisions. However, he admitted that «the leaders of 'Nashi' sometimes consult me when they make fundamental decisions» (Azar 2012).

were posted in June of 2013. Still, new projects are in the pipelines of the Presidential Administration: most recently, a Artur Omarov, another former Nashi commissar, founded an organization called Network (*Set'*) with considerable financial means (Khachatrian 2013).

The priorities of projects like Set' and of Russian youth policy in general, however, are less clear today than ever. The question of how to involve and engage the country's youth remains a vital issue for the Russian government. Russia is struggling with a difficult demographic situation, and every year a large number of young Russians, particularly those who are well educated, leave the country to work in Western Europe or the United States. Simple appeals to their patriotism will not stem this tide. Instead, red tape, corruption and frequent distrust of entrepreneurial activity suffocate creative and talented youth.

Too often, officials in Russia see youth as a potential force for instability that must be subdued and channeled. Nashi may provide its activists with educational and financial opportunities, but it continues to function within a strictly hierarchical framework. Researchers like Elena Omel'chenko believe that state youth policy has to recognize youth as subjects rather than objects before the young Russians truly feel they have a stake in the current system (Omel'chenko 2006: 16).

Nashi's promises of upward social mobility and less government corruption have remained mostly unattainable because of the organization's strict loyalty to the government. Criticism has rarely been voiced beyond the framework of official government discourse. Nashi consistently contributed to the suppression and vilification of more fundamental criticism. At the same time, it raised hopes for change and modernization, particularly under Medvedev. The fact that little has happened explains why the vast majority of young Russians lost interest in official youth organizations.

Nonetheless, criticism and dissatisfaction with Russia's political system have not disappeared. They reemerged after the Duma elections in December 2011, when hundreds of thousands of Russians took to the streets in large and peaceful demonstrations in Moscow, St. Petersburg and other Russian cities. These protests reflected urban and educated Russians' disappointment in the political system established by Vladimir Putin. Medvedev's refusal to run for president and his admission that he had always planned to step down in favor of Putin undermined the credibility of Medvedev's reform and modernization rhetoric.

Organizers and participants in the demonstrations surrounding the Duma elections in December 2011 are the same young people that Nashi tried to mobilize for participation in official youth politics. Nashi, however, opposed the protest movement and tried to present it as a new threat to Russia.[113] Putin ridiculed the protesters and presented them as agents of Western influence. Almost no attempt was made to engage with the political issues of the demonstrators.

Since then, the protesters struggled to keep up their momentum; most of them resigned and express their discontent through the Internet, as before. The opposition is too fragmented and weak to oppose Putin, who is perhaps now more firmly in power than ever before. Because of the country's oil wealth and Putin's conservative and mostly provincial constituency, the period of «normalized» political stability may last for many years.

Without the engagement of the younger generation, however, this stability is unlikely to provide visions for Russia's future development. Currently, Russia's economic model based on high oil prices continues to yield enough benefits for broad sectors of the elite and the conservative segments of the population that form Putin's base.

Nevertheless, falling growth rates, unresolved social, political and ethnic problems in the Russian Federation ensure that real and perceived enemies will continue to threaten «stability», the main political value holding Russia together under Putin. The case of Nashi illustrates one thing, which can also serve as a lesson to Putin: it is easier to mobilize support in times of perceived external threat and instability than to keep up this momentum in «peacetime». The political leadership's real task, however, should be to solve the country's «normal» structural problems, for which it needs the participation of its young, educated citizens.

---

113 On 6 December, Nashi activists demonstrated in support of Putin and Medvedev. As in 2005, Nashi had to «defend» the country against its enemies: «'Nashi' does not allow [the opposition] to turn the results of the all-Russian elections into a farce and to discredit free and democratic elections.» (Nashi 2011c)

Bibliography

Primary Sources Nashi

Nashi. 2005a. «Manifest». http://Nashi.su/projects [accessed 15 August 2011].

—— 2005b. «Neobyknovennyi Fashizm». http://en.bookfi.org/book/738535 [accessed 2 January 2012].

—— 2005c. «'NASHI' Zaiavili, Chto Prinimaiut Estafetu Bor'by u Veteranov». http://www.Nashi.su/news/140 [accessed 15 August 2011].

—— 2005d. «'NASHA POBEDA': Veterany Peredali 'NASHIMI' Estafetu Bor'by za Nezavisimost' Rossii». http://www.Nashi.su/news/138 [accessed 15 August 2011].

—— 2005e. «NASHA POBEDA: Bolee 60 Tysiach Chelovek Priniali Uchastie v Patrioticheskoi Aktsii v Moskve». http://www.Nashi.su/news/137 [accessed 19 August 2011].

—— 2005f. «Sostoialas' Press-Konferentsiia Dvizheniia 'NASHI'.» http://www.Nashi.su/news/149 [accessed 22 August 2011].

—— 2006. «Estonskii Gosudarstvennyi Vandalizm» http://www.Nashi.su/news/8474 [accessed 15 August 2011].

—— 2007a. «Patriotizm». http://www.Nashi.su/patriotizm [accessed 16 July 2009].

—— 2007b. «300 Komissarov Gotovy Nesti Vakhtu Pamiati na Tsentral'noi Ploshchad Tallinna». http://www.Nashi.su/news/11375 [accessed 20 September 2011]

—— 2007c. «Opomnites'!». http://www.Nashi.su/news/16698 [accessed 20 September 2011].

—— 2007d. «'NASHI' Govorit Estonii: 'Net!'». http://Nashi.su/news/16748 [accessed 20 September 2011].

—— 2007e. «'NASHI' 'Zablokirovali' Posla Estonii v Ee Mashine». http://Nashi.su/news/16740 [accessed 20 September 2011].

—— 2007f. «8 'Nashikh' Byli Zaderzhan v Khode Bessrochnogo Piketa u Konsul'stva Estonii v Sankt-Peterburge». http://www.Nashi.su/news/16970 [accessed 15 August 2011].

—— 2007g. «Sankt-Peterburg: 'NASHI' Perekryvaiut Dorogu v Estoniiu». http://Nashi.su/news/17113 [accessed 20 September 2011].

―― 2007h. «Rukovodstvo 'Nashikh', 'Rossii Molodoi' i 'Mestnykh' Ob"iavili Ul'timatum Pravitel'stvu Estonii». http://Nashi.su/news/16918 [accessed 20 September 2011].
―― 2007i. «Ofitsial'noe Zaiavlenie Dvizheniia 'Nashi' po Povodu Istecheniia Sroka Ul'timatuma Estonskomu Pravitel'stvu». http://www.Nashi.su/news/17063 [accessed 20 September 2011].
―― 2007j. «Pamiat' Dmitriia Ganina. Ubit Fashistami...» http://www.Nashi.su/news/16962 [accessed 20 September 2011].
―― 2007k. «16 Chelovek Zaderzhany u Zdaniia Redaktsii 'AiF'». http://Nashi.su/news/17112 [accessed 20 September 2011].
―― 2007l. «Okhraniki Posla Estonii Primenili Protiv 'NASHIKH' Slezotochivyi Gaz». http://www.Nashi.su/news/17111 [accessed 16 August 2011].
―― 2007m. «Blokada Posol'stva Estonii Sniata». http://www.Nashi.su/news/17258 [accessed 21 September 2011].
―― 2007n. «Vasilii Iakemenko: 'SSHA i NATO luchshe by zaniat'sia svoimi delami'». http://www.Nashi.su/news/17214 [accessed 21 September 2011].
―― 2007o. «Russkie Uroki dlia Evrosoiuza». http://www.Nashi.su/news/17274 [accessed 16 August 2011].
―― 2007p. «Estoniia Deportiruet 'Zhivoi Pamiatnik'». http://www.Nashi.su/news/18109 [accessed 16 August 2011].
―― 2007q. «Vasilii Iakemenko Oproverg Slukhi o Vozmozhnykh Besporiadkakh na Forume 'Seliger-2007'». http://Nashi.su/news/20041 [accessed 27 July 2011].
―― 2007r. «Prazdnichnyi Kontsert Sobral na Krasnoi Ploshchadi Bolee 15 Tysiach 'NASHIKH'». http://Nashi.su/news/17535 [accessed 21 September 2011].
―― 2009a. «Nasha Ideologiia». http://www.Nashi.su/ideology/sources [accessed 1 August 2009].
―― 2009b. «Vladimir Putin: 'Spasibo Vsem, i Vashim, i Nashim, Pust' Vas Soprovozhdaet Udacha!'». http://www.Nashi.su/news/27119 [accessed 27 July 2011].
―― 2010. «Revoliutsiia Otmeniaetsia». http://Nashi.su/position/27690 [accessed 27 August 2011].
―― 2011a. «Proekty». http://Nashi.su/projects/66 [accessed 27 July 2011].
―― 2011b. «Manifest». http://Nashi.su/manifest [accessed 16 August 2011].
―― 2011c. «'Nashi' Zashchitili Vybor Millionov Rossiian». http://Nashi.su/news/37687 [accessed 14 February 2012].

―― 2012a. «Manifest s Kommentariiami». http://Nashi.su/projects [accessed 13 February 2012].

―― 2012b. «Molodezhnoe Patrioticheskoe Dvizhenie 'STAL'». http://Nashi.su/projects/51 [accessed 23 February 2012].

Monographs, Articles and Internet Sources

Afanas'ev, I. 2009a. *Echo Moskvy. Tsena Pobedy*, 25 May 2009.

―― 2009b. «Iurii Afanas'ev: Ia Khotel By Uvidet' Rossiiu Raskoldovannoi». *Novaia Gazeta*. 27 May. 5-6.

Alexandrova, L. 2007. «Reaction to Freedom House Report in Russia». ITAR-TASS Daily. 2 February. http://dlib.eastview.com/browse/doc/11459739 [accessed 14 December 2011].

Alekseevskikh, A. 2013. «Sperbank: Vasilii Iakemenko u Nas ne Rabotaet». *Izvestia*. 6 December. http://izvestia.ru/news/562066 [accessed 20 December 2013].

American Embassy. 2009. *Is Stalin's Ghost a Threat to Academic Freedom?* Available at: http://www.guardian.co.uk/world/us-embassy-cables-documents/232245 [accessed 30 January 2012].

Andreev, D. 2006. «Fenomen Molodezhnoi 'Upravliaemoi Passionarnosti' i Vozmozhnye Stsenarii ego Perspektiv». In *Molodezh' i Politika: Sovremennye Ochertaniia i Istoriia Problemy, Rol' Gosudarstva i Grazhdanskogo Obshchestva, Ozhidaniia i Prognozy*, edited by F. Bomsford and G. Bordiugov, 49-61. Moskva: Fond Fridrikha Naumanna, AIRO-XXI.

Andreev, D. and G. Bordiugov. 2005. *Prostranstvo Pamiati: Velikaia Pobeda i Vlast'*. Moskva: Airo XX.

Arel, D. 2005. «Is the Orange Revolution Fading?». *Current History* 104, 684. 325-330.

Arias-King, F. 2007a. «Orange People: A Brief History of Transnational Liberation Networks in East Central Europe». *Demokratizatsiya: The Journal of Post-Soviet Democratization*. 15, 1. 29-72.

―― 2007b. «A Revolution of the Mind: Interview with Yulia Malysheva». *Demokratizatsiya: The Journal of Post-Soviet Democratization*, 15, 1. 117-128.

Ashplant, T.G., G. Dawson, and M. Roper. 2000. «The Politics of War Memory and Commemoration: Contexts, Structures and Dynamics». In *The Politics of War Memory and Commemoration*, edited by T.G. Ashplant, G. Dawson, and M. Roper, 3-85. London & New York: Routledge.

Assmann, A. 1999. *Erinnerungsräume: Formen und Wandlungen des kulturellen Gedächtnisses*. München: Verlag C.H. Beck

Assmann, J. 1988. «Kollektives Gedächtnis und kulturelle Identität». In *Kultur und Gedächtnis*, edited by A. Assmann and T. Hölscher, 9-19. Frankfurt a.M.: Suhrkamp.

Associated Press. 2005. «Russian President: Soviet Collapse 'Greatest Geopolitical Catastrophe' of 20th Century». http://business.highbeam.com/62732/article-1P1-107848729/russian-president-soviet-collapse-greatest-geopolitical. [accessed 9 August 2011].

Atwal, M. 2009. «Evaluating Nashi's Sustainability: Autonomy, Agency and Activism». *Europe-Asia Studies* 61, 5. 743-758.

Azar, I. 2012. «Poka ne Zagriatsia Zdaniia». *Lenta.ru*. 17 January. http://lenta.ru/articles/2012/01/17/jakemenko [accessed 14 February 2012].

Bacon, E. 2002. «Reconsidering Brezhnev». In *Brezhnev Reconsidered*, edited by E. Bacon and M. Sandle, 1-21. Houndmills, Basingstoke, Hampshire: Palgrave Macmillan.

Bacon, E. et al. 2006. *Securitizing Russia: The Domestic Politics of Putin*. Manchester: Manchester University Press.

Baev, P.K. 2005. «Counter-Terrorism as a Building Block for Putin's Regime». In *Russia as a Great Power: Dimensions of Security under Putin*, edited by J. Hedenskog et al., 323-344. London & New York: Routledge.

Balmasov, S. 2006. «My Nash My Novyi Mir Postroim». *Vysshee Obrazovanie Segodnia* 1. 16-23.

Barthes, R. 1964 [1957]. *Mythen des Alltags*. Frankfurt a.M.: Suhrkamp.

BBC. 2004. «Estonia Unveils Nazi War Monument». 20 August. http://news.bbc.co.uk/2/hi/europe/3585272.stm [accessed 16 September 2011].

―――― 2007a. «Estonia Removes Soviet Memorial». 27 April. http://news.bbc.co.uk/2/hi/europe/6598269.stm [accessed 18 September 2011].

BBC Russia. 2009. «Obshchestvennaia Palata Dast Deneg 'Nashim'i Pravosashchitnikam». 8 September. http://www.bbc.co.uk/russian/russia/2009/09/090908_ngo_government_grant.shtml [accessed 19 December 2011].

Binns, C. 1980. «The Changing Face of Power: Revolution and Accommodation in the Development of the Soviet Ceremonial System: Part II». *Man* 15, 1. 170-187.

Blum, D. 2007. *National Identity and Globalization: Youth, State, and Society in Post-Soviet Eurasia*. Cambridge: Cambridge University Press.
Bol'shakov, I. 2006. «No Title». *Neprikosnovennyi Zapas* 1, 45. 118-121.
Borusiak, L. 2005. «'Naschi' i kak Uchat Spasat' Rossiiu». *Vestnik Obshchestvennogo Mneniia* 5, 79. 17-29.
Bowden, Z. 2008. «*Poriadok* and *Bardak* (Order and Chaos): The neo-Fascist Project of Articulating a Russian 'People'». *Journal of Language and Politics* 7, 2. 321–347.
Bratersky, A. 2010. «800 Foreign Youth Flock to Seliger Camp». The St. Petersburg Times. 13 July. http://www.sptimesrussia.com/index.php?action_id=2&story_id=31926 [accessed 20 December 2011].
Breslauer, G. and C. Dale. 1997. «Boris Yeltsin and the Invention of the Russian Nation State». *Post-Soviet Affairs* 13, 4. 303-332.
Brezhnev, L. 1965. *The Great Victory of the Soviet People*. Moscow: Novosti Press Agency Publishing House.
Brüggemann, K. 2004. «Kontinuität in der Revolution: Der russische Blick auf das Baltikum während der ‚Zeit der Wirren' 1917-1920 am Beispiel der weissen Bewegung». In *Estland und Russland: Aspekte der Beziehungen beider Länder*, edited by O. Mertelsmann, 127-156. Hamburg: Verlag Dr. Kovač.
——— 2008. «Denkmäler des Grolls: Estland und die Kriege des 20. Jahrhunderts». *Osteuropa* 58, 6. 129-146.
Buchacek, D. 2006. «NASHA Pravda, NASHE Delo: The Mobilization of the Nashi Generation in Contemporary Russia». *Carolina Papers in Democracy and Human Rights* 7. http://cgi.unc.edu/uploads/media_items/nasha-pravda-nashe-delo-the-mobilization-of-the-Nashi-generation-in-contemporary-russia.original.pdf [accessed 27 July 2011].
Butrin, D. 2007. «Tsena Voprosa». *Kommersant"*. 2 May. http://kommersant.ru/doc/763115 [accessed 26 January 2012].
Buzan, B., O. Wæver, and J. de Wilde. 1998. *Security: A New Framework for Analysis*. Boulder & London: Lynne Rienner Publishers. 1-47.
Casula, P. 2010. «'Primacy in Your Face': Changing Discourses of National Identity and National Interest in the United States and Russia after the Cold War». *Ab Imperio* 11, 3. 245-271.
——— 2011. *Politische und nationale Identitäten in Putins Russland*. Unpublished Dissertation. Universität Basel.
Clifford, J. 1990. «Notes on (Field)notes». In *Fieldnotes: The Makings of Anthropol-*

ogy, edited by R. Sanjek, 47-70. Ithaca & London: Cornell University Press.
Comai, G. 2012. «Youth camps in Post-Soviet Russia and the Northern Caucasus: the cases of Seliger and Mashuk 2010». *Anthropology of East Europe Review* 30, 1. 184-212.
Confino, A. 1997. «Collective Memory and Cultural History: Problems of Method». *The American Historical Review* 102, 5. 1386-1403.
Copsey, N. 2005. «Election Report: Popular Politics and the Ukrainian Presidential Election of 2004». *Politics* 25, 2. 99-106.
Cornell, S. 2005. «Russia's Gridlock in Chechnya: Normalization or Deterioration». *OSCE Yearbook 2004*. 267-276.
Dafflon, D. 2009. *Youth in Russia – The Portrait of a Generation in Transition*. http://www.sad.ch/Publikationen/Youth-in-Russia-The-Portait-of-a-Generation-in-Transition.html [accessed 27 July 2011].
Danilin, P. 2006. *Novaia Molodezhnaia Politika, 2003-2005*. Moskva: Evropa.
Demes, P. and J. Forbrig. 2006. «Pora – 'It's Time' for Democracy in Ukraine». In *Revolution in Orange: The Origins of Ukraine's Democratic Breakthrough*, edited by A. Åslund and M. McFaul, 85-101. Washington: Carnegie Endowment for International Peace
DeWalt, M. and B. DeWalt. 2002. *Participant Observation: A Guide for Fieldworkers*. Walnut Creek, Lanham & Oxford: AltaMira Press.
DPNI. 2006. «My – Khoziaeva v Sobstvennom Dome». http://www.benzol.us/index.php?2 [accessed 15 August 2011].
Dubin, B. 2007. «Bremia Pobedy. Boris Dubin o Politicheskom Upotreblenii Simvolov». *Kriticheskaia Massa* 2. http://magazines.russ.ru/km/2005/2/du6.html [accessed 27 July 2011].
Edinaia Rossiia. 2006. «Prezident Podderzhal Ideiu Suverennoi Demokratii». http://gov.cap.ru/hierarhy.asp?page=./75063/187503/255513 [accessed 27 July 2011].
Ehala, M. 2009. «The Bronze Soldier: Identity Threat and Maintenance in Estonia». *Journal of Baltic Studies*. 40, 1. 139-158.
Eremin, V. 2007. «S Kem i za Kogo Boriutsia 'Nashi' i 'Mestnye'?». *Rossiiskaia Federatsiia Segodnia* 18.
Ershov, E. 2012. «'Molodaia gvardiia' khochet oboitis' bez 'Nashikh' i 'Seligera'». *Izvestiia*. 14 February. http://www.izvestia.ru/news/515332 [accessed 8 May 2012].
Estonian Security Police. 2008. *Annual Review 2007*. Tallinn: Estonian Security Police.

Federal Agency for Youth Affairs. 2011. «Missiia Federal'nogo Agenstva po Delam Molodezhi». http://fadm.gov.ru/about/mission [accessed 20 December 2011].

Freedom House. 2010. «Freedom in the World 2010: Russia». http://www.freedomhouse.org/report/freedom-world/2010/russia [accessed 18 December 2013].

Fuller, D., 1999. «Part of the Action, or 'Going Native'? Learning to Cope with the 'Politics of Integration'». *Area* 31, 3. 221-227.

Galperin, V. and A. Chernykh. 2011. «Vasiliia Iakemenko Utsenili po Dostoinstvu». *Kommersant"*. 22 June. http://www.kommersant.ru/doc/1664567 [accessed 13 February 2012].

Gavrilov, Iu. 2006. «Molodezhnaia Politika i Molodezh', kak ee Sub"ekt». In *Molodezh' i Politika: Sovremennye Ochertaniia i Istoriia Problemy, Rol' Gosudarstva i Grazhdanskogo Obshchestva, Ozhidaniia i Prognozy*, edited by F. Bomsford and G. Bordiugov, 89-101. Moskva: Fond Fridrikha Naumanna, AIRO-XXI.

Gavrov, S. 2006. «Nashi i ne Nashi». *Lichnost'. Kul'tura. Obshchestvo* 1, 29. 352-357.

Giannone, D. 2010. «Political and Ideological Aspects in the Measurement of Democracy: The Freedom House Case». *Democratization* 17, 1. 68-97.

Gillis, J. 1994. «Memory and Identity: The History of a Relationship». In *Commemorations: The Politics of National Identity*, edited by J. Gillis, 3-24. Princeton: Princeton University Press.

Grani. 2006. «Prokuratura Chechni Zavela Delo na Ukrainskikh Natsionalistov». http://www.grani.ru/War/Chechnya/m.103254.html [accessed July 27 2011].

Gudkov, L. 2005. «Die Fesseln des Sieges: Russlands Identität aus der Erinnerung an den Krieg». Translated from Russian by Misha Gabovich. *Osteuropa* 55, 4-6. 56-73.

Gudkov, L. and B. Dubin. 2005. «Svoeobrazie Russkogo Natsionalizma: Pochemu v nem Otsutstvuet Mobilizuiushchee, Modernizatsennoe Nachalo». *Pro et Contra* 9, 2. 6-24.

Gurevich, P. 2005. «Politizatsiia ili Depolitizatsiia?». *Vestnik Analitiki* 3, 21. 21-29.

Hackmann, J. 2003. «Past Politics in North-Eastern Europe: The Role of History in Post-Cold War Identity Politics». In *Post-Cold War Identity Politics: Northern and Baltic Experiences*, edited by M. Lehti and D. Smith, 78-100. London: Frank Cass.

Hahn, G.M. 1994. «Opposition Politics in Russia». *Europe-Asia Studies* 46, 2. 305-335.

Halbwachs, M. 1985 [1925]. *Das kollektive Gedächtnis*. Frankfurt a. M.: Suhrkamp.

Hammersley, M. and P. Atkinson. 2007 [1983]. *Ethnography: Principles in Practice*. 3rd edition. London & New York: Routledge.

Hansen, L. 2006. *Security as Practice: Discourse Analysis and the Bosnian War*. London: Routledge.

Harrington, B. 2002. «Obtrusiveness as Strategy in Ethnographic Research». *Qualitative Sociology* 25, 1. 49-61.

Heller, R. 2008. «Die russische Jugendbewegung ‚Naši'. Aufstieg und Fall eines polittechnologischen Projektes in der Ära Putin». *Russland-Analysen* 168. 2-9. http://www.lander-analysen.de/dlcounter/dlcounter.php?url=../russland/pdf/Russlandanalysen168.pdf [accessed 28 July 2011]

Hemment, J. 2009. «Soviet-Style Neoliberalism? Nashi, Youth Voluntarism, and the Restructuring of Social Welfare in Russia. *Problems of Post-Communism* 56, 6. 36-50.

Henry, L. 2006. «Shaping Social Activism in Post-Soviet Russia: Leadership, Organizational Diversity, and Innovation». *Post-Soviet Affairs* 22, 2. 99-124.

Horvath, R. 2011. «Putin's 'Preventive Counter-Revolution': Post-Soviet Authoritarianism and the Spectre of Velvet Revolution. *Europe-Asia Studies* 63, 1. 1-25.

Hosking, G. 2006. *Rulers and Victims: The Russians in the Soviet Union*. Cambridge: The Belknap Press of Harvard University Press.

Hudson, V. 2009. «Sovereign Democracy as a Discourse of Russian Identity». In *Identities and Politics During the Putin Presidency: The Foundations of Russia's Stability*, edited by P. Casula and J. Perovic, 189-210. Stuttgart: ibidem-Verlag.

Iakemenko, V. 2010. «Kashin – Eto Lenin Segodnia». *LiveJournal*. 13 November. http://vg-vg.livejournal.com [accessed 13 February 2012].

Il'inskii, I. 2005. «Molodezh' kak Budushchee Rossii v Kategoriiakh Voiny». *Vestnik Analitiki* 3, 21. 34-45.

Il'iushchenko, M. 2005. «Partiia Pensionerov Vziala Magadan». *Kommersant"*. 23 May. http://www.kommersant.ru/Doc-rss/579777 [accessed 17 August 2011].

Indexmundi 2011. «Youth Unemployment Rate Russia». http://www.indexmundi.com/russia/youth-unemployment-rate.html [accessed 18 August 2011].

Interfax. 2007. «Nashi Leader Urges Activists to Vacate AiF Building». 2 May.

Itar-Tass. 2007. «Mironov Slams Nashi's Initiative to Remove Estonian Embassy». 8 May.

Johnston, L. and G. Trefgarne 2003. «ExxonMobil nears deal with Russians». *The Telegraph*. 3 October. http://www.telegraph.co.uk/finance/2864866/ExxonMobil-nears-deal-with-Russians.html [accessed 18 December 2011].

Judt, T. 2002. «The Past is Another Country: Myth and Memory in Post-War Europe». In *Memory and Power in Post-War Europe: Studies in the Presence of the Past*, edited by J.-W. Müller, 157-183. Cambridge: Cambridge University Press.

Kämpfer, F. 1994. «Vom Massengrab zum Heroen-Hügel: Akkulturationsfunktionen sowjetischer Kriegsdenkmäler». In *Kriegerdenkmäler in der Moderne*, edited by R. Koselleck and M. Jeismann, 327-349. München: Fink.

Kanet, R.E. and L. Homarac. 2007. «The US Challenge to Russian Influence in Central Asia and the Caucasus». In *Russia: Re-Emerging Great Power*, edited by R.E. Kanet, 173-194. Houndmills, Basingstoke & Hampshire: Palgrave MacMillan.

Kashin, O. 2005a. «Znat' 'Nashikh'». *Kommersant"*. 28 February. http://www.kommersant.ru/doc/550696 [accessed 18 August 2011].

—— 2005b. «'Nashi' Napisali Shkol'nuiu Programmu». *Kommersant"*. 12 May. http://www.kommersant.ru/doc/576585 [accessed 27 August 2011].

—— 2005c. «Obshchestvennye Organizatsii». *Kommersant"*. 2 March. http://www.kommersant.ru/doc/551411 [accessed 28 July 2011].

—— 2005d. «Moskva Uznala 'Nashikh'». *Kommersant"*. 16 May. http://www.kommersant.ru/doc/577825 [accessed 19 August 2011].

—— 2006. «Sezon Meteoritnykh Dozhdei». In *Novaia Molodezhnaia Politika 2003-2005*, P. Danilin, 3-7. Moskva: Evropa.

—— 2007. «Spor o Bertsovoi Kosti». *Nezavisimaia Gazeta*. 24 May. http://www.ng.ru/printed/78296 [accessed 18 September 2011].

Kassner, K. and P. Wassermann. 2005. «Nicht überall, wo Methode draufsteht, ist auch Methode drin: Zur Problematik der Fundierung von ExpertInneninterviews». In *Das Experteninterview. Theorie, Methode, Anwendung*, edited by A. Bogner, B. Littig and W. Menz, 95-111. Wiesbaden: Vs Verlag.

Kelstrup, M. 2004. «Globalisation and Societal Insecurity: The Securitization of Terrorism and Competing Strategies for Global Governance». In *Contemporary Security Analysis and Copenhagen Peace Research*, edited by S. Guzzini and D. Jung, 106-116. London: Routledge.

Khachatrian, D. 2013. «Otche NASHikh. Korrespondent 'Novoi' Diana Khachatrian Porabotala Instruktorom v Novom Kremlevskom Proekte». 13 December. http://www.novayagazeta.ru/politics/61437.html?print=1 [accessed 22 December 2013].

Kokorev, D. 2006. «Politizirovannaia Rossiiskaia Molodezh': Pokhmel'e Komsmolom − Beremennost' Grazhdanskim Obshchestvom». *Neprikosnovennyi Zapas* 1, 45. 89-94.

Kommersant" Vlast'. 2007. «A v Chem Koshchunstvo». 7 May. http://kommersant.ru/doc/763721?themeID=116 [accessed 21 September 2011].

König, H. 2008. «Erinnern und Vergessen: Vom Nutzen und Nachteil für die Politik». *Osteuropa* 58, 6. 27-40.

Konnander, V. 2005. «What Prospects for Russia in the Baltic Sea Region? Cooperation or Isolation?». In *Russia as a Great Power: Dimensions of Security under Putin*, edited by J. Hedenskog et al., 109-129. London & New York: Routledge.

Konovalova, E. 2007. «Russia: Reactionary Revolutionaries». *Transitions Online*. 15 May. http://www.ceeol.com [accessed 27 July 2011].

Kozenko 2010. «Seliger ne Druzhit s Golovami». *Kommersant"*. 28 July. http://www.kommersant.ru/doc/1477432 [accessed 19 December 2011].

Kozhevnikova, G. 2010. «Pod Znakom Politicheskogo Terrora: Radikal'nyi Natsionalizm v Rossii i Protivodeistvie emu v 2009 Godu». http://www.sovacenter.ru/racism-xenophobia/publications/2010/02/d17889 [accessed 27 August 2011].

Kudriashov, S., 2007. «Erinnerung und Erforschung des Krieges: Sowjetische und russische Erfahrung». In *Der Zweite Weltkrieg in Europa: Erfahrung und Erinnerung*, edited by S. Martens and J. Echternkamp, 113-141. Paderborn: Ferdinand Schöningh.

Kupriianova, G. 2002. «Molodezhnye i Detskie Obshchestvennye Ob"edineniia Rossii na Sovremennom Etape: Tendentsii i Problemy Razvitiia». In *Molodezhnye i Detskie Obshchestvennye Ob"edineniia: Problemy Preemstvennosti Deiatel'nosti i Issledovanii. Sbornik Dokladov i Vystuplenii*, edited by E. Kamaldinova et al., 3-11. Moskva: Logos.

Laclau, E. 1990. *New Reflections on the Revolution of Our Time*. London & New York: Verso.
—— 1996. *Emancipation(s)*. London: Verso.
Laclau, E. and C. Mouffe. 2001 [1985]. *Hegemony and Socialist Strategy: Towards a Radical Democratic Politics*. London & New York: Verso.
Laruelle, M. 2009. *In the Name of the Nation: Nationalism and Politics in Contemporary Russia*. Houndmills, Basingstoke & Hampshire: Palgrave MacMillan.
—— 2012a. «Introduction». In *Russian Nationalism, Foreign Policy, and Identity Debates in Putin's Russia: New Ideological Patterns after the Orange Revolution*, edited by M. Laruelle, 7-9. Stuttgart: ibidem-Verlag.
—— 2012b. «Negotiating History: Memory Wars in the Near Abroad and the Pro-Kremlin Youth Movements».In *Russian Nationalism, Foreign Policy, and Identity Debates in Putin's Russia: New Ideological Patterns after the Orange Revolution*, edited by M. Laruelle, 75-103. Stuttgart: ibidem-Verlag.
Lassila, J. 2012a. «Making Sense of Nashi's Political Style: The Bronze Soldier and the Counter-Orange Community». In *Russian Nationalism, Foreign Policy, and Identity Debates in Putin's Russia: New Ideological Patterns after the Orange Revolution*, edited by M. Laruelle, 105-138. Stuttgart: ibidem-Verlag.
—— 2012b. *The Quest for an Ideal Youth in Putin's Russia II: The Search for Distinctive Conformism in the Political Communication of Nashi, 2005-2009*. Stuttgart: ibidem-Verlag.
Leonova, A. 2003. «Nepriiazn' k Migrantam kak Forma Samozashchity». http://www.strana-oz.ru/?numid=19&article=921 [accessed 27 August 2011].
—— 2006. «'Nashi' i 'Fashisty': Novye Pravila Staroi Igry?». *Indeks/Dos'e na Tsenzuru* 23. 115-119.
Levada-Tsentr. 2005. «Politicheskie Molodezhnye Organizatsii». http://www.levada.ru/press/2005090502.html [accessed 30 August 2011].
Levada-Zentrum. 2004. «Russen über die Wahlen in der Ukraine». *Russland-Analysen* 48. 16-17. http://www.laender-analysen.de/dlcounter/dlcounter.php?url=../russland/pdf/Russlandanalysen048.pdf [accessed 28 July 2011]
Lipkovich, L.I., 2005. «Gosudarstvennaia Programma 'Patrioticheskoe Vospitanie Grazhdan Rossiiskoi Federatsii na 2001-2005 Gody': Predystoriia, Osnovnye Polozheniia i Shagi Realizatsii». In *Patriotizm i Patrioticheskoe Vospitanie: Teoriia, Istoriia, Praktika: Materialy Mezhvuzovskogo Nauchno-Prakticheskogo Seminara g. Orenburg 12-13 Maya 2005 g.*, edited by O.A. Smirnova et al., 2005, 91-99. Orenburg: DIMUR.

Loskutova, E. 2008. *Iunaia Politika: Istoriia Molodezhnykh Politicheskikh Organizatsii Sovremennoi Rossii*. Moskva: Panorama.

Lozowy, I. 2005. «Ukraine: Parading Against Reconciliation». *Transitions Online*. 11 May 2005. www.tol.org [accessed 10 August 2011].

Lukov, V. 2006. «Gosudarstvennaia Molodezhnaia Politika: Bitva Kontseptsii i Ozhidanie Rezul'tatov». In *Molodezh' i Politika: Sovremennye Ochertaniia i Istoriia Problemy, Rol' Gosudarstva i Grazhdanskogo Obshchestva, Ozhidaniia i Prognozy*, edited by F. Bomsford and G. Bordiugov, 73-88. Moskva: Fond Fridrikha Naumanna, AIRO-XXI.

Makarychev, A. 2008. «Politics, the State, and De-Politicization: Putin's Project Reassessed». *Problems of Post-Communism* 55, 5. 62-71.

Maksimovich, A. 2010. «Ozero Nadezhdy». *Interfax*. 30 July. http://www.interfax-russia.ru/Center/view.asp?id=162903 [accessed 19 December 2011].

Malinova, O. 2009. «Russian Political Discourse in the 1990s: Crisis of Identity and Conflicting Pluralism of Ideas». In *Identities and Politics During the Putin Presidency: The Foundations of Russia's Stability*, edited by P. Casula and J. Perovic, 94-111. Stuttgart: ibidem-Verlag.

Maripuu, M. 2004. «Kollaboration und Widerstand in Estland 1940-1944». In *Collaboration and Resistance During the Holocaust: Belarus, Estonia, Latvia, Lithuania*, edited by D. Gaunt et al., 403-419. Bern: Peter Lang.

Markowitz, F. 2000. *Coming of Age in post-Soviet Russia*. Urbana and Chicago: University of Illinois Press.

Martinez, K. 2010. «A Visit to Seliger 2010: Examining Shifts in Russian Nationalism». *Center for Strategic & International Studies*. 20 July. http://csis.org/print/26313 [accessed 20 December 2011].

Medvedev, D. 2009. «O Velikoi Otechestvennoi Voine, Istoricheskoi Istine i o Nashei Pamiati». http://blog.kremlin.ru/post/11/transcript [accessed 21 September 2011].

Memorial. 2008. «Nationale Geschichtsbilder: Das 20. Jahrhundert und der 'Krieg der Erinnerungen'». *Osteuropa* 58, 6. 77-84.

Meuser, M. and U. Nagel. 1994. «Experteninterview». In *Lexikon der Politik, Band 2: Politikwissenschaftliche Methoden*, edited by J. Kriz, D. Nohlen and R. Schultze, 123-124. München: Beck.

Meyer, E. 2008. «Memory and Politics». In *Cultural Memory Studies: An International and Interdisciplinary Handbook*, edited by A. Erll and A. Nünning, 173-180. Berlin & New York: Walter de Gruyter.

Mijnssen, I. 2009. An Old Myth for a New Society. In *Identities and Politics During the Putin Presidency: The Foundations of Russia's Stability*, edited by P. Casula and J. Perovic, 284-305. Stuttgart: ibidem-Verlag.

Molchanov, N. 2005. «Molodye Grozd'ia Gneva?». *Vestnik Analitiki* 3, 21. 17-21.

Morozov, V. 2004. «Russia in the Baltic Sea Region: Desecuritization or Deregionalization?». *Cooperation and Conflict* 39, 3. 317-331.

―――― 2008. «Sovereignty and Democracy in Contemporary Russia: A Modern Subject Faces the Post-Modern World». *Journal of International Relations and Development* 11, 2. 152-180.

Moskovskii Komsomolets. 2005. «Giperboloid Inzhenera Iakemenko». *Moskovskii Komsomolets*. 24 February 2005. http://www.mk.ru/editions/daily/article/2005/02/24/199477-giperboloid-inzhenera-yakemenko.html [accessed 16 August 2011].

Mouffe, C. 2005. *On the Political*. London: Routledge.

Mukhin, A. 2006. *Pokolenie 2008:* Nashi *i ne* Nashi. Moskva: Algoritm.

Müller, M. 2009a. *Making Great Power Identities in Russia: An Ethnographic Discourse Analysis of Education at a Russian Elite University*. Zürich & Berlin: Lit Verlag.

―――― 2009b. «Rethinking Identification with the Hegemonic Discourse of a 'Strong Russia' through Laclau and Mouffe». In *Identities and Politics During the Putin Presidency: The Foundations of Russia's Stability*, edited by P. Casula and J. Perovic, 327-347. Stuttgart: ibidem-Verlag.

Münch, F. 2008. *Diskriminierung durch Geschichte? Der Deutungsstreit um den 'Bronzenen Soldaten' im postsowjetischen Estland*. Marburg: Tectum Verlag.

Myers, S.L. 2007. «Tensions Worsen Between Russia and Estonia». *The New York Times*. 2 May. http://www.nytimes.com/2007/05/02/world/europe/02iht-estonia.4.5537016.html [accessed 20 September 2011].

Myers, S.L. and E. Arvedlund. 2003. «Oil Tycoon's Arrest Scares Russian Financial Markets». *The New York Times*. 28 October. http://www.nytimes.com/2003/10/28/world/oil-tycoon-s-arrest-scares-russian-financial-markets.html?src=pm [accessed 18 December 2011].

Nasha Obshchaia Pobeda 2010. «O Proekte». http://41-45.su/about [accessed 14 December 2011].

NATO 2007. «NATO Statement on Estonia». http://www.nato.int/cps/en/natolive/news_7270.htm?mode=pressrelease [accessed 21 September 2011].

NBP 2004a. «Kul'turnaia Sostavliaiushchaia Natsional-Bol'shevizma». http://theory. nazbol.ru/index.php?option=com_content&view=article&id=196:2010-01-09-11-15-33&catid=30:the-community&Itemid=49 [accessed 8 August 2011].

—— 2004b. «Programma NBP – 2004». http://www.nbp-info.ru/1574.html [accessed 8 August 2011].

Nekhorosheva, M. 2010. «Seligerskii Izgnannik». *Seliger Times.* July 3-5. 2.

Newsru. 2009. «SMI: Vserossiiskii Molodezhnyi Forum 'Seliger 2009' Nakhoditsia pod Ugrozoi Sryva». May 26. http://www.newsru.com/russia/26may2009/frm.html [accessed 27 July 2011].

—— 2011. «'Nashi' pri Pomoshchi Avtoruchek Napomnili o Vozmozhnoi Prichastnosti Iakemenko k Banditskoi Firme». 15 April. http://www. newsru.com/russia/15apr2011/akbarspens.html [accessed 14 February 2012].

—— 2012. «Sponsory Bol'she ne Khotiat Finansirovat' 'Seliger': Milliony na 'Pir vo Vremia Chumy' Budut Potracheny iz Kazny». 29 June. http://www.newsru.com/russia/29jun2012/seliger.html [accessed 19 December 2013].

Nora, P. 1990. *Zwischen Geschichte und Gedächtnis.* Translated from French by Wolfgang Kaiser. Berlin: Verlag Klaus Wagenbach. 11-33.

Novye Liudi 2007. «Rolevaia Igra 'Maidan na Seligere'». http://www.newpeople.ru/svd/cnt/arkhiv/rolevaja_igra_majdan_na_seligere_26072007 [accessed 27 July 2011].

Okara, A. 2007. «Sovereign Democracy: A New Russian Idea or a PR Project?». *Russia in Global Affairs* 5, 3. 8-20.

Oldberg, I. 2007. «Russia's Great Power Ambitions and Policy Under Putin». In *Russia: Re-Emerging Great Power*, edited by R.E. Kanet, 13-30. Houndmills, Basingstoke & Hampshire: Palgrave MacMillan.

Olick, J.K. 2008. «From Collective Memory to the Sociology of Mnemonic Practices and Products. In *Cultural Memory Studies: An International and Interdisciplinary Handbook*, edited by A. Erll and A. Nünning, 151-161. Berlin & New York: Walter de Gruyter.

Omel'chenko, E. 2006. «Molodezh' dlia Politikov vs Molodezh' dlia Sebia? Razmyshleniia o Tsennostiakh i Fobiiakh Rossiiskoi Molodezhi». In *Molodezh' i Politika: Sovremennye Ochertaniia i Istoriia Problemy, Rol' Gosudarstva i Grazhdanskogo Obshchestva, Ozhidaniia i Prognozy*, edited by F.

Bomsford and G. Bordiugov, 9-34. Moskva: Fond Fridrikha Naumanna, AIRO-XXI.

Onken, E.-C. 2007. «The Baltic States and Moscow's 9 May Commemoration: Analysing Memory Politics in Europe». *Europe-Asia Studies* 59, 1. 23-46.

Orlova, I. 2002. «Sotsial'no-pedagogicheskie Usloviia Formirovaniia Grazhdansko-patrioticheskikh Kachestv u Podrostkov i Molodezhi pri Vzaimodeistvii Obshchestvennykh Ob''edinenii i Voinskikh Chastei». In *Molodezhnye i Detskie Obshchestvennye Ob''edineniia: Problemy Preemstvennosti Deiatel'nosti i Issledovanii. Sbornik Dokladov i Vystuplenii*, edited by E. Kamaldinova et al., 101-104. Moskva: Logos.

Oushakine, S. 2009. *The Patriotism of Despair: Nation, War, and Loss in Russia*. Ithaca & New York: Cornell University Press.

Overy, R. 1998 [1997]. *Russia's War: A History of the Soviet War Effort: 1941-1945*. New York: Penguin Books.

Pääbo, H. 2008. «War of Memories: Explaining 'Memorials War' in Estonia». *Baltic Security & Defence Review* 10. 5-28.

Perovic, J. and P. Casula. 2009. «The Stabilization of Russia during the Putin Presidency: Critical Reflections». In *Identities and Politics During the Putin Presidency: The Foundations of Russia's Stability*, edited by P. Casula and J. Perovic, 19-30. Stuttgart: ibidem-Verlag.

Pervyi Kanal. 2011a. «Fabrika Zvezd' 4». http://www.1tv.ru/fabrika4 [accessed 20 December 2011].

—— 2011b. «Sokrovishche Natsii». http://www.1tv.ru/sprojects/si=5767 [accessed 20 December 2011].

—— 2011c. «Vse Uchastniki Fabrika Zvezd». http://www.vsefz.ru/fabrika_zvëzd_6/chelsi.html [accessed 20 December 2011].

Pilkington, H. 1994. *Russia's Youth and its Culture: A Nation's Constructors and Constructed*. London: Routledge.

Plokhy, S. 2008. *Ukraine and Russia: Representations of the Past*. Toronto: University of Toronto Press. 3-16.

Pravitel'stvo Rossiiskoi Federatsii. 2006. «Strategiia Gosudarstvennoi Molodezhnoi Politiki v Rossiiskoi Federatsii». http://www.timolod.ru/docs/som_doc/raspor_18.doc [accessed 20 April 2012].

President of Russia. 2007. «Press Statement and Answers to Questions During the Joint Press Conference with President of the European Commission Jose

Manuel Barroso and German Chancellor Angela Merkel Following the Russia-European Union Summit Meeting».
http://archive.kremlin.ru/eng/speeches/2007/05/18/2256_type82914type82915_129689.shtml [accessed 21 September 2011].

Prozorov, S. 2005. «Russian Conservatism in the Putin Presidency: The Dispersion of a Hegemonic Discourse». *Journal of Political Ideologies* 10, 2. 121-143.

Putin, V. 2003. «Opening Address at a Meeting with History Scholars, Moscow, Russian National Library, November 27, 2003».
http://www.ln.mid.ru/bl.nsf/5d5fc0348b8b2d26c3256def0051fa20/3fd1249accaead9a43256dec002db610?OpenDocument [accessed 20 August 2011].

――― 2007a. «Putin's Speech at the 43rd Munich Conference on Security Policy». http://www.informationliberation.com/?id=20164 [accessed 28 July 2011].

――― 2007b. «Speech at the Military Parade Celebrating the 62nd Anniversary of Victory in the Great Patriotic War».
http://archive.kremlin.ru/eng/speeches/2007/05/09/1432_type82912type127286_127675.shtml [accessed 21 September 2011].

――― 2008a. «Vystuplenie na Voennom Parade v Chest 60-y Godovshchiny Pobedy v Velikoi Otechestvennoi Voine». In *Izbrannye Rechi i Vystupleniia*, 291-294. Moskva: Knizhnii Mir.

――― 2008b. «Vystuplenie na Rasshirennom Zasedanii Gosudarstvennogo Soveta 'O Strategii Razvitiia Rossii do 2020 Goda'».
http://www.kremlin.ru/text/appears/2008/02/159528.shtml [accessed 27 July 2011].

Rahi-Tamm, A. 2005. «Population: Human Losses». In *The White Book: Losses Inflicted on the Estonian Nation by Occupation Regimes 1940-1991*, edited by the Estonian State Commission on Examination of the Policies of Repression, 25-46. Tallinn: Estonian Encyclopedia Publishers.

RBK. 2013. «Na 'Seliger-2014' Rosmolodezh' Potratit 240 mln Rub.» 16 December. http://top.rbc.ru/politics/16/12/2013/895014.shtml [accessed 19 December 2013].

Regions.ru. 2013. «Skandaly Vokrug Rosmolodezhi: Beriia, 'Seliger', Lageria v Anape». 19 November. http://regions.ru/news/2486808/ [accessed 22 December 2013].

Regnum. 2007. «Estonian Prime Minister: Drunken Looters are Buried under the Bronze Soldier Monument». 24 April.
http://www.regnum.ru/english/817953.html [accessed 20 September 2011].

Ria Novosti. 2007. «Estonia has no Evidence of Kremlin Involvement in Cyber Attacks». 9 June. http://en.rian.ru/world/20070906/76959190.html [accessed 20 September 2011].

—— 2010. «Russian Billionaire Prokhorov to Finance Kremlin's Youth Forum – Newspaper». 15 March. http://en.rian.ru/russia/20100315/158199960.html [accessed 19 December 2011].

Riigikogu. 2007. «Protection of War Graves Act». 10 January. http://www.legaltext.ee/et/andmebaas/tekst.asp?loc=text&dok=XX10006&pg=1&tyyp=X&query=S%F5jahaudade+kaitse+seadus&ptyyp=RT&keel=en [accessed 18 September 2011].

Robertson, G.B. 2009. «Managing Society: Protest, Civil Society, and Regime in Putin's Russia». *Slavic Review* 68, 3. 528-547.

Romanov, M. 2005. «Kasparova Odolela Doska». *Moskovskii Komsomolets*. 18 April. http://www.mk.ru/editions/daily/article/2005/04/18/197300-kasparova-odolela-doska.html [accessed 27 August 2011].

Rossiia Molodaia 2005. «Nash Vzgliad: 'Zdravomysliashchaia Molodezh' Rossii Dolzhna Ob"edinit'sia!'». http://rumol.ru/ideology/manifest.html [accessed 16 August 2011].

Rossiiskaia Gazeta. 2001. «Gosudarstvennaia Programma 'Patrioticheskoe Vospitanie Grazhdan Rossiiskoi Federatsii na 2001-2005 Gody'». *Rossiiskaia Gazeta*. 16 February. http://www.rg.ru/oficial/doc/postan_rf/122_1.shtm [accessed 27 July 2011].

—— 2005. «Interv'iu Non-Stop». *Rossiiskaia Gazeta*. 10 May. 3.

Rossiiskii Soiuz Molodezhi 2009. *Ob Organizatsii*. http://www.ruy.ru/activity.html [accessed 16 August 2011].

Rosvoentsentr. 2010. «Tret'ia (Novaia) Gosudarstvennaia Programma 'Patrioticheskoe Vospitanie Grazhdan Rossiiskoi Federatsii na 2011 – 2015 Gody'». http://www.rosvoencentr-rf.ru/index.php?option=com_content&view=article&id=308:-q-2011-2015-q&catid=86:-2011-2015-&Itemid=57 [accessed 27 February 2012].

Rozhnov, O. 2005. «Molodezhnaia Politika i Molodezhnoe Dvizhenie v Rossii: 15 Let Peremen». *Vestnik Analitiki* 3, 21. 30-33.

Russian Justice Initiative. 2011. «ECHR Cases from the North Caucasus». http://www.srji.org/en/legal/cases [accessed 15 August 2011].

Sakwa, R. 2008 [1993]. *Russian Politics and Society*. 4th edition. London & New York: Routledge. 205-448.

—— 2004. *Putin: Russia's choice*. London: Routledge. 40-43.

Samarina, A. 2004. «Moskovskie Degustatory Ukrainskogo Sala». *Nezavisimaia Gazeta*. 7 December. http://www.ng.ru/ideas/2004-12-07/1_pavlovskiy.html [accessed 18 August 2011].

―――― 2013. «Presidentu Rasskazhut Istoriiu, Priiatnuiu vo Vsekh Otnosheniiakh». *Nezavisimaia Gazeta*. 29 October. http://www.ng.ru/politics/2013-10-29/1_history.html [accessed 16 December 2013].

Samarina, A. and I. Rodin. 2009. «'Seligeru-2009' Krizis ne Strashen». *Nezavisimaia Gazeta*. 6 September. http://www.ng.ru/politics/2009-06-09/1_seliger.html [accessed 20 December 2011].

Sarasin, P. 2003. *Geschichtswissenschaft und Diskursanalyse*. Frankfurt a.M.: Suhrkamp. 7-60.

Sarv, E. and P. Varju. 2005. «Survey of Occupation Regimes». In *The White Book: Losses Inflicted on the Estonian Nation by Occupation Regimes 1940-1991*, edited by the Estonian State Commission on Examination of the Policies of Repression, 9-24. Tallinn: Estonian Encyclopedia Publishers.

Savina, E. 2007. «Stop. Sniato». *Kommersant"*. 4 May. http://kommersant.ru/doc/763409 [accessed 21 September 2011].

Savina, E. and A. Pushkarskaia. 2007. «Bronzovyi Soldat Sobral Boitsov». *Kommersant"*. 2 May. http://kommersant.ru/doc/763152?themeID=116 [accessed 20 September 2011].

Savina, E. and Yu. Sukhonina. 2007. «'Marsh Nesoglasnykh Zastrial v Ocheredi». *Kommersant"*. 3 April. http://www.kommersant.ru/doc/755394 [accessed 18 December 2011].

Scheide, C. 2008. «Erinnerungsbrüche: Baltische Erfahrungen und Europas Gedächtnis». *Osteuropa* 58, 6. 117-128.

Schmid, U. 2006. «Naši – Die Putin-Jugend». *Osteuropa* 56, 5. 5-18.

Schröder, H.-H. 2009. «What Kind of Political Regime Does Russia Have?». In *Identities and Politics During the Putin Presidency: The Foundations of Russia's Stability*, edited by P. Casula and J. Perovic, 67-93. Stuttgart: ibidem-Verlag.

Schwirtz, M. 2007. «Russia's Political Youths». *Demokratizatsiya: The Journal of Post-Soviet Democratization* 15, 1. 73-85.

―――― 2008. «Estonia Bans Travel for Kremlin Group». *The New York Times*. 30 January 2008. http://www.nytimes.com/2008/01/30/world/europe/30russia.html?_r=1&ref=world&oref=slogin [accessed 21 September 2011].

Seliger 2010a. «Mikhail Mamonov – What is IYF Seliger 2010?». http://www.seliger2010.com/index.php?id=1 [accessed 27 July 2011].

―――― 2010b. «Obrashchenie Predsedatelia Pravitel'stva RF». http://www.seliger2010.com/index.php?id=12 [accessed 16 August 2011].

Shcherbakova, I. 2010. «Wenn Stumme mit Tauben Reden: Generationendialog und Geschichtspolitik in Russland». *Osteuropa* 60, 5. 17-25.

Sheeter, L. 2007. «Latvia, Russia Sign Border Deal». *BBC*. 27 March. http://news.bbc.co.uk/2/hi/europe/6498049.stm [accessed 22 September 2011].

Shegedin, A. et al. 2007. «Estonia Perezakhoronit Otnosheniia s Rossiei». *Kommersant"*. 27 April. http://kommersant.ru/doc/762639 [accessed 18 September 2011].

Sherlock, T. 2007. *Historical Narratives in the Soviet Union and Post-Soviet Russia.* New York: Palgrave MacMillan. 1-27, 149-185.

Shevtsova, L. 2005 [2003]. *Putin's Russia*. Washington, D.C.: Carnegie Endowment for International Peace.

Shleinov, R. 2010. «Glava Rosmolodezhi i Osnovatel' Dvizheniia 'Nashi' Vasilii Iakemenko v 1990-e Gody Chislilsia Uchreditelem Firmy, Osnovannoi Banditami, Rubivshimi Liudiam Golovy i Ruki». *Vedomosti*. 29 November. http://www.compromat.ru/page_30141.htm [accessed 14 February 2012].

Simonov, S. 2009. Interviewed by the author. 12 May, St. Petersburg.

Sivkova, A. 2013. «Dvizhenie 'Nashi' Stanet Vserossiiskim Soobshchestvom Molodezhi». *Izvestiia*. 11 February. http://izvestia.ru/news/544620 [accessed 22 December 2013].

Smith, A. 1999. *Myths and Memories of the Nation*. Oxford: Oxford University Press.

Smith, K. 2002. *Mythmaking in the New Russia: Politics and Memory During the Yeltsin Era*. Ithaca & London: Cornell University Press.

Snyder, T. 2010. *Bloodlands: Europe Between Hitler and Stalin*. New York: Basic Books. 119-154.

Sokolov, M. 2005. «Nash Zheleznyi Frunt». *Ekspert* 19, 466. http://www.forum-tvs.ru/index.php?showtopic=11662 [accessed 28 July 2011].

Solov'ev, V. 2007a. «Mogila Izvestnogo Soldata». *Kommersant"*. 2 May. http://kommersant.ru/doc/763080 [accessed 20 September 2011].

―――― 2007b. «Zapad Prinial Estoniiu na Svoi Schet». *Kommersant"*. 4 May. http://kommersant.ru/doc/763429 [accessed 21 September 2011].

Solov'ev, V. and A. Shegedin. 2007. «Pred"iavila Rossii Vinovnykh». *Kommersant"*. 15 May. http://kommersant.ru/doc/765360 [accessed 20 September 2011].

Solov'ev, V. and Zygar', M. 2007. «Estoniia Zakliuchila Evrosoiuz Protiv Rossii». *Kommersant"*. 3 May. http://kommersant.ru/doc/763227?themeID=116 [accessed 21 September 2011].

Stäheli, U. 2001. «Die politische Theorie der Hegemonie: E. Laclau und Ch. Mouffe». In *Politische Theorie der Gegenwart II: Eine Einführung*, edited by A. Brodocz and G. Schaal, 193-223. Opladen: Leske & Budrich.

Stiftung Öffentliche Meinung. 2005. «Jugend und Politik». *Russland-Analysen* 83 7-10. http://www.laender-analysen.de/dlcounter/dlcounter.php?url=../russland/pdf/Russlandanalysen083.pdf [accessed 28 July 2011].

――― 2006. «Russland und die Ukraine nach dem Gasstreit». *Russland-Analysen* 87. 12-16. http://www.laender-analysen.de/dlcounter/dlcounter.php?url=../russland/pdf/Russlandanalysen087.pdf [accessed 28 July 2011].

Strelkova, I. 2006. «V Kakikh Rukakh Budushchee Rossii». *Nash Sovremennik* 1. 235-249.

Surkov, V. 2005. «Sekretnyi Doklad Vladislava Surkova: 'My Real'no Schitaem, chto Davat' Vlast' Liberal'nym 'Druziam' Opasno i Vredno dlia Strany; Chem Bol'she ia Rabotaiu, tem Bol'she ja Razocharovyvaius v Mire'». http://archive.svoboda.org/programs/tp/2005/tp.071105.asp [accessed 28 July 2011]

――― 2006a. «Suverenitet – Eto Politicheskii Sinonim Konkurento-Sposobnost'». In *Suverenitet. Sbornik*, edited by N. Garadzha, 43-79. Moskva: Evropa.

――― 2006b. «Natsionalizatsiia Budushchego». *Ekspert* 43, 537. http://www.expert.ru/printissues/expert/2006/43/nacionalizaciya_buduscheg o [accessed 28 July 2011]

S"ezd Narodnykh Deputatov SSSR. 1989. «Postanovlenie Snd SSSR ot 24.12.1989 n 979-1 o Politicheskoi i Pravovoi Otsenke Sovetsko-Germanskogo Dogovora o Nenapadenii ot 1939 Goda». http://www.lawmix.ru/docs_cccp.php?id=1241 [accessed 10 August 2011].

Taranova, Yu. 2010. «Bureaucracy Stymies Pro-Kremlin Youth Retreat». *The New York Times*. 5 July. http://www.nytimes.com/2010/07/06/world/europe/06Nashi.html?scp=1&sq=seliger&st=nyt [accessed 15 December 2011].

Temnitskii, A.L. 2010. «Human Potential and Civic Positions of Activists in Youth Associations (The Example of the Seliger–2008 Forum)». *Russian Education and Society* 52, 11. 41-58.

The Telegraph. 2010. «Russia Cuts off Gas Supply to Belarus over Unpaid Bill». 21 June. http://www.telegraph.co.uk/finance/newsbysector/energy/oilandgas/7842834/Russia-cuts-off-gas-supply-to-Belarus-over-unpaid-bill.html [accessed 22 December 2011].

Thompson, W.C. 1998. «Citizenship and Borders: Legacies of Soviet Empire in Estonia». *Journal of Baltic Studies* 29, 2. 109-134

Tishman, M. 2011. «Biografiia Pevtsa i Kompozitora Marka Tishmana». http://www.marktishman.ru/index/0-16 [accessed 20 December 2011].

Tkachuk, O. 2008. «With Friends Like These: Ethnic Nationalism, the Church and the State of Russia». *CJOG* 1, 1. 17-24.

Tolz, V. 2004. «The Search for a National Identity in the Russia of Yeltsin and Putin». In *Reconstructing post-Communist Russia*, edited by Y. Brudny, J. Frankel and S. Hoffman, 160-178. Cambridge: Cambridge University Press.

Torfing, J. 1999. *New Theories of Discourse: Laclau, Mouffe and Zizek*. Oxford & Malden: Blackwell Publishers.

Tsentr Politicheskoi Informatsii. 2005. «Kremlevskie Instrumenty Vliianiya: Molodezhnoe Demokraticheskoe Antifashistskoe Dvizhenie 'Nashi' i Obshchestvennaia Organizatsiia 'Idushchie vmeste'». *Informatsionno-analiticheskii Biulleten'* 8, 1-23.

Tsygankov, A. 1997. «From International Institutionalism to Revolutionary Expansionism: The Foreign Policy Discourse of Contemporary Russia». *Mershon International Studies Review* 41, 2. 247-268.

Tumarkin, N. 1994. *The Living and the Dead: The Rise and Fall of the Cult of World War II in Russia*. New York: BasicBooks.

Urban, M. 1998. «Remythologising the Russian State». *Europe-Asia Studies* 50, 6. 969-992.

Vasjunin, I. 2007. «Ofitser Sviazi s 'Edinoi Rossiei'». *Novaia Gazeta*, 19 February. http://www.novayagazeta.ru/data/2007/12/20.html [accessed 4 August 2009].

Vetik, R. and J. Helemae. 2010. *The Russian Second Generation in Tallinn and Kohtla-Jarve*. Amsterdam: Amsterdam University Press. 13-25.

Vihalemm, T. 2008. «Crystallizing and Emancipating Identities in Post-Communist Estonia». In *Identities, Nations and Politics after Communism*, edited by R.E. Kanet, 71-96. London & New York: Routledge.

Voice of America. 2006. «Polish Defense Minister's Pipeline Remark Angers Germany». 3 May. http://www.voanews.com/english/news/a-13-Polish-Defense-Minister-Pipeline-Remark-Angers-Germany.html [accessed 14 September 2011].

Weiner, A. 1996. «The Making of a Dominant Myth: The Second World War and the Construction of Political Identities within the Soviet Polity». *Russian Review* 55, 4. 638-660.

Williams, C., V. Chuprov and J. Zubok. 2003. *Youth, Risk and Russian Modernity*. Hampshire: Ashgate.

Winter, J. and E. Sivan. 1999. «Setting the framework». In *War and Remembrance in the Twentieth Century*, edited by J. Winter and E. Sivan, 6-39. Cambridge: Cambridge University Press.

Yasmann, V. 2005. «Russia: National Bolsheviks, The Party Of 'Direct Action'». *Radio Free Europe / Radio Liberty*. 29 April. http://www.rferl.org/content/article/1058689.html [accessed 15 August 2011].

────── 2007. «Monument Dispute with Estonia Gets Dirty». *Radio Free Europe / Radio Liberty*. 8 May. http://www.rferl.org/content/article/1347550.html [accessed 20 September 2011].

Yevtukh, V. 2005. «Der Orange Geist der Freiheit: Profile und Motive der Revolutionsbewegung». In *Zur Anatomie der Orange Revolution in der Ukraine: Wechsel des Elitenregimes oder Triumph des Parlamentarismus?*, edited by I. Bredies, 15-39. Stuttgart: ibidem-Verlag.

Yurchak, A. 2006. *Everything Was Forever, Until It Was No More: The Last Soviet Generation*. Princeton and Oxford: Princeton University Press.

Zarubin, P. 2005. «'Nashi': Literaturnyi Debiut». *Vesti*. 11 May. www.vesti.ru/doc.html?id=108369&tid=27933 [accessed 15 September 2011].

Zaks. 2006. «Estonskii 'Nochnoi Dozor' Schitaet Pskovskikh 'Molodogvardeitsev' Porazhentsami». *Zaks*. 7 December. http://www.zaks.ru/new/archive/view/25722 [accessed 18 September 2011].

Zavtra. 2009. «Dmitrii Linter: Za Pravo Zhit'». *Zavtra*. 21 October. http://www.zavtra.ru/cgi/veil/data/zavtra/09/831/61.html [accessed 18 September 2011].

Zubov, M. 2010. «Guliai, Vasia!». *Moskovskii Komsomolets*. 16 November. http://www.mk.ru/politics/article/2010/11/15/544227-gulyay-vasya.html [accessed 14 February 2012].

Zygar', M. 2007a. «Vozvrashchenie Estonii v Orbitu Vliianiia Rossii Nevozmozhno». *Kommersant" Vlast'*. 14 May. http://kommersant.ru/doc/764740?themeID=116 [accessed 18 September 2011].

——— 2007b. «Vos'moe Maia Protiv Deviatogo». *Kommersant"*. 8 May. http://kommersant.ru/doc/763997 [accessed 13 January 2012].

Zygar' et al. 2007a. «Estonii Vyrazili Bespokoistvo». *Kommersant"*. 28 April. http://kommersant.ru/doc/762932 [accessed 18 September 2011].

——— 2007b. «Rossiiskie Chinovniki Pritsenivaiutsia k Sanktsiiam». *Kommersant"*. 3 May. http://kommersant.ru/doc/763233 [accessed 20 September 2011].

Index

A

Ansip, Andrus, 104, 105, 106, 107, 108, 109, 115, 124, 125
antagonism, 58, 79, 83, 97

B

Belokonev, Sergei, 64, 173, 174, 183
Bronze Soldier, 22, 98, 102, 106, 107, 108, 110, 114, 115, 118ff., 126, 128, 133, 177, 178
  history, 103, 104, 105, 106
  symbolic significance, 103, 106, 109, 112, 113, 114, 125, 126

C

Chechnya, 31, 38, 47, 53, 78, 83, 85
commemoration, 25, 42, 44, 45, 49, 50, 51, 84, 91, 102, 103, 178
constitutive outside, 37, 38, 40, 47, 49, 58, 66, 80, 112, 180

D

Danilin, Pavel, 32, 53, 58, 59, 64, 87, 88, 94
defeatists, 81, 82, 180
discourse, 30, 35, 36, 43, 83, 84, 93, 125, 138
  analysis, 20, 21, 28, 29, 37, 51, 180
  hegemonic, 29, 30, 31, 41, 43, 44, 45, 114, 121, 123, 171
  Nashi, 114, 128
  of Nashi, 21, 26, 78, 79, 80, 81, 91, 92, 98, 106, 110, 112, 122, 124, 178, 179, 180, 181, 184
  official, 20, 22, 26, 31, 33, 40, 45, 50, 58, 60, 68, 78ff., 83, 89, 92, 97, 104, 122ff., 129, 134, 150, 151, 155, 168, 171, 172, 173, 177
dislocation, 25, 29, 30, 31, 34, 37, 41, 51, 58, 114, 122

E

Edinaia Rossiia (United Russia), 18, 26, 92, 93, 104, 133, 182
Estonia, 20, 22, 102, 103, 104, 105, 106, 107, 108, 110ff., 117, 118, 119ff., 177, 178
  ethnic Russians, 98, 100, 101, 103, 104, 106, 117, 118, 121
  identity, 98, 122, 126
  war history, 99, 101, 104
European Union, 98, 107, 114, 115, 117, 118, 119, 120, 121, 124, 179

F

fascism/fascist, 19, 66, 71, 72, 83, 84, 85, 88, 108, 109, 110, 112, 114, 115, 117, 123, 177, 178, 181
  as signifier, 22, 47, 81, 82, 85, 100, 108, 112, 119, 122, 124, 127
  unusual fascism, 85, 86, 87, 88
Federal Agency for Youth Affairs, 137, 138, 147, 155, 181
focal points, 20, 28, 177
Fursenko, Andrei, 62, 86

G

Ganin, Dmitrii, 113, 114, 119
Gorbachev, Mikhail, 30, 33, 43, 81
Great Patriotic War, 41, 42, 85, 92, 103
  commemoration, 17, 25, 26, 44, 45, 49, 50, 51, 52, 63, 65, 71, 84, 91, 103, 107, 126, 128, 130, 155
  history, 17, 69
  official narrative, 21, 22, 33, 65, 77, 93, 122, 124, 178
great power, 17, 21, 22, 36, 37, 45, 47, 51, 58, 76, 78, 80, 112, 130, 163, 178

H

hegemony/hegemonic, 20, 30, 72, 81, 91, 123, 125, 168
  concept of, 25, 37, 43
  myth, 51, 52
  response, 22, 58, 70

I

Iabloko (Apple - opposition party), 54, 71, 86, 91
Iakemenko, Vasilii, 63, 64, 71, 85, 92, 135, 137, 138, 147, 182, 183
  and violence, 88, 89, 136, 181, 182
  conflict with Estonia, 106, 111, 113, 116, 118, 127
  foundation Nashi, 18, 59, 60, 61, 63
Idushchie Vmeste (Going Together), 18, 59, 71
International Youth Forum Seliger, 23, 27, 134, 138, 140, 169, 171, 174, 177, 180

K

Kadyrov, Ramsan, 84, 136
Kaljurand, Marina, 110, 115, 116, 118
Kashin, Oleg, 18, 62, 64, 65, 86, 182, 183, 195
Komsomol, 18, 32, 52, 60, 61, 91

L

Lake Seliger, 20, 28, 64, 84, 92, 134, 138, 145, 150, 155, 179, 183

M

Mamonov, Mikhail, 141, 142, 144, 145, 152, 153, 160, 162, 169, 170, 173
managed passion, 19, 65, 127, 181
Medvedev, Dmitry, 93, 105, 128, 129, 133, 137, 142, 148, 157, 164, 169, 170, 175, 184, 185
Mestnye (Locals), 18, 105, 111, 136
MGIMO (Moscow State Institute of International Relations), 51, 138, 142, 156, 157
Molodaia Gvardiia (Young Guard), 18, 93, 105, 109, 111, 167, 182
Mutko, Vitalii, 141
myth, 22, 23, 44, 50, 51, 52, 66, 77, 90, 126, 130, 165

N

Nashi, 21, 22, 45, 63, 67, 81, 82, 84, 85, 90, 91, 97, 104, 129, 134, 135, 140, 146, 150, 151, 155, 167, 171, 172, 173, 184, 185
and enemies, 19, 64, 77, 79, 80, 84, 85, 86, 87, 88, 89, 93, 108, 123, 136, 178, 180, 181, 182
and government, 18, 20, 23, 69, 94, 95, 120, 133, 156, 174, 177
commissars, 27, 60, 61, 62, 63, 73, 75, 79, 80, 89, 92, 93, 109, 126, 135, 136, 162, 179, 183, 184
conflict with Estonia, 105, 106, 108, 109, 110, 111, 112, 113, 115, 116, 117, 118, 119, 120, 123, 124, 126, 178, 179
continuity of generations, 65, 81, 178
finances, 64, 133, 182, 183
foundation, 17, 18, 20, 25, 26, 32, 52, 54, 58, 60, 61, 62, 71
manifesto, 72, 73, 76, 82, 83, 147, 165, 168
modernization, 80, 133, 134, 139, 163, 181
national identity, 21, 32, 44, 50, 73, 92
NBP (National Bolshevik Party), 54, 60, 71, 86, 87, 88, 89, 90, 91
Nochnoi Dozor (Night Watch), 104, 105, 106, 107, 128
nodal point, 80, 122, 149, 178
Novye Liudi (New People), 136

O

Orange Revolution, 48, 54, 55, 56, 58, 59, 60, 61, 64, 65, 68, 71, 75, 90, 97
foundation of youth groups, 28, 93, 133, 135, 178
Russian perception, 18, 56, 57, 58, 156

P

participant observation, 134, 138, 140
patriotic education, 22, 34, 35, 52, 61, 64, 66, 68, 69, 85, 137, 155
patriotism, 22, 37, 44, 52, 81, 84, 137, 146, 152, 171
political identity, 20, 21, 25, 31, 32, 34, 36, 40, 43, 44, 50, 52, 58, 70, 75, 78, 81, 91, 98, 114, 122, 125
Putin, Vladimir, 17, 26, 34, 36, 44, 67, 68, 70, 74, 83, 93, 122, 129, 137, 151, 163, 166, 179
and criticism, 53, 76, 86, 87, 88, 185
and Nashi, 17, 26, 45, 49, 64, 73, 82, 85, 94, 112, 125
and security, 38, 39, 40, 77, 78, 95, 123
hegemonic project, 20, 25, 37, 41, 51, 65, 82, 92, 114, 177
international relations, 47, 48, 78, 102, 115, 119
Prime Minister, 138, 142
regime, 18, 19, 20, 21, 25, 38, 44, 50, 53, 54, 78, 157, 184, 185
third term, 172, 174, 175, 185
Victory Day, 45, 46, 47, 48, 49, 63, 127

R

Red Army, 42, 43, 45, 49, 99, 101, 103, 125, 126
Rossiia Molodaia (Young Russia), 105, 136

S

securitization, 21, 22, 25, 38, 39, 40, 58, 70, 88, 90, 98, 123
signifier, 22, 31, 35, 37, 47, 50, 58, 81, 84, 106, 108, 122, 129
Sovereign Democracy, 18, 21, 22, 23, 26, 48, 74, 75, 76, 77, 123, 157, 178
Soviet Union, 32, 33, 42, 48, 50, 61, 74, 97, 114, 124, 130, 179
and Nashi, 62, 72, 126
collapse, 20, 25, 28, 30, 33, 36, 42, 45
war history, 17, 42, 43, 46, 84, 98, 99, 122, 125, 127
Spravedlivaia Rossiia (Just Russia), 90, 157
SPS (Union of Right Forces - opposition party), 54, 86, 91
stability, 22, 29, 30, 34, 38, 69, 185
stabilization, 25, 38, 39, 40
Surkov, Vladislav, 22, 26, 57, 58, 59, 62, 74, 76, 78, 79, 80, 81, 84, 95, 123, 157
and Nashi, 18, 26, 74, 75, 76, 79, 135, 178
and Putin, 26, 93, 182

T

Tallinn, 22, 28, 100, 101, 103, 104, 106, 107, 108, 109, 110, 115, 119, 121, 125, 133, 178
terrorism, 47, 58, 77, 78, 83
Tönismägi, 103, 106, 108, 109

U

Ukraine, 22, 28, 49, 54, 55, 56, 57, 58, 60, 61, 66, 68, 78, 164
United States, 46, 47, 48, 56, 57, 68, 78, 79, 80, 104, 121, 128, 156, 163, 164, 165, 168, 171, 179

V

veterans, 17, 42, 44, 45, 63, 92, 108, 155, 178, 181
Victory Day, 17, 42, 45, 46, 48, 49, 63, 85, 127, 128, 129, 179
Volodin, Viacheslav, 93, 182, 183

Y

Yeltsin, Boris, 20, 31, 36, 44, 61, 68, 81, 111, 113
Yushchenko, Viktor, 48, 55, 56, 57, 59

ПРОГРАММА ПО БОРЬБЕ С ФАШИЗМОМ

НЕОБЫКНОВЕННЫЙ ФАШИЗМ

ФАШИЗМ ГОТОВИТ УДАР

9 мая мы отмечаем 60-летие Великой Победы. В 1945 году Россия разгромила гитлеровскую Германию и освободила Европу от «коричневой чумы». Но сегодня, в 2005 году, в России поднимает голову новый фашизм. Правда, это фашизм необыкновенный.

Да и каким может быть фашизм в стране, сломавшей хребет гитлеровским ордам? Только необыкновенный, привнесенный, тщательно взращиваемый всевозможными политическими интриганами и эмигрантами!

Новые фашисты лицемерно заявляют, что они выступают за свободу, якобы ущемляемую российским государством. Посмотрим правде в глаза: как можно называть партию, члены которой называют друг друга «партайгеноссе», а председатели региональных исполкомов называются «гауляйтерами»? Как можно называть партию, которая активно использует нацистскую символику и стилистику, как не фашистской?

ПРОГРАММА ПО БОРЬБЕ С ФАШИЗМОМ

Взгляните, как точно униформа, обряды и плакаты Национал-большевистской партии (НБП) копируют символику Национал-социалистической рабочей партии Германии (НСДАП) 1920-х годов.

Слева – агитационные плакаты НБП, справа – плакаты фашистской Германии. Как говорится, найдите пять отличий...

Организация «Пора!», призывающая к «оранжевой революции» в России, своей эмблемой избрала ...свастику.

Партийный флаг НБП тоже вызывает вполне определенные ассоциации. Слева - флаг НСДАП, ставший впоследствии символом фашизма. Справа - флаг НБП.

ПРОГРАММА ПО БОРЬБЕ С ФАШИЗМОМ

Фашисты из НБП своих убеждений не скрывают.

Вот, что они говорят:

«*Товарищи фашисты, приверженцы идеологии РНЕ и жесткого национализма, радикальные люди, пришло наше время! Давайте объединимся в этой священной, народной борьбе против происков капиталистических ублюдков и сжирания достояния нации!*
Товарищ! Не ссы! Вступай в НБП!»

(*http://nbp-klin.narod.ru*)

ПРОГРАММА ПО БОРЬБЕ С ФАШИЗМОМ

НБП – ТОТАЛИТАРНАЯ СЕКТА

НБП, по своей сути, является не политической организацией, а тоталитарной сектой.

Как известно, тоталитарная секта – это организация, главный смысл существования которой – власть, деньги и слава для лидера и его приближенных.

Главными признаками тоталитарной секты являются обожествление лидеров и использование особых методик по зомбированию ее членов.

Подтверждают это и сами нацболы.

Вот, что они говорят:

«Мы сектанты... Мы верим в Партию... Каждый полдень мы смотрим на солнце и начинаем молитву нацбола... Все наши встречи начинаются и заканчиваются словами «Слава Партии!». Этими же словами сопровождается каждый прием пищи. Все эти ритуалы выработались за годы борьбы, и не кажутся нам противоестественными. Это для нас в порядке вещей...»

(«Русский журнал», 01.03.2005)

ПРОГРАММА ПО БОРЬБЕ С ФАШИЗМОМ

ФАШИЗМ В ЕДИНОЙ ЕВРОПЕ

Нацизм поднимает голову не только в России. По городам Латвии, освобождённым Советской Армией от фашизма, торжественно маршируют вражеские недобитки из легионов «Ваффен – СС».

Ветеран ВОВ Василий Кононов отсидел в тюрьме за борьбу с фашизмом

В последнее десятилетие профашистские позиции и риторика в Прибалтике вошли в политический язык. Президенты Эстонии и Литвы Арнольд Руутел и Валдас Адамкус, идя на поводу у местных фашистов, отменили поездку в Москву на празднование 60-летия Великой Победы.

Президент Литвы Валдас Адамкус

А скандально известная Президент Латвии Вайра Вике-Фрейберга, прожившая, кстати, всю жизнь в Канаде, в интервью западным СМИ осуществляет политическое прикрытие пересмотра итогов Второй Мировой войны:

«9 мая – дата неоднозначная... Половина стран Европы остались под советским господством, будучи оккупированными, как прибалтийские государства... Три прибалтийских государства совершенно единодушны в том, что этот день означал для нас утрату свободы и начало неописуемых страданий нашего народа».

(«Frankfurter Allgemeine Zeitung», 23.03.2005)

ПРОГРАММА ПО БОРЬБЕ С ФАШИЗМОМ

СОЧУВСТВУЮЩИЕ ФАШИСТАМ В РОССИИ

Сегодня откровенных нацистов поддерживают обанкротившиеся «либералы и демократы», «Комитет-2008», партии «Яблоко» и «Наш выбор», Молодежный союз правых сил.

Ирина Хакамада, как наиболее раскрученный из «либеральной» тусовки политик, открыто поддерживает фашиствующих лимоновцев. Вот, что она говорит в их поддержку в интервью газете НБП «Генеральная линия / Лимонка»:

«Вы справедливо протестуете... Когда вы, врываетесь в кабинеты министров – это не может не вызвать симпатии... Поэтому необходимо объединение всех сил. Тем более, таких как у вас, пассионарных и оппозиционных. Вместе будет легче действовать... Вы делаете периодические партизанские вылазки, молодежное «Яблоко» начинает двигаться в этом направлении, и я это приветствую».

Дела не отстают от слов. Посмотрите: нацболы и яблочники уже маршируют вместе!

Молодой яблочник И. Яшин открыто выступает на фашистских митингах НБП.

ПРОГРАММА ПО БОРЬБЕ С ФАШИЗМОМ

СОЧУВСТВУЮЩИЕ ФАШИСТАМ В РОССИИ

Сегодня откровенных нацистов поддерживают обанкротившиеся «либералы и демократы», «Комитет-2008», партии «Яблоко» и «Наш выбор», Молодежный союз правых сил.

Ирина Хакамада, как наиболее раскрученный из «либеральной» тусовки политик, открыто поддерживает фашиствующих лимоновцев. Вот, что она говорит в их поддержку в интервью газете НБП «Генеральная линия / Лимонка»:

«Вы справедливо протестуете… Когда вы, врываетесь в кабинеты министров – это не может не вызвать симпатии… Поэтому необходимо объединение всех сил. Тем более, таких как у вас, пассионарных и оппозиционных. Вместе будет легче действовать… Вы делаете периодические партизанские вылазки, молодежное «Яблоко» начинает двигаться в этом направлении, и я это приветствую».

Дела не отстают от слов. Посмотрите: нацболы и яблочники уже маршируют вместе!

Молодой яблочник И. Яшин открыто выступает на фашистских митингах НБП.

ПРОГРАММА ПО БОРЬБЕ С ФАШИЗМОМ

Пресс-секретарь Молодежного союза правых сил Н.Каримова позирует фотографу с повязкой НБП на руке.

Не отстают от Н. Каримовой и «боевые подруги» самих нацистов. В НБП обычной практикой является позирование обнаженных подростков на фоне фашистской символики. Порнографические открытки – один из нехитрых приемов агитации и пополнения партийной кассы.

Финансовую и информационную поддержку так называемым «либералам и демократам» намеренны оказывать беглые олигархи.

Они заявляют об этом открыто. Вот, например, что говорит скрывающийся в Израиле от российского правосудия экс-совладелец «Юкоса» Л. Невзлин...

«Безусловно, я себя считаю частью оппозиции и содержательной, и организационной, и материальной... Хакамада – это человек, которого я поддерживал и буду всегда поддерживать. Не важно – содержательно или материально, как договоримся».

(«Коммерсант-Власть», 07.03.2005)

«Контуры демократической оппозиции появились, и я обращаюсь к этим людям... Рыжков и Каспаров, та же Ира Хакамада. Есть еще, например, молодое «Яблоко», очень перспективный Яшин – насколько я могу судить, глядя отсюда».

(«Коммерсант-Власть», 07.03.2005)

ПРОГРАММА ПО БОРЬБЕ С ФАШИЗМОМ

ФАШИСТ ЛИМОНОВ – ЕДИНЫЙ КАНДИДАТ?

В последнее время фашисты в России стали находить поддержку у некоторых политических спекулянтов, представленных в парламенте.

Рогозинская «Родина», зюгановская КПРФ открыто сотрудничают с фашиствующими отморозками, вступая в союзы и осуществляя взаимную поддержку.

Москва, апрель 2005 г., Г. Зюганов, Д. Рогозин, С. Глазьев вместе в с Э. Лимоновым на собрании инициативной группы по проведению всероссийского референдума.

Эти факты, наряду с терактами, «цветными» бандитскими переворотами, грязными интригами олигарха Б. Березовского и К°, являются звеньями одной цепи, единой кампанией против России.

ПРОГРАММА ПО БОРЬБЕ С ФАШИЗМОМ

КТО ТАКОЙ ЛИМОНОВ

На фото слева – молодая жертва лимоновских политических извращений. Справа – «автор»...

О нравах, царящих в так называемой «молодежной оппозиции», можно судить, например, по автобиографической книге Э. Лимонова «Это я, Эдичка!»:

«Я стащил с себя брюки, мне хотелось, чтобы он меня вые...л. Я стащил с себя брюки, стащил сапоги. Трусы я приказал ему разорвать на мне, мне хотелось, чтоб он именно разорвал, и он послушно разорвал на мне мои красные трусики. Я отшвырнул их далеко в сторону.

В этот момент я действительно был женщиной, капризной, требовательной и, наверное, соблазнительной, потому что я помню себя игриво вихляющим своей попкой, упершись руками в песок...»

Пишет smolyak (smolyak)

Re:Объяснить то можно, было бы желание понять.
Лимонов – великий писатель!!! НБП – великая партия!!!
Но голосовать все равно буду за «ЯБЛОКО»

И автора подобного рода «литературы» наши «либералы» называют «великим»!..

А ведь Павел Смоляк – член Центрального совета санкт-петербургского молодежного союза «Яблоко».

Видимо, такие «молодые демократы» и предлагают сделать Э. Лимонова руководителем страны...

Родители! Берегите своих детей от политического растлителя малолетних – Э. Лимонова!

ПРОГРАММА ПО БОРЬБЕ С ФАШИЗМОМ

ПРОГРАММА ПО БОРЬБЕ С ФАШИЗМОМ

ФАШИСТОВ-СЕКТАНТОВ И ПРИМКНУВШИХ К НИМ «ДЕМОКРАТОВ» НЕОБХОДИМО ОСТАНОВИТЬ!

Василий Якеменко, Федеральный комиссар движения «НАШИ»:

— В канун 60-летия Победы России в Великой Отечественной войне, ряд региональных молодежных организаций выступили с инициативой о создании широкого демократического антифашистского движения. Это здоровая реакция на растущую популярность в псевдоинтеллигентских кругах политического растлителя малолетних Лимонова и его недоношенных нацистов.

Под фашистскими флагами национал-социализма, которыми размахивают национал-большевики, собрались Хакамада и ее «Комитет-2008», молодежное «Яблоко», Березовский, Макашов и прочие безнравственные личности.

Для нас открытые выступления и безнаказанность переносчиков чумы XX-го века, погубившей 28 миллионов русских, татар, белорусов, евреев, являются личным оскорблением. Мы положим конец противоестественному союзу олигархов и антисемитов, нацистов и либералов.

ОНИ НЕ ПРОЙДУТ! ПОБЕДА БУДЕТ ЗА НАМИ!

Этот буклет создан в рамках программы по борьбе с фашизмом Молодежного демократического антифашистского движения «НАШИ» совместно с союзами ветеранов Великой Отечественной войны. Программа реализуется в год 60-летия Великой Победы в честь памяти павших в борьбе за независимость нашей Родины.

Информационный Центр «НАШИ», (095) 953-73-25, info@nashi.su

www.nashi.su

НЕСКОЛЬКО НЕУДОБНЫХ ВОПРОСОВ РОССИЙСКОЙ ВЛАСТИ

- Путин за время своего нахождения у власти ничего не сделал, только зря потерял время и не подготовился к кризису...

Это совершенно несправедливо. Практически все экономические показатели стремительно летели вниз до прихода Путина к власти, и наоборот, все они росли стабильно весь срок его правления. Кризис, безусловно, ударил по России, как и по многим другим странам, но именно запас прочности созданный Путиным и его командой позволил России пережить мировой кризис. А теперь только цифры: за период 2000-2007 г. ВВП России увеличился на 70% и составил по итогам 2007 года около 33 трлн. рублей. Россия обогнала Италию по объему ВВП, рассчитанному по паритету покупательной способности, и занимает 8 место в мире. За 2000-2007 гг. ВВП на душу населения в долларах в России вырос почти в 5 раз. Так быстро не росла ни одна страна за исключением Азербайджана (5,5), Китай, который все очень хвалят, сумел увеличить доходы на душу населения всего в 2,5 раза. ВВП на душу населения по текущему курсу в 2007 году превысил 9 тыс. долл., что приблизительно соответствует аналогичному показателю в Чили (9,6), Литве (10,2) Мексике (8,4), Венесуэле (8,2). По итогам 1999 г. этот показатель был на уровне 1340 долларов, и мы находились в группе следующих стран: Египет, Эквадор, Самоа, Свазиленд, Вануату, значительно уступая Намибии и Суринаму. Инвестиции в основной капитал за время правления Путина выросли в 2,6 раза, иностранные инвестиции – в 13,6 раза. В 1999 г. дефицит федерального бюджета составил 51,4 млрд. руб. (1,1% ВВП), в 2006 г. наблюдался профицит в размере 1994,1 млрд. руб. (7,5% ВВП), а в 2007 г. около 3,6% ВВП. Объем золотовалютных резервов на 1.01.2000 составил 12,5 млрд. долл., на конец 2007 г. – 476,4 млрд. долл. Государственный внешний долг за 2000 – 2006 гг. сократился со 148,5 млрд. долл. (75,9% ВВП) до 48,6 млрд. долл. (4,9% ВВП). На 1.01.2008 долг составил 2,3% от ВВП. В 1999 г. государственный внешний долг превышал экспорт товаров и услуг в 1,6 раза, в 2000 г. – они были равны, а в 2007 составлял от экспорта всего около 13%.

- Коррупция достигла катастрофических размеров. Россия по уровню мздоимства находится среди самых отсталых африканских стран и занимает 146-е место в рейтинге Transparency International. Почему власть не борется с коррупцией? Ей это не выгодно, потому что она же ею занимается?

Во-первых, по мнению Transparency International., «индекс коррупции» РФ держится все время примерно на одном уровне (вообще он выражается числом от 0 до 10) – около 2,5. Россия «скатывается» к последним местам, от 47-ого при Ельцине до 146-ого при Путине просто потому, что количество стран в этом рейтинге поначалу было всего 54, а потом его постепенно расширили до 180. Так что никуда Россия не скатывается, просто рейтинг расширяется. Во-вторых, что еще смешнее – **этот рейтинг вовсе не измеряет уровня коррупции**. И он вообще не позволяет сравнивать объективно уровни коррупции в разных странах, и это даже сами создатели TI отмечают. Этот индекс является всего лишь измерителем, как сами граждане страны воспринимают/оценивают коррумпированность. Это исключительно субъективная оценка ситуации, как ее воспринимают люди в своей стране, а не сравнительный объективный показатель.

Одним словом, рейтинг устойчиво показывает, что сами россияне озабочены этой проблемой больше, чем другие народы. Одна из причин этого, возможно, в том, что наш менталитет воспринимает коррупцию как болезнь, как порок, а вот во многих, особенно восточных обществах, это норма. Сейчас не существует объективного уровня оценки коррупции, но очевидно, что почти во всех латиноамериканских странах она выше, она выше почти во всех ближневосточных и среднеазиатских странах, она выше почти во всех африканских странах, коррупция выше в Китае, коррупция выше в большинстве бывших стран СССР, и она на таком же уровне как в странах Восточной Европы. Одним словом, в плане коррупции лучше, чем у нас, дела обстоят не более чем в 20 странах из 200! И, конечно, это не означает, что власть может и не обращать на проблему внимания. Наоборот, именно власть первой и затеяла масштабный разговор об этой проблеме, поставила тему коррупции в повестку дня СМИ. И не только затеяла разговор, но предприняла ряд мер: еще в 2008 году президент Медведев подписал указ о создании Национального плана по борьбе с коррупцией. Согласно этому плану чиновники и их родственники теперь публикуют свои налоговые декларации, они так же обязаны сообщать о всех случаях предложения взяток и мн. др. В России ведется борьба с коррупцией правоохранительными органами. И тут тоже есть серьезные достижения. Так, Глава СКП России Александр Бастрыкин привел следующую статистику: «За 2009 год было расследовано более 40 тысяч преступлений, совершенных чиновниками, из них преступлений против государственной власти и интересов государственной службы и службы в органах местного самоуправления - почти 25 тысяч. В основном это служебный подлог - около 9 тысяч, получение взятки - 6880, злоупотребление должностными полномочиями - 5226, нецелевое расходование бюджетных средств - около 300. Всего за минувший год поймано за руку более 8 тысяч чиновников, совершивших преступления против государственной власти, интересов службы. Уголовные дела о 16 тысячах преступлений направлены в суды. Одна треть - 5448 преступлений - это взятки. По ним к уголовной ответственности привлечено 3512 человек».

- В России огромный чиновничий аппарат, который паразитирует на теле общества. Почему количество чиновников растет год от года?

Крайне часто можно услышать от представителей оппозиции или просто незнающих людей, что в нашей стране неимоверно большое число чиновников. Что вся вина во всех бедах России именно в них, этих бюрократах, «штаныпросиживателях» и «бюджетопроедателях». Увы, но и тут оппозицию придется огорчить. Вот лишь небольшая статистика по этому вопросу. Так, по данным Росстата, на конец 2009 года в федеральных органах государственной власти РФ должности занимали 878 тысяч чиновников, из них на региональном уровне - 830,7 тысячи человек, то есть 94,6% от общего числа сотрудников. При этом общее количество чиновников в стране (в федеральной, региональной власти и органах местного самоуправления) составило около 1,7 миллиона человек. Среднемесячная начисленная зарплата служащих федеральных органов власти на региональном уровне составила на конец 2009 года 25,7 тысячи рублей. По данным Всемирного банка, доля федеральных и региональных чиновников по отношению к численности населения в нашей стране составляет менее 1%, что значительно меньше, чем в развитых странах мира. Доля подобных чиновников в населении Бразилии составляет 1,5%, Чили — 1%, Китая — 1,6%. В развитых странах в госаппарате занято гораздо больше: в Германии — 6,1 % населения, США — 6,8%, Швеции — 11,7%. Сейчас в России на тысячу жителей приходятся в среднем 7 чиновников, тогда как в Австрии соответствующий показатель составляет 14, в Америке -7,8, в Великобритании - 8,8, во Франции - 12,4, а в Швеции - целых 16,8! Выходит, что нам необходимо не сокращать, а, наоборот, в перспективе увеличивать количество чиновников, если мы хотим идти вровень с развитыми и цивилизованными странами! Тем не менее, сейчас в кризисных условиях даже при нехватке чиновников, Президент принял решение о необходимости сокращения их числа на 20%. В 2009 году, кстати, было аналогичное сокращение на 10%.

- Почему ОМОН разгоняет «марши несогласных» оппозиции и почему нарушается 31-ая статья Конституции?

Любимая тема для выпадов в адрес власти со стороны оппозиции – это обвинения относительно, якобы, нарушения 31-ой статьи Конституции России, которая гласит: «Граждане Российской Федерации имеют право собираться мирно без оружия, проводить собрания, митинги и демонстрации, шествия и пикетирование». При этом оппозиция любит предоставлять различные фото- и видеоматериалы о том, как «бесчинствующий» ОМОН разгоняет «мирных» протестующих. Что же на самом деле это за «мирные» протестующие, и почему их разгоняет ОМОН?! Вот, представьте себе, что Вы – председатель профсоюза какой-либо организации. У Вашего профсоюза возникли какие-то проблемы, например, с зарплатой, и Вы хотите провести митинг, ну, скажем, 31 мая на Триумфальной площади с требованиями, чтобы зарплату все же подняли. Вот, идете Вы в мэрию Москвы, относите необходимые документы и получаете соответствующее разрешение на митинг. 31 мая. Вы со своими соратниками идете митинговать. Подходите к Триумфальной площади, а тут... Молодые люди с повязками на лице кидаются камнями в милиционеров, в витрины и вообще, во все, что движется; кто-то бегает с плакатом «Поддержим Ходорковского»; а какая-то полоумная бабка «горланит» на всю площадь «Путина в отставку»! Нет, это не съемки фильма «В нашем дурдоме день открытых дверей» - это «марш несогласных», а также Ваш испорченный день, ну или митинг.

Разгоняет ОМОН все эти хулиганские сборища под названием «марши несогласных» не потому что он плохой или власть плохая, а потому что сборища незаконны. Во всех развитых странах, в том числе и в России, для того, чтобы провести публичное мероприятие – необходимо заранее уведомить муниципалитет, на территории которого это мероприятие будет проводиться. Так, в соответствии с Законом Франции, порядок организации и проведения массовых мероприятий граждан и их объединений (манифестаций) связан с обязанностью их организаторов заблаговременно информировать власти о готовящихся массовых выступлениях. В противном случае проведение подобных мероприятий запрещено. В Германии действует закон «О собраниях» от 24 июня 1953 года, в котором, в частности, закреплено: «...тот, кто намеревается организовать общественное собрание под открытым небом или демонстрацию, шествие и иные мероприятия с участием людей, должен заявить об этом компетентным органам не позднее, чем за 48 часов до публичного объявления о своем намерении». В столице США, Вашингтоне, правила проведения массовых мероприятий на улицах устанавливаются местным муниципалитетом. Они предусматривают обязательную подачу на рассмотрение властей специальной анкеты - заявления не позднее, чем за 4 дня (исключая выходные и праздничные дни) до даты проведения планируемого массового мероприятия.

Также, если в России все эти незаконно «марширующие» «несогласные», как максимум, получат штраф от 500 до 1 500 рублей за нарушение общественного порядка, то в других странах могут обойтись с такими куда суровей. В Саудовской Аравии, например, за подстрекательства ко всяким таким «несогласным» шествиям могут казнить. Согласно французским законам, подстрекательство к проведению митинга или демонстрации, с выкрикиванием или произнесением публичных речей, а также распространение разного рода печатной либо аудиовизуальной продукции, в соответствии со ст. 431-6 наказывается лишением свободы на срок до 1 года и штрафом до 15 тысяч евро. В случае, если призывы к проведению демонстрации привели к желаемому результату, предусмотрено наказание до 7 лет лишения свободы и штраф до 100 тысяч евро. А после отказа разойтись гражданин, добровольно принимающий участие в демонстрации подвергается наказанию в виде лишения свободы на срок до 1 года и штрафу до 15 тысяч евро (ст. УК Французской республики № 431-4). В случае, если задержанный участник демонстрации частично или полностью скрывал свое лицо, то он подвергается наказанию до 3-х лет лишения свободы и штрафу до 45 тысяч евро. В США законы примерно такие же. Не слабо, а?! Это по сравнению с нашими-то 500 рублями!

- *Зачем понадобилось тратить деньги на Сколково – это неуклюжее подобие американской Силиконовой долины? Для того, чтобы изображать видимость инновационной деятельности или для того, чтобы опять «распилить» бюджетные деньги?*

Оппозиция годами критиковала власть за то, что она слишком большое внимание уделяет нефтегазовому сектору и не занимается наукоемкими отраслями. И вот с 2008 года власть усиленно начинает заниматься поддержкой инноваций. Что мы видим со стороны оппозиции? Радостные приветствия? Нет, опять одни упреки! Создается впечатление, что чтобы не делала власть – все будет раскритиковано, даже если власть будет выполнять требования самой же оппозиции.

Итак, в России наконец-то представители власти серьезно обратили свой взгляд на науку. Началось строительство первого иннограда в Сколково, а также начат курс на модернизацию российской экономики. Сразу же из-за всяких оппозиционных щелей параллельно с этим начались «писки» о том, что проект Сколково – это «распил» бюджетных средств. Что модернизация России не нужна. Что все эти начинания – утопия и прочий подобный бред. Теперь же адекватно оценим проект в Сколково в рамках начала системной модернизации российской экономики. Во-первых, проект в Сколково уникален. Это начинание, почему-то, ошибочно сравнивают с советскими наукоградами, вроде Королева. Но в наукоградах просто жили и работали ученые, как правило, по одному направлению. В Сколково же планируется построить не город для ученых, а центр инноваций в самых различных отраслях; мощнейшую экономическую площадку, стимулированную налоговыми льготами; образовательный центр нового поколения, как для ученых, инженеров и инноваторов, так и для экономистов, политиков и финансистов. Во-вторых, проект в Сколково весьма представителен. Какой смысл приглашать иностранных ученых и менеджеров в руководство, если хотят создать «видимость»? И будут ли знаменитые ученые и менеджеры в этом участвовать? Да и как Президент будет выглядеть перед народом, если Сколково не получится?! А ведь 19 июня Президент России Дмитрий Медведев решил лично возглавить Попечительский совет «Сколково» и, тем самым, приобщиться к проекту. Научным руководителем проекта инограда в Сколково стал Нобелевский лауреат Жорес Алферов, а большую часть финансирования проекта взял на себя российский бизнесмен Виктор Вексельберг, который также выразил желание активно участвовать и в жизни инограда. В-третьих, в Сколково никакой «распил» бюджетных средств, как про это говорят отдельные «всезнайки», в принципе невозможен. Большую часть финансирования проекта взял на себя частный бизнес. Так, проект в Сколково будут финансировать: «Ренова», «НОКИА», американские и европейские компании. Вряд ли эти серьезные организации собираются создать проект под «распил» своих же собственных средств.

Что же касается сути проекта, то Сколково – это только начало. Для России необходимо взять старт в модернизации свой экономики с чего-то одного, а потом развиваться дальше. Виктор Вексельберг уверен, что таких инновационных центров, как Сколково в России должно быть много. Да и потенциал у России для подобных инициатив просто безграничный. Кто же против модернизации, смело может записать себя в ряды отъявленных коллаборационистов, взять 100 рублей «премии» у Касьянова, пойти «митинговать» против «проклятой власти» и заслуженно получить резиновой дубинкой по одному месту за очередную незаконную сходку на Триумфальной площади – этот алгоритм действий для «несогласных» хорошо уже известен!

- *Почему Стабилизационный фонд хранится в американских ценных бумагах и долларах?*

Многие несведущие люди, когда читают предоставленную Центральным Банком России статистику относительно размещения вкладов России за рубежом, состава бивалютной корзины, золотовалютных резервов, Стабилизационного фонда и т.д., начинают недоумевать, почему наша страна размещает свои вклады за границей, да еще в иностранной валюте и иностранных ценных бумагах. Да, это, действительно, так происходит, и на это есть свои причины. Но о них чуть попозже, а сейчас посмотрим немного статистики.

На 30 апреля 2010 года объем валютных резервов России составлял 460,7 миллиарда долларов, а запас золота – 523,7 тонны. По этому показателю Россия занимает 3 место в мире после Китая и Японии, если не рассматривать Европейский Союз, как единое государство. Как распределены эти резервы, можно узнать из брошюры Центрального Банка России под названием «Обзор деятельности Банка России по управлению валютными активами». На начало октября 2009 года в процентном отношении по видам валют валютные резервы Центрального Банка были распределены так:

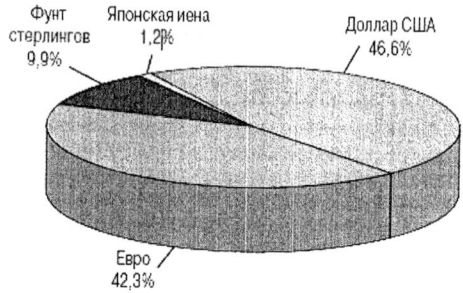

Распределение валютных резервов Центрального Банка по географическому признаку на начало октября 2009 года выглядело так:

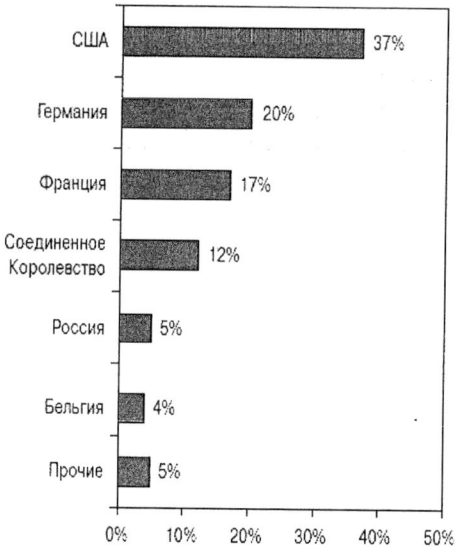

Как мы видим, действительно, большая часть резервов размещена в иностранной валюте и хранится в США, Германии, Франции, Англии и т.д. В принципе, так поступают все нормальные государства. Дело в том, что одной из важнейших задач Центрального Банка является не допустить того, чтобы резервы стремительно сокращались. А это возможно сделать только в том случае, если вложить эти резервы в наиболее надежные финансовые инструменты. Таких инструментов в мире пока, увы, не много. Из валютных инструментов – это доллар, евро и фунт стерлингов. Из ценных бумаг – это американские казначейские облигации и акции крупных американских компаний. Как правило, именно использование этих финансовых инструментов, даже не смотря на все кризисы, позволит сохранить, а то и приумножить валютные резервы страны. Так, в 2005 году в портфеле резервов Центрального Банка России, доллар США приносил 3,2% годовых, евро – 2,2%, а фунты стерлингов – 4,8%. Причем эти вклады весьма ликвидны. То есть, в любой момент наша страна может вернуть свои деньги.

Можно, конечно, хранить деньги в любой другой валюте или товаре, только, когда они тебе внезапно понадобятся, тебе надо будет долго искать, кто купит эту валюту или этот товар и даст тебе ту валюту, которая тебе нужна, а времени может и не быть... Действительно, США извлекают прибыль из того, что Россия, и не только Россия, а весь мир, то есть и Китай, и Япония, и ЕС, и другие страны хранят свои сбережения в американских ценных бумагах и долларах – эта прибыль своего рода плата Америке за «услугу» по обеспечению функционирования мировой валютной системы. Мы, как и другие, страны, могли бы отказаться от этих услуг, если бы, была иная система. Ее нет, а создать ее сами мы пока не в состоянии. Сейчас пока есть план превращения рубля в региональную и резервную валюту. Публицист Н.Стариков так объясняет, почему мы держим наш Стабилизационный фонд в долларах: мы платим дань мировой Орде. Если продолжать эту мысль, то можно сказать, что для того, чтобы сокрушить Орду нужно время. В разное время нужны Александр Невский, который установил с Ордой союз и договорился о дани, Иван Калита, который платил дань, но скапливал сокровища для будущего экономического рывка, Дмитрий Донской, которая первым бил монголов, но еще только под видом того, что он воюет за законную власть хана Тохтамыша против сепаратиста Мамая, и, наконец Иван Третий, которая разорвал ханскую грамоту и отказался от дани окончательно. Только имея силы навязать свой порядок, можно выступать против мирового порядка, в противном случае, издержки твоей борьбы будут выше для народа, чем нынешние потери от того, что мы пользуемся чужой валютой.

- В России нет свободных СМИ, все контролируется Кремлем!

В настоящее время в Министерстве печати зарегистрированы 6 616 электронных СМИ, в том числе, 868 электронных периодических изданий в Интернете, 3 267 телепрограмм и 2 378 радиопрограмм. Число же зарегистрированных печатных изданий составляет 37 425. Из них 22 181 — газеты; 12 726 — журналы. Вряд ли все СМИ из этого многообразия контролируются напрямую из Кремля, и как только где-то что-то нехорошее пишется, то к редактору проштрафившейся газетенки сразу приезжает «черный воронок», и больше после этого его никто не видит. Чтобы контролировать такое количество СМИ и журналистов, надо, как минимум создать аппарат чиновников такой же численности только по контролю над каждым журналистом, что абсурдно. В чем же дело? Действительно, часто на плакатах оппозиции можно увидеть лозунги «Свободу СМИ!». Также наши именитые оппозиционеры любят в прямом эфире радиостанций «Эхо Москвы», «Радио Свобода» или в интервью по телевидению заявить, что как же российские СМИ-то сильно притесняются свободы им, понимаешь, не дают. Вот, в качестве наглядного примера такой либерально-оппозиционной мысли можно привести слова из интервью для «Радио Свобода» доктора юридических наук Михаила Федотова: «Сегодня у государства есть юридическая возможность просто в одночасье закрыть все неугодные СМИ. Понятие экстремизма крайне широкое и неопределенное, а механизм закрытия СМИ по обвинению в экстремизме элементарно простой». Но, как мы видим, независимые СМИ не закрыты, иначе, где выступает М.Федотов?! Почему его не обвинили в экстремизме и не закрыли?! Наверное, потому, что власть вовсе не собирается закрывать оппозиционные СМИ!

Действительно, на выборах в Государственную Думу партии, придерживающиеся «либеральных» взглядов получили менее 5% голосов, но СМИ, которые отражают точку зрения этих 5% в России гораздо больше. Им же хочется вещать на всех телеканалах. С какой стати? В 90-ые годы вся либералы имели власть и все телеканалы, – и потеряли доверие народа. Сейчас их не приглашают в центральные СМИ, не потому что есть какой-то запрет, а потому что они не интересны массовому читателю или зрителю, всем заранее известно, что они скажут.

Поэтому не свободы вообще хочет оппозиция, а свободы для себя и только для себя. Точно так же проблему раздувают иностранные некоммерческие организации в интересах других стран. Эти рейтинги не имеют ничего общего с действительностью, а служат лишь элементами информационной войны против России. Есть, например, мировой рейтинг, созданный организацией «Репортеры без границ», в котором Россию по уровню свободы СМИ поставили аж на 153 место. Это сразу после Туниса и перед тихоокеанским государством Фиджи, в котором-то и СМИ, как таковых, наверное, штуки три не наберется. К слову, такие полностью «демократические» государства, как Афганистан, Грузия, Ирак и Буркина-Фасо «Репортеры без границ» поставили на 149, 81, 145 и 57 места, соответственно. То есть, во всех этих странах, где до сих пор идут или тлеют серьезные военные конфликты, а власть вообще не контролирует часть территории страны, свобода СМИ ущемляется меньше, чем в России! Искренне жаль будет этих «безграничных (если только в своем неведении) репортеров», если они попадут в беспредельно «демократическое», стоящее в их рейтинге даже на 57 месте африканское государство Буркина-Фасо, которое по совместительству является одним из беднейших в мире, а по уровню безопасности для иностранцев хуже него могут быть разве что только Сомали и Судан!

Что же касается опусов многоуважаемого Михаила Федотова, который так ратует на «Радио Свобода» о «последних баррикадах из «независимых» СМИ», то он без проблем может взять билет во все тоже Буркина-Фасо. Там, с этим, в смысле с баррикадами, как-то проще, как в прямом, так и в переносном смысле.

- *Россия, по версии международной правозащитной организации «Freedom House» снова оказалась в списке самых несвободных стран, в которых не соблюдаются права человека. Так, по политическим правам у России оценка 6 (из семи возможных), а по гражданским свободам — 5 (чем больше балл, тем не свободнее страна). Стоит отметить, что немногим хуже рейтинг по шкале свободы также получили такие страны, как Белоруссия, Чад, Китай, Куба, Гвинея, Лаос, Саудовская Аравия, Сирия, Южная Осетия и Западная Сахара. «Эти страны и территории предлагают весьма ограниченные возможности для свободы слова, жестоко притесняют политическую оппозицию, в них действует цензура» - написано в соответствующем докладе данной международной организации.*

Сравнивать Белоруссию и Западную Сахару – это все равно, что сравнивать Президента США с БОМЖом от Курского вокзала. Просто нет на свете такого состоявшегося государства, как Западная Сахара. Есть просто небольшой участок земли вдоль побережья Атлантического океана между Марокко и Мавританией. Там нет органов власти, идет многолетняя гражданская война и, скорее всего, там даже не знают о существовании такой организации, как «Freedom House». Но зато всякого рода оппозиционеры и «правозащитники» с гордо поднятой головой теперь смогут заявить, что, дескать, экономически развитая «авторитарная» Белоруссия под «жестким диктатом» Александра Лукашенко; динамично развивающийся, на отлично проведший Олимпийские игры в 2008 году «деспотический» Китай или там, начавшая системную модернизацию «авторитарная» Россия под «тиранией» Владимира Путина стоят на одном уровне с такими «светочами» африканской демократии, как не вылезающие из десятилетиями идущих гражданских войн, голода и геноцида Чад, Западная Сахара и еще там какое-нибудь Сомали в качестве «полезной» нагрузки....

Увы, но подобные рейтинги делаются, априори, предвзято. Похоже, нарождается такая новая мировая тенденция, что, если динамично развивающаяся страна угодила во всяких там рейтингах, составленных «Freedom House» по уровню прав и свобод на уровень «недосформировавшихся африканских придатков», то, значит, дела в этом государстве, наоборот, идут хорошо. Просто это «хорошо» кому-то очень уж слишком мешает. По поводу этого «кому-то» догадаться не сложно, узнав, кто же финансирует всякие там «Freedom House», дает гранты оппозиции «на развитие демократии в России» и занимается в мире прочими деструктивными вещами. А гранты на существование «Freedom House» дает Правительство США. Это, собственно, все и объясняет.

- За что посадили М. Ходорковского? Он имел смелость выступить против власти и оказался в тюрьме...

Давайте для начала присмотримся к биографии Ходорковского. Бывший глава объединения «Менатеп», бывший Председатель Совета директоров «Роспром», бывший владелец нефтяной империи «ЮКОС». Типичный представитель т.наз. *олигархии.* Родился в 1963 г. в Москве в семье инженеров. С 1981 по 1986 гг. учился в Московском химико-технологическом институте имени Д.И. Менделеева. В 1988 году окончил Московский институт народного хозяйства им. Г.В. Плеханова. Активно занимался комсомольской работой (замсекретаря комсомольского комитета МХТИ, член Свердловского райкома ВЛКСМ, замсекретаря Фрунзенского райкома ВЛКСМ). Был членом КПСС. В 1987 г. участвовал в создании при Фрунзенском райкоме комсомола Центра научно-технического творчества молодежи, переименованного впоследствии в Центр межотраслевых научно-технических программ и далее сократившего свое название до «Менатеп». В 1988 г. при Центре был создан ряд кооперативов и Коммерческий инновационный банк научно-технического прогресса (с 1990 г. – банк «Менатеп»). В начале 1989 г. Ходорковский знакомится с В. Дубовым, через родителей которого получает выходы на ряд крупных чиновников в высших эшелонах власти - вплоть до М. Горбачева, с разрешения которого в банке «Менатеп» были открыты счета Фонда ликвидации последствий аварии на Чернобыльской АЭС. Около 60% средств Фонда разошлось по различным структурам «Менатепа». Благодаря опеке Госкомитета по науке и технике,

«Менатеп» одним из первых начал проводить валютные операции и торговать собственными ценными бумагами. Примечательно, что не «МММ», а именно «Менатеп» впервые стал широко продавать свои акции населению, в массе своей так и не увидевшей никаких дивидендов.

В 1989-1990 гг. Ходорковский создает фирмы за рубежом – в Швейцарии, Гибралтаре, Будапеште, Париже, учреждает Торговый дом «Менатеп-Импекс», ставший главной уполномоченной структурой по ввозу в Россию кубинского сахара, в снабжении Москвы продовольствием, начинает ставить под контроль промышленные предприятия. В 1992 г. Совет директоров «Менатепа» объявил о переходе от чисто банковского бизнеса к созданию финасово-промышленной группы. Ходорковский назначен Председателем Инвестиционного фонда содействия топливно-энергетической промышленности с правами Заместителя министра топлива и энергетики России (!!!), а в марте 1993 г. – замминистра топлива и энергетики.

В 1994-1995 гг. «Менатеп» взамен раздаваемых чиновникам «обещаний инвестиций» получает в актив пакеты акций АО «Апатит» и «Воскресенские минеральные удобрения», «Уралэлектромедь», Среднеуральского и Кировоградского медеплавильного заводов, Усть-Илимского лесопромышленного комбината, Красноярского металлургического, Волжского трубного и др. – всего более ста предприятий. Для управления ими создается холдинг-компания «Роспром». Инвестиции на предприятия так и не поступили, большая часть пакетов была потом дороже перепродана другим собственникам.

В 1995 г. Ходорковский активно участвует в разработке и проведении т.наз. **залоговых аукционов**, в результате чего «Менатеп» через подставные фирмы приобрел 78% госпакета акций нефтяной компании ЮКОС за сумму, почти в сто раз меньшую их реальной рыночной стоимости. С июня 1996 г. Ходорковский – Председатель Совета директоров АО Нефтяная компания «ЮКОС». С приходом «Менатепа» на предприятиях ЮКОСа («Юганскнефтегаз», «Томскнефтегаз», «Самаранефтегаз») было уволено до 70% рабочих, социальная сфера была передана на баланс местным властям. Благодаря изящно разработанной афере с покупкой у собственных подразделений нефти под видом «скваженной жидкости» и ее последующей продажей уже как собственной нефти, Ходорковскому удалось в 9-10 раз снизить долю сырьевых налогов, взимаемых от цены продукта.

Передел нефтяной отрасли был связан с большим количеством заказных убийств, за некоторые из них уже осужден начальник службы охраны «ЮКОСА» – Пичугин. В 1998 г. инициируется создание нефтяного холдинга «ЮКСИ» (так и не состоявшееся объединение компаний «ЮКОС» и «Сибнефть»). В начале 2000-х гг. Ходорковский стремится избавиться от репутации предпринимателя, связанного с криминальным миром, и переходит к западному стандарту прозрачности в финасовых операциях компании. В то же время «ЮКОС» приобретает 68% акций Восточно-Сибирской нефтегазовой компании и Ангарскую нефтехимическую компанию. Все это приводит к росту цен на акции «ЮКОСа». Ходорковский попадает в списки «Forbes» как самый богатый человек России (в 2002 г. - $8 млрд., в 2004 г. – $15,2 млрд.) и заявляет о президентских амбициях.

В 2001 году он основывает фонд «Открытая Россия» и открывает по всей стране «Школы публичной политики», предназначенные для «формирования человеческого ресурса». Одновременно разрабатываются механизмы «скупки» депутатов всех представленных в Госдуме партий – «для формирования правительства парламентского большинства». Для того, чтобы сделать свои капиталы полностью неуязвимыми, Ходорковский планирует продажу новой объединенной компании «ЮКСИ» американскому концерну «Эксон-Мобайл». Если бы это произошло, около трети российской нефтяной отрасли оказалась бы под контролем американцев как раз перед самым взлетом цен на нефть, стратегическая безопасность России оказалась бы под угрозой.

Смысл шахматной партии, выстроенной Ходорковским прозрачен донельзя: из российского миллиардера, состояние которого на 99% заключено в скважинах и инфраструктуре нефтяной отрасли, он задумал превратиться в миллиардера настоящего, владеющего ликвидными миллиардами на Западе. На самом деле, Ходорковский продает вовсе не «ЮКОС». В этом нетрудно убедиться: «ЮКОС», особенно, вместе с «Сибнефтью» - это треть нефтяной отрасли России. Доходы только от экспорта нефти по оценкам специалистов в бюджете составляют 13-14%. Но есть еще доходы от внутреннего налогообложения. В совокупности, с учетом «смежников», то есть производств, косвенно работающих на нее, нефтяная отрасль приносит до 30-40% бюджета страны. Следовательно, «ЮКОС» (особенно с «Сибнефтью») обеспечивает до 15% бюджета. Это сопоставимо с госзатратами на оборону, а какой-нибудь науки на этом фоне и вообще не видно. Даже если брать в расчет только экспортную выручку, доля «ЮКОСа» в бюджете составляет около пяти процентов. Практически, это означает, что власть в России, если сделка осуществится, переходит к новому владельцу «ЮКОСа», и Россия живет и существует исключительно по его воле и с его разрешения, ибо власть 10% бюджета страны - это полная власть над страной.

Достаточно представить себе, что иностранный владелец - нормальная, между прочим, бизнес-практика - возьмет, да и пригрозит закрыть «ЮКОС». Мало того, что 100000 работников самого «ЮКОСа» выйдут на улицы. Они потянут за собой еще и миллионы тех, кто работает на «ЮКОС» в других отраслях. Закрытие «ЮКОСа» - это полная дестабилизация страны, возврат ее к гиперинфляции, и окончательное разрушение экономики. Иными словами, в руках у владельцев «ЮКОСа» окажется мощнейший рычаг для создания крупномасштабных политических кризисов в любой желаемый момент, рычаг беспрецедентного давления на российскую власть. И противопоставить этому давлению власти будет нечего. Даже национализировать эту собственность будет невозможно, так как - и это правильно, - собственность священна, - США получат полное моральное и юридическое право собственность своих граждан защищать любыми способами, вплоть до военных. Отступные же обойдутся России куда как больше, чем в 25 миллиардов, что и само по себе немало.

Надо ясно понимать - власть над 10% бюджета - это власть абсолютная. Иными словами, пресловутые 25 миллиардов долларов, за которые Ходорковский хотел продать треть российской нефтянки – это не цена «ЮКОСа» - это посреднические деньги за приобретение власти над Россией третьей силой. Правительство РФ предупредило Ходорковского о несогласии с этой сделкой, но переговоры продолжались. Тем временем, правоохранительные органы заводят уголовные дела на П. Лебедева, Л. Невзлина, А. Пичугина.

25 октября 2003 г. Ходорковский, пытавшийся получить «депутатскую неприкосновенность», выдвинувшись сенатором от Эвенкии, был взят под стражу и помещен в СИЗО «Матросская тишина». Генпрокуратура предъявила ему обвинение по семи статьям, в том числе «мошенничество, совершенное оргруппой в крупном размере» (за завладение обманным путем 20% акций ОАО «Апатит» на сумму 500 млрд. руб.), уклонение от уплаты налогов, подделку документов и пр. Показания против Ходорковского дали его бывшие бухгалтера и топ-менеджеры, были раскрыты сложнейшие оффшорные схемы ухода от

налогов. Следствию помогло и то, что во время обыска у Ходорковского был найден компьютер, в котором содержались конфиденциальные данные о незаконных сделках. В 2005 г. Мещанский районный суд г. Москвы признал М. Ходорковского виновным по шести статьям УК и приговорил к 9 годам лишения свободы (решением Мосгорсуда срок снижен до 8 лет). Ныне Ходорковский отбывает наказание в колонии г. Краснокаменска Читинской обл. Так называемая «демократическая оппозиция» на деньги бежавшего в Израиль Л. Невзлина и западных НГО и НКО издает статьи и книги, в которых старается представить Ходорковского жертвой «кровавого чекистского режима». Имущество «ЮКОСа», находящегося на грани банкротства из-за предъявленных налоговых претензий было продано на аукционе компании, контролируемой государством.

- Россия вымирает: смертность в стране значительно превосходит рождаемость. Из этой «демографической ямы» России уже не выбраться. Разве можно сказать, что власть работает на благо населения после этого?!

Демографическая проблема, действительно, одна из острейших проблем современной России. Страна до сих пор пожинает плоды либеральных и экономических «экспериментов» Гайдара-Ельцина 1990-х гг. Именно на это время пришелся пик демографической катастрофы. За счет избыточной смертности и сокращения рождаемости страна потеряла 20 млн. человек – 18,9% взрослого населения! При сохранении прежних темпов рождаемости мы должны были за эти годы прибавить 15 млн. человек, а не потерять 5 млн. И это при том, что объем иммиграции в РФ из стран СНГ преобладал над эмиграцией из РФ. Т.о., «деколлективизация» 1990-х гг. обошлась в большую «цену», чем коллективизация, голод и репрессии 1930-х гг. Падение роста рождаемости в СССР, особенно в европейской части, наблюдалось уже с 1960 г. Но только в начале 1990-х этот процесс приобрел катастрофический характер. С 1991 г. население России ежегодно сокращалось на 500-700 тысяч чел., причинами чего были низкая рождаемость, локальные войны, алкоголизм, отсталая медицина, низкий уровень жизни россиян.

Однако, к настоящему времени ряд из этих проблем удалось решить. Россия больше не ведет войны, в стране реализуется национальный проект «Здоровье», который подразумевает повышение доступности и качества медицинской помощи для широких слоев населения при сохранении гарантий бесплатной медицинской помощи. По инициативе Путина был принят закон о радикальном увеличении т.наз. материнского капитала – до 250 тысяч рублей за рождение второго ребенка. Помимо материального поощрения родившим матерям, улучшения медицинского обслуживания, на улучшение демографической ситуации работает и совершенствование миграционной политики, побуждающей выходцев из России возвращаться на свою историческую родину. По данным ученых, конкретные шаги последних лет по улучшению качества медицинского обслуживания уже привели к тому, что средняя продолжительность жизни в России увеличилась на один год и составила 67 лет.

Снижается естественная убыль населения – по оценке Росстата, в январе-апреле 2010 г. она уменьшилась по сравнению с соответствующим периодом 2009 г. на 24,2 тыс. человек. Таким образом, надежда на улучшение демографической ситуации в Российской Федерации есть. По мнению разработчиков Национальной программы демографического развития России, введение, помимо уже действующих, дополнительных мер государственной поддержки семей, имеющих детей, в том числе, в решении жилищных проблем, позволит стабилизировать к 2015 г. численность населения России на уровне 140-142 млн. человек, и созданы предпосылки для роста населения в будущем. Цена вопроса – 560 млрд. рублей в год, или 2% ВВП.

Огромной проблемой являются аборты. По их количеству (от 3 до 6 млн. в год) Россия с 1990-х гг. занимает первое место в мире. Во многом это является результатом подрывной деятельностью ряда западных НГО/НКО, прежде всего американского «Комитета планирования семьи» (бывшая «Лига контроля над рождаемостью», финансируемая Фондом Рокфеллера). Свою доктрину «демографической коррекции», основанную на трех столпах: контрацепция, аборт, стерилизация, они активно внедряли в России на самом высоком уровне. С их подачи под эгидой Министерства здравоохранения в России с 1992 г. было открыто 300 государственных центров «планирования семьи», 52 филиала общественной организации РАПС – Российской ассоциации планирования семьи, 40 региональных представительств Международного фонда охраны здоровья матери и ребенка, многочисленные филиалы Российского общества контрацепции и международных женских центров. В 1998 г. Минздрав издал положение, предписывающее открыть кабинеты «планирования семьи» во всех женских консультациях и медицинских учреждениях. На аборты тратилась половина бюджетных средств по статьям, относящимся к акушерству и гинекологии. В российских школах внедрялись подготовленные и щедро финансируемые Фондом народонаселения ООН программы по половому воспитанию, провозглашающие стерилизацию самым надежным методом контрацепции. Борьба с абортами может стать решающим шагом к исправлению демографической ситуации, и в этом направлении уже делаются первые шаги.

Успехи в выправлении демографической ситуации обеспечены усиленным вниманием Правительства к здравоохранению. Медицинскую помощь в рамках

Программы государственных гарантий оказывают 12,4 тыс. учреждений, в том числе федеральных – 0,8 тыс., субъектов Российской Федерации – 4,1 тыс., муниципальных – 7,2 тыс., частных – 0,2 тыс. В них работают более 614 тыс. врачей и 1354 тыс. средних медицинских работников.

С 2006 г. реализуется национальный приоритетный проект «Здоровье». Улучшилось качество и доступность первичной медико-санитарной медицинской помощи: увеличилась численность участковых врачей на 6 тысяч человек, в том числе врачей общей практики. Снизился коэффициент совместительства участковых врачей с 1,6 до 1,3. На участки пришли работать 1,9 тыс. молодых специалистов. Доля врачей пенсионного возраста снизилась на 10 %, медицинских сестер - на 12%. Увеличен средний уровень оплаты труда медицинских работников первичного звена в 2,7 раза, врачей – специалистов, работающих в поликлиниках, в 2,1 раза (в целом по проекту 690 тысяч медицинским работникам повышена оплата труда, рост средней заработной платы в здравоохранении составил 56,6%); более чем в 2 раза увеличилась доля медицинских работников участковой службы, прошедших обязательную переподготовку (до 75%); сократилось время ожидания диагностических обследований в муниципальных поликлиниках в среднем с 10 до 7 дней. Повысилась эффективность оказания скорой медицинской помощи. Сократилось время ожидания больными скорой помощи с 35 до 25 минут. В среднем на 70% обновлен парк машин скорой помощи. Снижена инфекционная заболеваемость, в том числе, дифтерией в 5 раз, корью в 3,7 раза, краснухой в 2,6 раз, эпидемическим паротитом на 30,7%, коклюшем на 30%. Заболеваемость гепатитом «В» снижена на 24%. Вспышек и эпидемий гриппа, коревой краснухи, вирусных гепатитов в 2006 - 2007 г.г. не было. Это стало результатом крупномасштабной вакцинации почти 77 млн. человек. Снижаются риски распространения ВИЧ-инфекции. Полным курсом профилактики охвачено 19,93 тыс. граждан, входящих в группу риска. Все ВИЧ–инфицированные беременные женщины получают специфическое лечение с целью снижения рисков передачи инфекции новорожденным. Выявлено более 60,3 тыс. новых случаев ВИЧ-инфекции. Проводится лечение антиретровирусными препаратами 35,0 тысяч ВИЧ-инфицированных; Проведены дополнительная диспансеризация и медицинские осмотры 7,4 млн. человек трудоспособного возраста, из них 5,0 млн. работающих в бюджетной сфере (почти 30 % от всех работающих); Почти в 3,5 раза увеличен ежегодный объем высокотехнологичной медицинской помощи (в 2007 г. – 170,0 тыс. человек, в 2005 г. - 60,0 тыс. человек).

Начато строительство 14 федеральных центров высоких медицинских технологий в регионах. Предполагается строительство 23 перинатальных центров. В 19 субъектах Российской Федерации реализуются «пилотные» проекты. Отрабатываются механизмы повышения мотивации медицинских работников к качественному труду, внедрению систем оплаты труда, увязанных с качеством и результатами труда, методов оплаты медицинской помощи. Основными тенденциями развития здравоохранения на среднесрочную перспективу являются: завершение перехода к одноканальному финансированию медицинской помощи и оплаты ее по результатам деятельности; модернизация системы обязательного медицинского страхования; развитие новых организационно-правовых форм; развитие правовых отношений в здравоохранении (пациент-врач – учреждение).

- *Российские вооруженные силы небоеспособны. Реформы армии проводятся вразрез с интересами страны. Заключенный в апреле 2010 г. договор СНВ-3 подписан целиком на американских условиях, что предельно ослабило обороноспособность России. Наше руководство сдает Россию?*

Миф о низкой боеготовности российской армии усиленно насаживается Западом и российской «пятой колонной» еще со времен развала СССР. В 1990-х гг. Россия, в самом деле, являлась «колоссом на глиняных ногах», что, в частности, продемонстрировали неудачи нашей армии в первой чеченской войне (1994-96 гг.) В 2006 г. В Послании Федеральному собранию РФ президент В. Путин признал, что сама структура вооруженных сил была неадекватна существующим реалиям – так, в 1999 г., когда возникла необходимость противостоять масштабной агрессии международного терроризма на Северном Кавказе, из всей почти полуторамиллионной армии невозможно было собрать группировку численностью 65 тыс. человек.

Огромный провал существовал и в оснащении армии и флота современными средствами вооруженной борьбы: в период с 1996 по 2000 г. не было заложено ни одного корабля, а на вооружение было принято всего 40 образцов военной техники. С середины 2000-х гг. ситуация в армии стала качественно меняться. Введенный в 2006 г. План перевооружения армии и флота отличается не только резко возросшим объемом финансирования, но существенным изменением самой структуры расходов. Если предыдущая программа, которая составлялась в условиях жесточайшего дефицита государственного бюджета, была ориентирована преимущественно на создание новых образцов вооружений и военной техники, то новый документ предполагает серийные закупки новейших образцов вооружений и военной техники, которые составят основу системы вооружения вплоть до 2020 года. С 2006 г. начались массовые серийные закупки техники для нужд Министерства обороны России. Реанимировано военное кораблестроение, строятся боевые корабли практически всех типов. В 2008 г. спущен на воду подводный крейсер нового поколения «Юрий Долгорукий», оснащенный ракетными комплексами «Булава» и «Тополь-М». В 2010-11 гг. стратегические силы ядерного сдерживания России пополнятся еще двумя атомными субмаринами этого класса («Александр Невский» и «Владимир Мономах»), а всего до 2017 г. планируется построить 8 ракетоносцев класса «Борей». Ни одной лодки подобного типа с 1990 г. в России не строили.

В конце 2005 г. был развернут новый стратегический ракетный полк, вооруженный системами подземного базирования «Тополь-М». В ближайшие годы будут поставлены на вооружение мобильные системы «Тополь-М» (SS-X-27), не имеющие сегодня аналогов в мире, вооруженная баллистическими ракетами подводного запуска «Булава-30» (SS-NX-30). Продолжается модернизация в целом ракетных войск стратегического назначения. На вооружении есть ракетные установки, траектория полета ракет которых не по зубам никакой ПРО. В январе 2010 г. состоялся подъем в воздух истребителя пятого поколения, разработанного компанией «Сухой». К 2015 г. современных видов вооружений в войсках должно быть не менее 30%, а к 2020 г. – не менее 70%. В связи с этим идет рост оборонных расходов России, обусловленный как новыми вызовами и угрозами, появившимся в последнее время (в т.ч. международный терроризм), так и необходимостью реагировать на усиление военной мощи Китая и США, а также неуклонное продвижение НАТО к российским границам.

Если в 2010 году расходы на оборону составили 2,6% ВВП России, то в 2011 году объем финансирования составит 2,9%, в 2012 году - 3% с последующим выходом на 3,2%. Красноречивой демонстрацией боеспособности российских войск стала пятидневная кампания по принуждению Грузии к миру в 2008 г., когда введенные в Южную Осетию части российской армии показали полное превосходство над многократно превосходящей по численности и оснащенной самым современным оружием грузинской армией. Россия, на протяжении всех 1990-х гг. шедшая на уступки США в области сокращения вооружения, теперь неуклонно защищает свои интересы. Заключенный 8 апреля 2010 г. в Праге Договор между Российской Федерацией и Соединенными Штатами Америки о мерах по дальнейшему сокращению и ограничению стратегических наступательных вооружений (СНВ-3), ставит преграду усилению дисбаланса в области ядерного вооружения и упрочивает безопасность не только России и США, но и всего мирового сообщества. По словам президента Академии геополитических проблем Леонида Ивашова, «Россия не поддалась давлению американцев и заключила выгодный для себя договор. Во-первых, нам удалось сбросить с себя „контролирующие оковы", когда американцы зорко следили не только за производством наших баллистических ракет, например, на том же

Воткинском заводе, но и даже отслеживали маршруты передвижения мобильных ракетных комплексов. Теперь, по условиям договора, этого не будет». Ярким доказательством того, что Россия не поступилась собственными интересами при заключении договора СНВ-3, является яростная критика в американских кругах президента США Барака Обамы, обвиняемого в том, что он подписал договор на российских условиях.

— Не является ли несправедливым, что Россия самостоятельно распоряжается своими ресурсами, прежде всего, нефтью и газом? Почему Россия не исходит из общемировых интересов и не позволяет участвовать в разработке и распределении своих природных ресурсов другим странам?

Подобные аргументы приводятся оппонентами России для подготовки общественного мнения к принятию идеи о необходимости расчленения России и превращения ее в сырьевой придаток Запада. При этом данные аргументы касаются только России: свои ресурсы, как природные, так производственные и финансовые, политики западных держав перераспределять в пользу других стран отнюдь не собираются. Признавая права своих стран на свои национальные богатства, они отказывают в этих правах нашей. Справедливо ли, что ресурсы России принадлежат ей и только ей? Безусловно! За все эти богатства было заплачено большой кровью и огромным трудом предков, веками осваивавших едва пригодные для жизни территории, отстаивавших их в многочисленных войнах.

Право государств на свои недра закреплено международными актами — а отказ той или иной стране в этом праве не что иное, как колониализм. Манипулятивным является и утверждение о «нефтяном проклятии» России, которое тормозит технологическое перевооружение державы и не мобилизует страну на поиски альтернативных форм участия в международной кооперации. Нефть и газ являются главными экспортными товарами России, за счет продажи которых финансируются наука, образование, медицина и пр. Если мы лишимся доходов от их продажи, то обречем нацию на вымирание. Кроме того, несправедливой предполагается дискриминация нашего основного экспортного товара по сравнению с экспортными товарами других стран. С точки зрения рынка, нет товара «плохого» и «хорошего», нефть ничем не уступает в сложности производства продуктам легкой промышленности или, скажем, труда программиста или кинорежиссера. Природные богатства не приносят пользы тем странам, которые не обладают достаточным суверенитетом для того, чтобы эффективно использовать их для развития собственной экономики. Бывшая бельгийская колония Конго обладает колоссальными природными богатствами и, в отличие от России, великолепными условиями для ведения сельского хозяйства — и при этом остается одной из беднейших стран мира. Напротив, Канаде и

Норвегии, минеральные и природные ресурсы, значительная часть которых находится в северных районах, помогли стать странами с одним из самых высоких уровней жизни на планете. При этом добыча углеводородов, особенно в условиях Крайнего Севера, является не отсталым производством, а, напротив, высокотехнологичным: оно требует наличия развитых технологий по оснащению скважин, глубоководному и пр. бурению, строительству трубопроводов, развитой нефтегазоперерабатывающей, нефтехимической и пр. промышленности.

Нефтегазовая отрасль остается локомотивом российской экономики — рост дополнительных экспортных доходов преобразовывается в увеличение, как инвестиционного, так и потребительского спроса, что в свою очередь стимулирует рост отечественного производства, в том числе, инновационного.

- Внешняя политика России неконструктивна. За последние годы мы умудрились испортить отношения со всеми странами!

Оставляют желать лучшего наши отношения лишь с ближайшими соседями – Грузией, Молдавией, странами Прибалтики – теми странами, которые до сих пор испытывают комплекс «лимитрофов», не могут простить России «десятилетий оккупации», предъявляют к нашей стране финансовые претензии и т.д. Причем нельзя не заметить, что эти настроения разделяют далеко не все граждане этих стран. А с рядом стран, еще недавно находившихся с нами «на ножах» – например, Польшей и Украиной – за последний год отношения резко нормализовались.

С западными странами отношения и были не столь плохими, как это пытались продемонстрировать некоторые оппозиционные журналисты. Германия, Франция, Италия были и остаются нашими партнерами, во многих вопросах, они склонны консолидироваться именно с российской стороной. Даже в таком остром вопросе, как признание в Грузино-Югоосетинском конфликте 2008 г. агрессором Грузии европейские страны заняли со временем верную позицию, сняв с России все обвинения в попытке аннексии грузинских территорий. Не вполне дружественную позицию демонстрирует (традиционно) лишь Великобритания, однако пик напряженности, пришедшийся на середину 2000-х гг., уже прошел, и отношения наши постепенно теплеют. Заметно улучшились отношения и с США – чему свидетельствует объявление политики «перезагрузки», с энтузиазмом поддержанной как американской элитой, так и большинством населения этой страны.

После реальных провалов во внешнеполитической деятельности в 1990-х гг., Россия всерьез заявила о своей способности на деле проводить самостоятельную внешнюю политику, активно участвовать в формировании и реализации международной повестки дня, заслужив уважение со стороны мировой общественности. Это лишний раз подтвердили и результаты репрезентативного опроса, проведенного в сентябре 2007 г. немецким Фондом Бертельсмана в США, России, Бразилии, Китае, Индии, Японии, Германии, Франции и Великобритании, согласно которым Россию относят к числу великих держав 58% россиян и 39% граждан других ведущих стран мира. Авторитет нашей страны вырос, прежде всего, в Китае (плюс 24%), Великобритании (плюс 22%) и Германии (плюс 20%). В этой связи совсем неудивительным является и тот факт, что журнал The Time в 2007 г. назвал Владимира Путина «Человеком года» – именно с ним, прежде всего, во всем мире ассоциируется рост международного авторитета и влиятельности России, а также формирование стабильного политического режима внутри страны.

- В 2005 г. указом Президента В. Путина в России были отменены прямые выборы высших руководителей в регионах – теперь они избираются по представлению Президента узкой группой региональных депутатов. Не является эта реформа отходом от принципов демократии и не несет ли она в себе угрозы «кумовщины» и коррупции?

Т.н. «Реформа 13 сентября» была обусловлена нуждами времени. Достигнув политической стабильности в стране, необходимо было провести институциональную реформу для мобилизации к активной политической жизни партий, региональных элит, бизнеса, институтов гражданского общества. 13 сентября 2004 г. на расширенном заседании Правительства В. Путин объявил о предстоящих институциональных реформах. Суть реформ: осуществлять экспертизу законопроектов России через новый орган – Общественную палату, перейти к пропорциональной системе выборов в парламент страны, избирать высших руководителей субъектов Федерации региональными парламентами по представлению Президента страны. Изменение порядка формирования исполнительной власти в субъектах Федерации было призвано повысить ответственность местных элит за своего губернатора, и губернатора – перед своей партией, превратить региональные политические сообщества в активных субъектов политического процесса, создать эффективный механизм ускорения социальных и экономических реформ.

Представители оппозиции выразили свое недовольство, находя, что законопроект написан под «Единую Россию», и воспользоваться им сможет лишь она одна. «Это имитация демократической процедуры, – заявил, например, зампред партии «Яблоко» Сергей Митрохин. – Она носит чисто пиаровский характер и нужна лишь для того, чтобы легитимировать в глазах общественного мнения назначение губернаторов». На самом деле, предложение Президента выглядело, скорее уж, неким реверансом в сторону оппозиции. Напомним, что политические ценности Путина несовместимы с однопартийной системой. То, что «Единой России» была гарантирована победа во всех российских регионах, вовсе не являлось самоочевидным фактом. Например, в Корякском и Ненецком автономных округах своего кандидата в губернаторы выдвигала КПРФ, в Алтайском крае – блок коммунистов и аграриев, в Амурской области – блок «Российской партии жизни» и «Яблока», а на Сахалине – блок Аграрной партии и партии «Народная воля».

Изначально, до 1995-96 гг. губернаторы в России назначались Президентом России. Потом, в течение нескольких лет эта должность была выборной. Каждый раз выборы превращались в соревнование финансово-промышленных групп, во время которого ситуация в регионе резко дестабилизировалась, фактически это приводило к безвластию. Кризисом пользовались криминальные структуры, террористические организации (особенно, на Кавказе). В результате, на пост главы региона приходили и криминальные субъекты, и популисты, и люди без высшего образования, и люди без опыта работы в народном хозяйстве или на государственной службе, то есть, попросту некомпетентные. Каждый раз такой «всенародно избранный» руководитель вставал в позицию «переговоров» с федеральной властью, отказывался подчиняться, выполнять свои функции, торговался, угрожал сепаратизмом. Институциональная реформа стала своего рода заслоном для таких людей и уже сегодня очевидно, что качественный состав региональных элит значительно улучшился. Помимо России высшие региональные руководители назначаются во Франции, в Испании, в Германии, на Украине и т.д. – то есть, в странах, которые во всем мире считаются демократическими.

Разговор о «демократичности» и «недемократичности» назначения губернаторов – сугубо абстрактный, хотя бы просто потому, что существует огромное количество форм народовластия, имеющих национальную и историческую специфику. Кроме конкурентной (представительской) демократии в современных обществах существуют и другие формы демократии: прямая, плебисцитарная, электронная демократия и т.д., каждая из которых предполагает участие народа в политической жизни, принятие им решений по принципиальным вопросам, осуществление им своей власти либо непосредственно, либо через представительные органы, а стало быть, подпадает под определение демократии.

Как таковой «демократии» не существует, как не существует в обществе универсальных моделей и законов, подобных законам природы.

- Нынешней властью в России проповедуется великодержавный русский шовинизм, ущемляются права других народов. Не удивительно, что по улицам ходят скинхеды, которые совершают убийства представителей других народов и даже иностранцев.

Национальная тема для России является крайне острой. И ее подогрев различными провокаторами, вроде «русских скинхедов» или «якутских националистов» губителен для страны. А это, прежде всего, выгодно нашим врагам, например, ЦРУ. Так, в докладе Центрального разведывательного управления США «Глобальные тенденции до 2015 года» в числе всего прочего говориться, о том, что еще до 2015 года Россию ждет полный экономический коллапс, в результате которого она распадется на 8 отдельных государств. Планы наших врагов озвучены ясно. Кто же после этого все эти «якутские националисты» и «русские бритоголовые» для нашей страны?! Провокаторы и не более того.

Если рассмотреть по национальному составу на всех уровнях класс высших чиновников в России, то можно убедиться в следующем. В Правительстве, Государственной Думе, Совете Федерации, Администрации Президента работают как русские, так и представители почти всех других национальностей России. Владимир Путин, например, полностью русский. А Сергей Шойгу – тувинец. Сергей Миронов, Сергей Нарышкин и Борис Грызлов – русские, а Рашид Нургалиев и Эльвира Набиуллина – коренные татары. Если рассматривать региональные уровни, то там элита состоит, как правило, в большинстве своем из представителей той национальности, которая преобладает в том или ином регионе. В Ингушетии – Президент ингуш, в Чечне – чеченец, в Приморье – русский, в Новгородской области – русский, в Якутии – якут, в Туве – тувинец и т.д. Многие российские регионы имели губернаторов не русских по этническому происхождению – Россель в Свердловской области, Амангельды Тулеев – в Кузбассе и так далее. Это все же справедливое разделение по национальному признаку среди элиты в многонациональной стране.

Жалобы на российским империализм совершенно безосновательны не только потому, что империализм предполагает политические ограничения прав малых народов, чего у нас нет, но и экономическую эксплуатацию метрополией своих национальных колоний. У нас же в экономической области ситуация обратная – практические все национальные республики являются не донорами бюджета, а реципиентами, то есть на 50-90% содержатся за счет «русских» регионов. По всем международным меркам, страна, где 80% населения относят себя к одной национальности (а в России эта цифра даже больше) считается мононациональной, и, тем не менее, Россия продолжает считать себя многонациональной страной и делает все для развития культуры и защиты прав малых народов.

Это, кстати, говоря, раздражает еще одну группу националистов, теперь уже русских, которые заявляют, что русских у нас все ущемляют, что «титульная» нация находится в рабах у национальных меньшинств: евреев, чеченцев, масонов, гуманоидов с Проксимы Центавра – список «поработителей» можно продолжить. Пользуются такой риторикой, как правило, правые радикалы, приспешники всяких КОБов и КПЕ. Как бы они ни желали субъективно блага русскому народу, они объективно работают на разжигание национальной розни, на разрушение государства, на осуществление планов ЦРУ по расколу России. Скинхеды так же своими действиями портят имидж России в мире и русских внутри страны, то есть, по сути, работают против России и русских. Все преступления скинхедов расследуются с особой тщательностью, берутся под контроль руководителями субъектов Федерации, виновные получают длительные сроки. Это лишний раз свидетельствует, что власть не поощряет шовинизм, а борется с ним.

- Почему в России нет свободных выборов, почему власть всегда подтасовывает результаты выборов в пользу «Единой России»?

В стране ежегодно проходят 25 миллионов гражданских судебных процессов. Следовательно, есть 25 миллионов выигравших сторон и 25 миллионов проигравших. Как вы думаете, что говорят адвокаты проигравшей стороны своим клиентам? Что они сразу были не правы, что, мы, адвокаты, плохо работали? Нет, они говорят, что противоположная сторона просто подкупила суд. Большая часть разговоров о всемирной коррупции идет по этой причине.

Теперь давайте возьмем выборы. На выборах, в отличие от суда, где есть один истец и один ответчик, то есть всего 2 стороны, участвует по десятку кандидатов или партий. Следовательно, победителей всегда меньше, чем побежденных. Что говорят побежденные и их политтехнологи? Что их идей не понравились избирателям? Что они не правы? Что они не умеют работать с народом? Нет, они говорят, что власть подтасовала выборы... Наверное, самая обожаемая «фенечка» для любого оппозиционера – это заявлять о том, что результаты выборов «подтасованы» властью. Дескать, вот у нас в Кремле сейчас какие-то Самосы «засели», которые только и живут по принципу «Выигрывает выборы не тот, кто наберет больше голосов, а тот, кто больше себе насчитает!». Для чего это делается? Все просто: оппозиция подталкивает людей к тому — чтобы они не участвовали в выборах, шли на улицы и делали «цветные революции». Небезызвестный Борис Березовский прямо говорит: «Поскольку процесс публичных дебатов в России сегодня кастрирован, а Кремль в состоянии осуществить подтасовку выборов, смена режима - единственный путь для тех, кто хочет спасти демократическую идею в России: Сегодня вопрос о власти в России уже не может быть решен только на избирательных участках. Как это случилось когда-то на Украине, в Ливане и Кыргызстане, он будет решаться на улицах» Не будем рассматривать тот факт, что только за призывы к насильственной смене власти Березовского самого необходимо осудить, согласно УК РФ. Просто вдумаемся в логику мысли Бориса Абрамовича. Кремль кастрировал в России процесс публичных дебатов. Благодаря этому Кремль сможет осуществить подтасовку выборов. И выход из-за этого у народа многострадальной Руси один — брать топоры и вилы, и идти стеной на «треклятый» Кремль! Не понимая сам, что говорит, Березовский, по сути, обвиняет Кремль в том, что он сам готовит против себя восстание. Естественно, что в отличие от Лондона, в Кремле не дураки сидят и понимают, что если выборы, действительно, подтасовывать и лишать партии и кандидатов возможности бороться честно, то власть будет нелегитимной и в любой момент все может кончиться бунтом.

Именно поэтому Президент Медведев неоднократно предостерегал и партии, и власть против использования административного ресурса. Что касается самих публичных дебатов, то у нас их массово никогда и не было. Было только «пустопорожнее балабольство» в период перестройки, да кидание стаканами и кулачные бои в Думе в эпоху «развитой либерализации». Более-менее какая-то практика дискуссионных клубов начала появляться только сейчас.

Теперь же рассмотрим процедуру выборов серьезно. Во-первых, за любыми крупными выборами в России наблюдает очень много человек. Это и иностранные наблюдатели, и наблюдатели от партий, а также независимые наблюдатели. Всех их купить, запугать или как-то заставить не заметить подтасовку результатов голосования сейчас уже просто невозможно. Да и члены избирательных комиссий знают, что фальсификация выборов – уголовное преступление. А кому нужна судимость?

Партия «Единая Россия», которую, обычно, и клеймят во всех мыслимых и немыслимых грехах, получила на выборах в Государственную Думу в декабре 2007 года 70,08% голосов. В принципе, победа «Единой России» и большинство мест в Думе были бы гарантированы даже при 50%. Смысла в «подтасовке» уже просто не было – победа итак очевидна. Или же все свои 70% «Единая Россия» получила благодаря «подтасовке»? Ну, тогда вообще пришлось бы чуть ли не за каждого проголосовавшего бюллетень подменять. Такое даже Герберту Уэлсу в голову не пришло бы! Но вот нашим оппозиционерам приходит.

Еще наши оппозиционеры упорно не замечают, что время от времени та же «Единая Россия» проигрывает выборы. В 2010 г. единороссы проиграли выборы мэров Иркутска и Братска, аж на 20 % снизили свой результат в Свердловской области, в которой всегда были одними из лучших.. В 2009 году единорссы проиграли выборы мэров Смоленска и Мурманска. И это только из крупных городов! Райцентры проигрываются десятками, хотя там фальсифицировать выборы гораздо легче. О чем говорят эти поражения? Что вдруг разучились фальсифицировать? Нет, просто халатно отнеслись к агитации, вот и все. И обвинили потом себя - сняли региональных секретарей «Единой России», а не стали говорить, что оппозиция подкупила все избирательные комиссии.

- За десять лет число терактов по некоторым данным выросло более чем в 6 раз. Ориентация на коррумпированные кланы Кавказа привела к фактической потере контроля над Северо-Кавказскими республиками, при этом федеральная власть продолжает их дотировать на уровне $5–6 млрд. в год.

Секундочку. 10 лет назад вообще-то на Кавказе шла вторая чеченская. Она у оппозиции как не считается? Одним длинным терактом? Как можно сравнивать масштабные боевые действия при участии десятков тысяч комбатантов с нынешними обстрелами постов ДПС в Ингушетии (каждый из которых проходит как теракт)? 10 лет назад каждый день и каждую ночь были не просто обстрелы, а убитые и раненые. Да и теракты, по своему, если так можно выразиться, качеству, куда более значительны: один «Норд-Ост» чего стоит... Как можно сравнивать количество терактов, не задаваясь вопросом, захват это целого города или обстрел полицейского поста?! Как можно в здравом уме и твердой памяти, по сути, утверждать, что 10 лет назад обстановка на Кавказе была лучше? И как можно говорить о **потере контроля** – а в 90-х что, там был какой-то лучший контроль?

Кавказ был территорией, где вообще отсутствовала какая–либо власть. 10 лет назад боевики, по сути, независимой Ичкерии (независимой, потому что неконтролируемой, и этот контроль, действительно, потеряли в 90-ые, когда Немцов и ему подобные правили бал) захватывали Дагестан и полноценная война обходилась бюджету не в 5 или 6 миллиардов долларов, а в разы дороже. Раньше, во время войны деньги разворовывались, «война все спишет», теперь же видны действительные результаты. Например, заново отстроен г. Грозный. В других республиках быстрыми темпами развивается туристическая инфраструктура. Сейчас, по указанию Медведева создан новый Кавказский федеральный округ, назначен полпред А. Хлопонин в ранге Вице-премьера

Правительства. Ему поручено экономическое развитие Кавказа, что уменьшит дотации из федерального бюджета.

Вообще же – странная логика обвинять в терактах власть, а не террористов. Не власть же теракты совершает, в самом деле! А количество их может расти просто потому, что внешние силы, видя успехи наших властей просто увеличивают финансирование боевиков. Организаторами терактов выступают, как правило, религиозные фанатики, исповедующие радикальное учение секты ваххабитов. Сам ваххабизм был придуман в 18-ом веке Мухаммадом ибн Абд аль-Ваххабом. Секта ваххабитов сейчас активно действует на Северном Кавказе России, вербуя наемников из числа малообеспеченного местного населения. Затем наемники проходят жесткую психологическую обработку. Фактически, людей готовят к самоубийству ради борьбы с «неверными». К слову, «неверные» - это мы с вами. Кстати, многие последователи канонического ислама тоже относятся к ваххабитам к числу «неверных» или же гауров. Кто финансирует ваххабитов?! Изначально радикальное религиозное подполье для расшатывания ситуации на Северном Кавказе в Российской Империи готовили Великобритания и Турция. Ведь еще в 19 веке в Англии создавались черкесские комитеты. И точно такие же «ахмеды закаевы» сидели в Лондоне и вещали на весь мир о царском империализме и борьбе с неверными. Затем для расшатывания ситуации в СССР и в Афганистане кадры готовило ЦРУ. Идеологи ваххабизма готовились в Иране до момента исламской революции. После того, как США потеряли контроль над Ираном – ваххабитов стали готовить в Пакистане. Сейчас бандитское подполье на Северном Кавказе финансируется через международные террористические движения вроде «Всемирного джихада». Деньги на их деятельность идут, как правило, из Саудовской Аравии. Ранее, по информации из ряда источников, деньги давали египетские и иорданские бизнесмены. Психологические методы обработки наемников позаимствованы из ЦРУ. Американские спецслужбы специально разрабатывали технологии психологической обработки наемников для применения в «горячих точках», начиная еще с проекта «MK-ULTRA». Также на Северном Кавказе нередки случаи, когда ваххабиты и иностранные спецслужбы вообще не имеют к произошедшему теракту никакого отношения. Часто там друг друга взрывают, расстреливают и поджигают враждующие кланы и преступные группировки во время «разборок» между собой.

- *Зачем мы поссорились с братским народом Белоруссии? Стоило ли начинать против них «газовую войну» по украинскому сценарию?*

Причины «газовой войны» 2010 г. лежат исключительно в политической плоскости. На просьбу оплатить долги за поставку газа ($192 млн. – сумма, вполне посильная для Белоруссии) официальный Минск выступил со встречным иском, потребовав, чтобы Кремль уплатил транзитные $260 млн. «Газпром» ограничил поставки газа в Белоруссию на 30%, а Минск, в свою очередь, перекрыл транзит через РБ и начал отбор транзитного газа с целью «поддержки газотранспортной системы».

Даже когда было найдено компромиссное решение проблемы (подняли цену транзита), белорусское правительство, преследуя популистские цели, продолжало спекулировать на «газовой теме». Лукашенко привык требовать преференций в отношении цен на энергоносители, забывая при этом, что именно благодаря беспрецедентной помощи России (в т.ч. предоставления энергоносителей по дотационным ценам – в 2-4 раза ниже рыночных) Белоруссия сумела добиться существенных экономических успехов. Ежегодно белорусские НПЗ получали по льготным ценам более 20 млн. тонн нефти из России. При этом потребности самой республики в нефтепродуктах составляют 6-8 млн. тонн. Остальная продукция реализовывалась на западных рынках, в первую очередь, в Нидерландах и Великобритании, что приносило Беларуси ежегодно до $3,5 млрд. Беларусь долгое время оставалась единственной страной на постсоветском пространстве, уровень экономического развития которой превысил уровень 1990 г. Так, по данным на 2005 г. уровень ВВП по отношению к 1990 г. составил в Белоруссии 127%, на Украине — 66,7%, в России — 89,5%, а уровень развития промышленности — 153%, 76% и 96%, соответственно.

Между тем, спекулируя на теме дружбы двух государств, Лукашенко одновременно постоянно устраивает различные демарши, не сдерживает обещаний, не выполняет условий соглашений. Тормозятся интеграционные процессы между Россией и Белоруссией, не была введена, как было обещано Лукашенко, единая валюта, не решается вопрос о создании совместного газотранспортного консорциума. Стремясь склонить Россию к уступкам в отношении цен на газ, Лукашенко не раз делал заявления о готовности отвернуться от России и начать сотрудничество с Западом и Китаем. В ответ на это Россия предложила покупать у нее газ и нефть по мировым ценам, уплачивая положенную пошлину, что вызвало волну антироссийской пропаганды со стороны Лукашенко и активизировало ранее ослабленные националистические силы. Беларусь до сих пор не признала независимость Южной Осетии и Абхазии, чего Россия добивается от Минска с августа 2008 г. Вместе с тем, весной 2009 г. Россия предоставила Минску кредит, чтобы компенсировать повышение цен на газ, и помогает Белоруссии бороться с последствиями глобального финансового кризиса, который мог привести к падению белорусского экспорта на 45%. Минск продолжает затягивание всех внутренних процедур, связанных со вступлением Беларуси в Таможенный союз, существующий в настоящее время не как союз трех государств – России, Казахстана, Беларуси, а как союз только двух первых.

В апреле 2010 г. президент А. Лукашенко предоставил политическое убежище Курманбеку Бакиеву как главе правительства Киргизии в изгнании, хотя и такие действия обыкновенно в рамках союза принято согласовывать. Тем самым, президент Белоруссии фактически простимулировал гражданскую войну в Киргизии – «подбрюшье» России. С некоторых пор советником Лукашенко стал «опальный олигарх» Б. Березовский - враг России. Ссора с провокатором и истериком А. Лукашенко – это не ссора с белорусским народом, к которому мы продолжаем испытывать самые теплые чувства.

- Если бы не выросли цены на нефть на мировом рынке, никакого «путинского благополучия» бы не было. Правительство ничего не делало, только проедало нефтяные доходы... А надо было нефтяные доходы вложить в нашу экономику...

Радует уже то, что хоть тут признается некое «путинское благополучие», а то у нас оппозиция такая: в одной строчке говорит, что при Путине было плохо, а в другой, что было хорошо, но из-за нефти, в третьей – называет нефть – проклятием России. Кажется, ничего не поймешь в их логике. На самом деле, еще психолог З. Фрейд приводил пример «логики бессознательного»: «во-первых, я вообще не брал ваш чайник, во-вторых, когда я его вам вернул, он был без дырки, в–третьих, когда вы мне его давали, он был с дыркой». Понятно, что герой рассказа всеми силами пытается оправдаться за то, что сделал, испортил данный ему чайник, и каждое его оправдание само опровергает другое. Так и наша оппозиция, опровергает сама себя, а цель ее противоречивых утверждений всегда одна - вернуться к власти и делать с Россией то, что уже было сделано в 90-ые.

Утверждение, что цены на нефть просто обрушились на нас, а мы всего лишь пользовались этим, увы, поверхностно. Во-первых, надо сказать, что сам наш экономический рост, в свою очередь способствовал, спросу на нефть, а, следовательно, и росту цены на нее. Пусть в масштабах мира это не много, но все же. Во-вторых, надо понимать, что цена на нефть в мире давно уже не является рыночной. Еще в 1980-ые годы США могли легко уговаривать арабов снизить цены на нефть в несколько раз и за счет этого прикончить СССР. С чего же это вдруг американцы, которые разрушали СССР и легко манипулировали ценами, теперь дают России набирать мощь и цены не контролируют? На самом деле, и американский президент Буш, который вышел из нефтяного бизнеса, и арабы, хотели повысить мировые цены на нефть, сверхприбыли же они собирались делить без России. В частности, накануне нефтяного бума, консорциум американских банков, хотел купить у Ходорковского (который в то же время покупал нефтяную компанию у Абрамовича) треть российской нефтяной отрасли. Путин сумел сесть за стол переговоров как равноправный партнер с основными нефтяными игроками - это раз. Во-вторых, Путин сумел добиться того, что недра России оказались под контролем государства, как раз в период нефтяного бума. В-третьих, путин обеспечил, чтобы сверхдоходы от нефти не разворовывались, как при Ельцине, а пошли на отдачу государственных долгов России и в Стабилизационный фонд государства, что позволило нам амортизировать удар от мирового кризиса.

Мало ли где и на каких рынках росли какие цены - вопрос в том, сумело ли то или иное государство этим воспользоваться: обеспечить добычу и транспортировку, продажу продукта? Сумело ли конвертировать полученные доходы в блага для страны? Оппозиция часто любит приводить совпадающие графики роста цен на нефть и роста благосостояния России. Дескать, видите, благосостояние растет только из-за цен! Так это хорошо, что графики совпадают и показывают тем самым, что нефть работает на государство. А разве было бы лучше, если бы график роста благосостояния отличался бы от графика роста цен, и благосостояние бы отставало от этого роста?

Разговор о том, что нефтяные доходы можно было бы влить в экономику страны – экономически безграмотен. Как нельзя влить ведро воды в стакан, так нельзя влить лишние деньги в экономику. Мы сами видели, как росли цены на недвижимость у нас из-за лишних денег, мы видели вывоз капитала, экономика не справлялась с потоком денег. Вообще рост экономики в 10-12 % в год – предельный, выше этого начинается мобилизационная экономика, которая ведет к надрыву общества и плохим последствиям. Правительство Путина обеспечивало в среднем 7% роста в год. Да, несколько меньше требуемого, но не критично. Гораздо хуже, если бы мы «переборщили» с вливанием денег, и недвижимость выросла бы еще в 2 раза (хотя Москва и так уже догнала по стоимости Париж и Лондон), и все накопленное нами просто утекло бы заграницу. Кроме того, возникшая инфляция сделала бы нестабильным бизнес, сделала бы невозможными инвестиции, планирование, банки не смогли бы выдавать кредиты при низкой норме резервирования. То есть не работали бы так называемые денежные мультипликаторы.

Центральный банк создает денежную базу, а коммерческие банки за ее счет выдают кредиты, которые в сумме в несколько раз больше денежной базы (отношение денежной базы к сумме кредитов и называется кредитным мультипликатором). При этом считается, что чем больше кредитный мультипликатор, тем более развитой является экономика, и тем более эффективной является денежная эмиссия. У Китая мультипликатор равен 1:10, у США 1:6, а у России – 1:3. То есть, в Китае эмиссия одного юаня приводит к увеличению выпуска товаров и услуг сразу на 10 юаней, в США эмиссия одного доллара приводит к увеличению выпуска на 6 долларов, а в России эмиссия одного рубля приводит к увеличению выпуска только на 3 рубля. И вот как раз в том, что у российской экономики слишком короткий мультипликатор, во всяком случае, по сравнению с другими развитыми странами, Министр финансов и видит основную (но не единственную) проблему нашего развития. Денежная эмиссия Центрального банка у нас не является высокоэффективной, потому что она приводит к слишком незначительному увеличению выпуска продукции и услуг. И поэтому расширение денежной эмиссии, как способ стимулирования экономического роста не является стратегией, адекватной российским реалиям. Главная задача экономической политики государства – чтобы рос мультипликатор. Доверие на рынке конвертируется в мультипликатор. Среда задается макроэкономикой, администрированием государства, защитой собственности. То есть ключевыми факторами являются климат, спокойствие, доверие, администрирование и, конечно, защита собственности. Тогда деньги перестают бегать туда-сюда и превращаются в длинные деньги, а это означает, говоря иначе, что все меньшая часть доходов, полученных факторами производства, держится в высоколиквидной форме, а все большая часть сберегается. И вот за счет этой сберегаемой части доходов, как легко понять, и происходит инвестирование в экономику, следствием которого и будет растущий мультипликатор. Вливание лишних денег, действительно, бы сделало нас страной рантье, а не производителей, так что некий искусственный голод и самоограничение пошли нам на пользу.

- За годы правления Путина социальное расслоение в стране выросло на 15%. В кризисный 2009 год число долларовых миллиардеров удвоилось, при этом 18,5 млн. человек живут за чертой бедности, безработица достигла уровня 9%, а зарплаты бюджетников заморожены.

Сама по себе эта цифра в 15% ничего не говорит. Скажем, если обеднели нижние слои на 15%, а верхние остались при своих – это плохо. Если разбогатели верхние на 25%, а нижние разбогатели на 10% - ничего страшного (цифры условны). Теперь смотрим, что у нас там с миллиардерами вышло. Но по данным журнала «Форбс» в кризис число миллиардеров как раз сократилось. И что характерно - именно в два раза.

Теперь давайте посмотрим на зарплаты и доходы населения. В 2000-2007 годах устойчиво росли все основные показатели, характеризующие уровень жизни граждан страны. Реальные располагаемые денежные доходы граждан росли в среднем на 10% процентов в год. По сравнению с 1999 годом они в реальном выражении выросли в 2,3 раза. В номинально выражении рост еще более существенен: в 1999 г. душевые доходы составляли 1659 рублей в месяц, а по итогам 2007 года – превысили 12 тысяч рублей в месяц. Как результат, почти вдвое снизилась бедность. В 1999 г. за чертой бедности проживал 41,6 млн. человек (28% населения), в I полугодии 2007 года 22,3 млн. человек (16%). Реальная заработная плата выросла по сравнению с 1999 г. в 3 раза (с 1,5 тыс. рублей до более чем 12 тысяч рублей в месяц в номинальном выражении). При этом рост заработной платы коснулся работников всех отраслей экономики, включая и сельское хозяйство, и отрасли бюджетной сферы. Так, в сельском хозяйстве заработная плата в 1999 г. составляла лишь 629 рублей в месяц, а в 2007 году – достигла 6 тысяч рублей. В образовании заработная плата выросла с 885 рублей до более чем 8,5 тысяч рублей. В здравоохранении заработная плата выросла с 975 рублей до почти 10 тысяч рублей. К 2007 г. практически полностью ликвидировано такое явление, как задолженность по заработной плате (в 1999 году задолженность составляла 77 млрд. рублей в 132 тысячах организаций).

Установленный законом минимальный размер оплаты труда был повышен со 83,49 коп. в месяц до 2,3 тыс. рублей (т.е. в 27,5 раз). В настоящее время величина МРОТ составляет более 50% от прожиточного минимума трудоспособного населения (в 1999 г. – лишь 10%). Теми же темпами (или даже быстрее за счет проведения структурных реформ) растет оплата труда работников бюджетных отраслей. Только с 1 февраля 2008 г. она увеличена на 14%. Средний размер пенсии в 2007 году вырос по сравнению с 1999 г. с 449 рублей до 3100 рублей. Реальный рост составил 2,4 раза. Средняя пенсия превысила величину прожиточного минимума пенсионера (а в 1999 г. она составляла лишь 70% от прожиточного минимума). В 2007-2009 годах продолжился рост пенсий на 65% за три года. Существенно выросло потребление, по отдельным группам товаров – в разы. Потребление мяса и птицы выросло в 2 раза, сыров – в 3 раза, растительных масел – в 2,3 раза, медикаментов – в 2,7 раза, стиральных машин – в 3,4 раза, телевизоров – в 3,8 раза. Возросла обеспеченность населения товарами длительного пользования. В 2000 г. только 48% семей имели видеомагнитофоны, в 2005 г. (более поздних данных нет) – 66% семей. Обеспеченность компьютерами возросла с 6% до 26%.

Повсеместное распространение получила сотовая связь. Растет автомобилизация населения. Сегодня автомобиль имеется уже в 35% российских семей.

- Сельское хозяйство России за время правления Путина уничтожено, мы полностью зависим от импорта.

Сельское хозяйство было уничтожено не за время правления Путина, а в 90-ые годы из-за реформ по насаждению фермерства и открытия всех рынков западным товарам. За время правления Путина началось возрождение села. С 1999 г. по ноябрь 2007 г. индекс производства продукции сельского хозяйства в сопоставимых ценах вырос более чем на 33%. С 1999 г. по 2006 г. положительная динамика наблюдается как в растениеводстве (объем производства зерна вырос на 43,7%, сахарной свеклы – на 102,7%, семян подсолнечника – на 62,7%, картофеля – на 23%, овощей – на 27,3%), так и в животноводстве (объем производства скота и птицы вырос на 20,3%, яиц – на 14,5%).Правительством Российской Федерации 14 июля 2007 г. утверждена Государственная программа развития сельского хозяйства и регулирования рынков сельскохозяйственной продукции, сырья и продовольствия на 2008-2012 годы (далее – Госпрограмма), основными целями которой являются:

- устойчивое развитие сельских территорий, повышение занятости и уровня жизни сельского населения;

- повышение конкурентоспособности отечественной сельскохозяйственной продукции на основе финансовой устойчивости и модернизации сельского хозяйства, ускоренного развития приоритетных подотраслей сельского хозяйства с целью импортозамещения

- сохранение и воспроизводство используемых в сельскохозяйственном производстве земельных и других природных ресурсов.

Из федерального бюджета в 2008-2012 годах на реализацию Госпрограммы будет направлено 551,3 млрд. рублей, софинансирование со стороны бюджетов субъектов Российской Федерации будет осуществляться в сопоставимых размерах (544,3 млрд. рублей). Импортозависимость по некоторым отраслям сократилась с 80% до 40%, то есть в 2 раза.

SOVIET AND POST-SOVIET POLITICS AND SOCIETY

Edited by Dr. Andreas Umland

ISSN 1614-3515

1   *Андреас Умланд (ред.)*
Воплощение Европейской конвенции по правам человека в России
Философские, юридические и эмпирические исследования
ISBN 3-89821-387-0

2   *Christian Wipperfürth*
Russland – ein vertrauenswürdiger Partner?
Grundlagen, Hintergründe und Praxis gegenwärtiger russischer Außenpolitik
Mit einem Vorwort von Heinz Timmermann
ISBN 3-89821-401-X

3   *Manja Hussner*
Die Übernahme internationalen Rechts in die russische und deutsche Rechtsordnung
Eine vergleichende Analyse zur Völkerrechtsfreundlichkeit der Verfassungen der Russländischen Föderation und der Bundesrepublik Deutschland
Mit einem Vorwort von Rainer Arnold
ISBN 3-89821-438-9

4   *Matthew Tejada*
Bulgaria's Democratic Consolidation and the Kozloduy Nuclear Power Plant (KNPP)
The Unattainability of Closure
With a foreword by Richard J. Crampton
ISBN 3-89821-439-7

5   *Марк Григорьевич Меерович*
Квадратные метры, определяющие сознание
Государственная жилищная политика в СССР. 1921 – 1941 гг
ISBN 3-89821-474-5

6   *Andrei P. Tsygankov, Pavel A.Tsygankov (Eds.)*
New Directions in Russian International Studies
ISBN 3-89821-422-2

7   *Марк Григорьевич Меерович*
Как власть народ к труду приучала
Жилище в СССР – средство управления людьми. 1917 – 1941 гг.
С предисловием Елены Осокиной
ISBN 3-89821-495-8

8   *David J. Galbreath*
Nation-Building and Minority Politics in Post-Socialist States
Interests, Influence and Identities in Estonia and Latvia
With a foreword by David J. Smith
ISBN 3-89821-467-2

9   *Алексей Юрьевич Безугольный*
Народы Кавказа в Вооруженных силах СССР в годы Великой Отечественной войны 1941-1945 гг.
С предисловием Николая Бугая
ISBN 3-89821-475-3

10   *Вячеслав Лихачев и Владимир Прибыловский (ред.)*
Русское Национальное Единство, 1990-2000. В 2-х томах
ISBN 3-89821-523-7

11   *Николай Бугай (ред.)*
Народы стран Балтии в условиях сталинизма (1940-е – 1950-е годы)
Документированная история
ISBN 3-89821-525-3

12   *Ingmar Bredies (Hrsg.)*
Zur Anatomie der Orange Revolution in der Ukraine
Wechsel des Elitenregimes oder Triumph des Parlamentarismus?
ISBN 3-89821-524-5

13   *Anastasia V. Mitrofanova*
The Politicization of Russian Orthodoxy
Actors and Ideas
With a foreword by William C. Gay
ISBN 3-89821-481-8

14 Nathan D. Larson
    Alexander Solzhenitsyn and the
    Russo-Jewish Question
    ISBN 3-89821-483-4

15 Guido Houben
    Kulturpolitik und Ethnizität
    Staatliche Kunstförderung im Russland der
    neunziger Jahre
    Mit einem Vorwort von Gert Weisskirchen
    ISBN 3-89821-542-3

16 Leonid Luks
    Der russische „Sonderweg"?
    Aufsätze zur neuesten Geschichte Russlands
    im europäischen Kontext
    ISBN 3-89821-496-6

17 Евгений Мороз
    История «Мёртвой воды» – от
    страшной сказки к большой
    политике
    Политическое неоязычество в
    постсоветской России
    ISBN 3-89821-551-2

18 Александр Верховский и Галина
    Кожевникова (ред.)
    Этническая и религиозная
    интолерантность в российских СМИ
    Результаты мониторинга 2001-2004 гг.
    ISBN 3-89821-569-5

19 Christian Ganzer
    Sowjetisches Erbe und ukrainische
    Nation
    Das Museum der Geschichte des Zaporoger
    Kosakentums auf der Insel Chortycja
    Mit einem Vorwort von Frank Golczewski
    ISBN 3-89821-504-0

20 Эльза-Баир Гучинова
    Помнить нельзя забыть
    Антропология депортационной травмы
    калмыков
    С предисловием Кэролайн Хамфри
    ISBN 3-89821-506-7

21 Юлия Лидерман
    Мотивы «проверки» и «испытания»
    в постсоветской культуре
    Советское прошлое в российском
    кинематографе 1990-х годов
    С предисловием Евгения Марголита
    ISBN 3-89821-511-3

22 Tanya Lokshina, Ray Thomas, Mary
    Mayer (Eds.)
    The Imposition of a Fake Political
    Settlement in the Northern Caucasus
    The 2003 Chechen Presidential Election
    ISBN 3-89821-436-2

23 Timothy McCajor Hall, Rosie Read
    (Eds.)
    Changes in the Heart of Europe
    Recent Ethnographies of Czechs, Slovaks,
    Roma, and Sorbs
    With an afterword by Zdeněk Salzmann
    ISBN 3-89821-606-3

24 Christian Autengruber
    Die politischen Parteien in Bulgarien
    und Rumänien
    Eine vergleichende Analyse seit Beginn der
    90er Jahre
    Mit einem Vorwort von Dorothée de Nève
    ISBN 3-89821-476-1

25 Annette Freyberg-Inan with Radu
    Cristescu
    The Ghosts in Our Classrooms, or:
    John Dewey Meets Ceauşescu
    The Promise and the Failures of Civic
    Education in Romania
    ISBN 3-89821-416-8

26 John B. Dunlop
    The 2002 Dubrovka and 2004 Beslan
    Hostage Crises
    A Critique of Russian Counter-Terrorism
    With a foreword by Donald N. Jensen
    ISBN 3-89821-608-X

27 Peter Koller
    Das touristische Potenzial von
    Kam''janec'-Podil's'kyj
    Eine fremdenverkehrsgeographische
    Untersuchung der Zukunftsperspektiven und
    Maßnahmenplanung zur
    Destinationsentwicklung des „ukrainischen
    Rothenburg"
    Mit einem Vorwort von Kristiane Klemm
    ISBN 3-89821-640-3

28 Françoise Daucé, Elisabeth Sieca-
    Kozlowski (Eds.)
    Dedovshchina in the Post-Soviet
    Military
    Hazing of Russian Army Conscripts in a
    Comparative Perspective
    With a foreword by Dale Herspring
    ISBN 3-89821-616-0

29 Florian Strasser
Zivilgesellschaftliche Einflüsse auf die Orange Revolution
Die gewaltlose Massenbewegung und die ukrainische Wahlkrise 2004
Mit einem Vorwort von Egbert Jahn
ISBN 3-89821-648-9

30 Rebecca S. Katz
The Georgian Regime Crisis of 2003-2004
A Case Study in Post-Soviet Media Representation of Politics, Crime and Corruption
ISBN 3-89821-413-3

31 Vladimir Kantor
Willkür oder Freiheit
Beiträge zur russischen Geschichtsphilosophie
Ediert von Dagmar Herrmann sowie mit einem Vorwort versehen von Leonid Luks
ISBN 3-89821-589-X

32 Laura A. Victoir
The Russian Land Estate Today
A Case Study of Cultural Politics in Post-Soviet Russia
With a foreword by Priscilla Roosevelt
ISBN 3-89821-426-5

33 Ivan Katchanovski
Cleft Countries
Regional Political Divisions and Cultures in Post-Soviet Ukraine and Moldova
With a foreword by Francis Fukuyama
ISBN 3-89821-558-X

34 Florian Mühlfried
Postsowjetische Feiern
Das Georgische Bankett im Wandel
Mit einem Vorwort von Kevin Tuite
ISBN 3-89821-601-2

35 Roger Griffin, Werner Loh, Andreas Umland (Eds.)
Fascism Past and Present, West and East
An International Debate on Concepts and Cases in the Comparative Study of the Extreme Right
With an afterword by Walter Laqueur
ISBN 3-89821-674-8

36 Sebastian Schlegel
Der „Weiße Archipel"
Sowjetische Atomstädte 1945-1991
Mit einem Geleitwort von Thomas Bohn
ISBN 3-89821-679-9

37 Vyacheslav Likhachev
Political Anti-Semitism in Post-Soviet Russia
Actors and Ideas in 1991-2003
Edited and translated from Russian by Eugene Veklerov
ISBN 3-89821-529-6

38 Josette Baer (Ed.)
Preparing Liberty in Central Europe
Political Texts from the Spring of Nations 1848 to the Spring of Prague 1968
With a foreword by Zdeněk V. David
ISBN 3-89821-546-6

39 Михаил Лукьянов
Российский консерватизм и реформа, 1907-1914
С предисловием Марка Д. Стейнберга
ISBN 3-89821-503-2

40 Nicola Melloni
Market Without Economy
The 1998 Russian Financial Crisis
With a foreword by Eiji Furukawa
ISBN 3-89821-407-9

41 Dmitrij Chmelnizki
Die Architektur Stalins
Bd. 1: Studien zu Ideologie und Stil
Bd. 2: Bilddokumentation
Mit einem Vorwort von Bruno Flierl
ISBN 3-89821-515-6

42 Katja Yafimava
Post-Soviet Russian-Belarussian Relationships
The Role of Gas Transit Pipelines
With a foreword by Jonathan P. Stern
ISBN 3-89821-655-1

43 Boris Chavkin
Verflechtungen der deutschen und russischen Zeitgeschichte
Aufsätze und Archivfunde zu den Beziehungen Deutschlands und der Sowjetunion von 1917 bis 1991
Ediert von Markus Edlinger sowie mit einem Vorwort versehen von Leonid Luks
ISBN 3-89821-756-6

44 Anastasija Grynenko in Zusammenarbeit mit Claudia Dathe
Die Terminologie des Gerichtswesens der Ukraine und Deutschlands im Vergleich
Eine übersetzungswissenschaftliche Analyse juristischer Fachbegriffe im Deutschen, Ukrainischen und Russischen
Mit einem Vorwort von Ulrich Hartmann
ISBN 3-89821-691-8

45 Anton Burkov
The Impact of the European Convention on Human Rights on Russian Law
Legislation and Application in 1996-2006
With a foreword by Françoise Hampson
ISBN 978-3-89821-639-5

46 Stina Torjesen, Indra Overland (Eds.)
International Election Observers in Post-Soviet Azerbaijan
Geopolitical Pawns or Agents of Change?
ISBN 978-3-89821-743-9

47 Taras Kuzio
Ukraine – Crimea – Russia
Triangle of Conflict
ISBN 978-3-89821-761-3

48 Claudia Šabić
"Ich erinnere mich nicht, aber L'viv!"
Zur Funktion kultureller Faktoren für die Institutionalisierung und Entwicklung einer ukrainischen Region
Mit einem Vorwort von Melanie Tatur
ISBN 978-3-89821-752-1

49 Marlies Bilz
Tatarstan in der Transformation
Nationaler Diskurs und Politische Praxis 1988-1994
Mit einem Vorwort von Frank Golczewski
ISBN 978-3-89821-722-4

50 Марлен Ларюэль (ред.)
Современные интерпретации русского национализма
ISBN 978-3-89821-795-8

51 Sonja Schüler
Die ethnische Dimension der Armut
Roma im postsozialistischen Rumänien
Mit einem Vorwort von Anton Sterbling
ISBN 978-3-89821-776-7

52 Галина Кожевникова
Радикальный национализм в России и противодействие ему
Сборник докладов Центра «Сова» за 2004-2007 гг.
С предисловием Александра Верховского
ISBN 978-3-89821-721-7

53 Галина Кожевникова и Владимир Прибыловский
Российская власть в биографиях I
Высшие должностные лица РФ в 2004 г.
ISBN 978-3-89821-796-5

54 Галина Кожевникова и Владимир Прибыловский
Российская власть в биографиях II
Члены Правительства РФ в 2004 г.
ISBN 978-3-89821-797-2

55 Галина Кожевникова и Владимир Прибыловский
Российская власть в биографиях III
Руководители федеральных служб и агентств РФ в 2004 г.
ISBN 978-3-89821-798-9

56 Ileana Petroniu
Privatisierung in Transformationsökonomien
Determinanten der Restrukturierungs-Bereitschaft am Beispiel Polens, Rumäniens und der Ukraine
Mit einem Vorwort von Rainer W. Schäfer
ISBN 978-3-89821-790-3

57 Christian Wipperfürth
Russland und seine GUS-Nachbarn
Hintergründe, aktuelle Entwicklungen und Konflikte in einer ressourcenreichen Region
ISBN 978-3-89821-801-6

58 Togzhan Kassenova
From Antagonism to Partnership
The Uneasy Path of the U.S.-Russian Cooperative Threat Reduction
With a foreword by Christoph Bluth
ISBN 978-3-89821-707-1

59 Alexander Höllwerth
Das sakrale eurasische Imperium des Aleksandr Dugin
Eine Diskursanalyse zum postsowjetischen russischen Rechtsextremismus
Mit einem Vorwort von Dirk Uffelmann
ISBN 978-3-89821-813-9

60   Олег Рябов
      «Россия-Матушка»
      Национализм, гендер и война в России XX
      века
      С предисловием Елены Гощило
      ISBN 978-3-89821-487-2

61   Ivan Maistrenko
      Borot'bism
      A Chapter in the History of the Ukrainian
      Revolution
      With a new introduction by Chris Ford
      Translated by George S. N. Luckyj with the
      assistance of Ivan L. Rudnytsky
      ISBN 978-3-89821-697-5

62   Maryna Romanets
      Anamorphosic Texts and
      Reconfigured Visions
      Improvised Traditions in Contemporary
      Ukrainian and Irish Literature
      ISBN 978-3-89821-576-3

63   Paul D'Anieri and Taras Kuzio (Eds.)
      Aspects of the Orange Revolution I
      Democratization and Elections in Post-
      Communist Ukraine
      ISBN 978-3-89821-698-2

64   Bohdan Harasymiw in collaboration
      with Oleh S. Ilnytzkyj (Eds.)
      Aspects of the Orange Revolution II
      Information and Manipulation Strategies in
      the 2004 Ukrainian Presidential Elections
      ISBN 978-3-89821-699-9

65   Ingmar Bredies, Andreas Umland and
      Valentin Yakushik (Eds.)
      Aspects of the Orange Revolution III
      The Context and Dynamics of the 2004
      Ukrainian Presidential Elections
      ISBN 978-3-89821-803-0

66   Ingmar Bredies, Andreas Umland and
      Valentin Yakushik (Eds.)
      Aspects of the Orange Revolution IV
      Foreign Assistance and Civic Action in the
      2004 Ukrainian Presidential Elections
      ISBN 978-3-89821-808-5

67   Ingmar Bredies, Andreas Umland and
      Valentin Yakushik (Eds.)
      Aspects of the Orange Revolution V
      Institutional Observation Reports on the 2004
      Ukrainian Presidential Elections
      ISBN 978-3-89821-809-2

68   Taras Kuzio (Ed.)
      Aspects of the Orange Revolution VI
      Post-Communist Democratic Revolutions in
      Comparative Perspective
      ISBN 978-3-89821-820-7

69   Tim Bohse
      Autoritarismus statt Selbstverwaltung
      Die Transformation der kommunalen Politik
      in der Stadt Kaliningrad 1990-2005
      Mit einem Geleitwort von Stefan Troebst
      ISBN 978-3-89821-782-8

70   David Rupp
      Die Rußländische Föderation und die
      russischsprachige Minderheit in
      Lettland
      Eine Fallstudie zur Anwaltspolitik Moskaus
      gegenüber den russophonen Minderheiten im
      „Nahen Ausland" von 1991 bis 2002
      Mit einem Vorwort von Helmut Wagner
      ISBN 978-3-89821-778-1

71   Taras Kuzio
      Theoretical and Comparative
      Perspectives on Nationalism
      New Directions in Cross-Cultural and Post-
      Communist Studies
      With a foreword by Paul Robert Magocsi
      ISBN 978-3-89821-815-3

72   Christine Teichmann
      Die Hochschultransformation im
      heutigen Osteuropa
      Kontinuität und Wandel bei der Entwicklung
      des postkommunistischen Universitätswesens
      Mit einem Vorwort von Oskar Anweiler
      ISBN 978-3-89821-842-9

73   Julia Kusznir
      Der politische Einfluss von
      Wirtschaftseliten in russischen
      Regionen
      Eine Analyse am Beispiel der Erdöl- und
      Erdgasindustrie, 1992-2005
      Mit einem Vorwort von Wolfgang Eichwede
      ISBN 978-3-89821-821-4

74   Alena Vysotskaya
      Russland, Belarus und die EU-
      Osterweiterung
      Zur Minderheitenfrage und zum Problem der
      Freizügigkeit des Personenverkehrs
      Mit einem Vorwort von Katlijn Malfliet
      ISBN 978-3-89821-822-1

75 Heiko Pleines (Hrsg.)
Corporate Governance in post-
sozialistischen Volkswirtschaften
ISBN 978-3-89821-766-8

76 Stefan Ihrig
Wer sind die Moldawier?
Rumänismus versus Moldowanismus in
Historiographie und Schulbüchern der
Republik Moldova, 1991-2006
Mit einem Vorwort von Holm Sundhaussen
ISBN 978-3-89821-466-7

77 Galina Kozhevnikova in collaboration
with Alexander Verkhovsky and
Eugene Veklerov
Ultra-Nationalism and Hate Crimes in
Contemporary Russia
The 2004-2006 Annual Reports of Moscow's
SOVA Center
With a foreword by Stephen D. Shenfield
ISBN 978-3-89821-868-9

78 Florian Küchler
The Role of the European Union in
Moldova's Transnistria Conflict
With a foreword by Christopher Hill
ISBN 978-3-89821-850-4

79 Bernd Rechel
The Long Way Back to Europe
Minority Protection in Bulgaria
With a foreword by Richard Crampton
ISBN 978-3-89821-863-4

80 Peter W. Rodgers
Nation, Region and History in Post-
Communist Transitions
Identity Politics in Ukraine, 1991-2006
With a foreword by Vera Tolz
ISBN 978-3-89821-903-7

81 Stephanie Solywoda
The Life and Work of
Semen L. Frank
A Study of Russian Religious Philosophy
With a foreword by Philip Walters
ISBN 978-3-89821-457-5

82 Vera Sokolova
Cultural Politics of Ethnicity
Discourses on Roma in Communist
Czechoslovakia
ISBN 978-3-89821-864-1

83 Natalya Shevchik Ketenci
Kazakhstani Enterprises in Transition
The Role of Historical Regional Development
in Kazakhstan's Post-Soviet Economic
Transformation
ISBN 978-3-89821-831-3

84 Martin Malek, Anna Schor-
Tschudnowskaja (Hrsg.)
Europa im Tschetschenienkrieg
Zwischen politischer Ohnmacht und
Gleichgültigkeit
Mit einem Vorwort von Lipchan Basajewa
ISBN 978-3-89821-676-0

85 Stefan Meister
Das postsowjetische Universitätswesen
zwischen nationalem und
internationalem Wandel
Die Entwicklung der regionalen Hochschule
in Russland als Gradmesser der
Systemtransformation
Mit einem Vorwort von Joan DeBardeleben
ISBN 978-3-89821-891-7

86 Konstantin Sheiko in collaboration
with Stephen Brown
Nationalist Imaginings of the
Russian Past
Anatolii Fomenko and the Rise of Alternative
History in Post-Communist Russia
With a foreword by Donald Ostrowski
ISBN 978-3-89821-915-0

87 Sabine Jenni
Wie stark ist das „Einige Russland"?
Zur Parteibindung der Eliten und zum
Wahlerfolg der Machtpartei
im Dezember 2007
Mit einem Vorwort von Klaus Armingeon
ISBN 978-3-89821-961-7

88 Thomas Borén
Meeting-Places of Transformation
Urban Identity, Spatial Representations and
Local Politics in Post-Soviet St Petersburg
ISBN 978-3-89821-739-2

89 Aygul Ashirova
Stalinismus und Stalin-Kult in
Zentralasien
Turkmenistan 1924-1953
Mit einem Vorwort von Leonid Luks
ISBN 978-3-89821-987-7

90 Leonid Luks
Freiheit oder imperiale Größe?
Essays zu einem russischen Dilemma
ISBN 978-3-8382-0011-8

91 Christopher Gilley
The 'Change of Signposts' in the Ukrainian Emigration
A Contribution to the History of Sovietophilism in the 1920s
With a foreword by Frank Golczewski
ISBN 978-3-89821-965-5

92 Philipp Casula, Jeronim Perovic (Eds.)
Identities and Politics During the Putin Presidency
The Discursive Foundations of Russia's Stability
With a foreword by Heiko Haumann
ISBN 978-3-8382-0015-6

93 Marcel Viëtor
Europa und die Frage nach seinen Grenzen im Osten
Zur Konstruktion ‚europäischer Identität' in Geschichte und Gegenwart
Mit einem Vorwort von Albrecht Lehmann
ISBN 978-3-8382-0045-3

94 Ben Hellman, Andrei Rogachevskii
Filming the Unfilmable
Casper Wrede's 'One Day in the Life of Ivan Denisovich'
ISBN 978-3-8382-0044-6

95 Eva Fuchslocher
Vaterland, Sprache, Glaube
Orthodoxie und Nationenbildung am Beispiel Georgiens
Mit einem Vorwort von Christina von Braun
ISBN 978-3-89821-884-9

96 Vladimir Kantor
Das Westlertum und der Weg Russlands
Zur Entwicklung der russischen Literatur und Philosophie
Ediert von Dagmar Herrmann
Mit einem Beitrag von Nikolaus Lobkowicz
ISBN 978-3-8382-0102-3

97 Kamran Musayev
Die postsowjetische Transformation im Baltikum und Südkaukasus
Eine vergleichende Untersuchung der politischen Entwicklung Lettlands und Aserbaidschans 1985-2009
Mit einem Vorwort von Leonid Luks
Ediert von Sandro Henschel
ISBN 978-3-8382-0103-0

98 Tatiana Zhurzhenko
Borderlands into Bordered Lands
Geopolitics of Identity in Post-Soviet Ukraine
With a foreword by Dieter Segert
ISBN 978-3-8382-0042-2

99 Кирилл Галушко, Лидия Смола (ред.)
Пределы падения – варианты украинского будущего
Аналитико-прогностические исследования
ISBN 978-3-8382-0148-1

100 Michael Minkenberg (ed.)
Historical Legacies and the Radical Right in Post-Cold War Central and Eastern Europe
With an afterword by Sabrina P. Ramet
ISBN 978-3-8382-0124-5

101 David-Emil Wickström
"Okna otkroi!" – "Open the Windows!"
Transcultural Flows and Identity Politics in the St. Petersburg Popular Music Scene
With a foreword by Yngvar B. Steinholt
ISBN 978-3-8382-0100-9

102 Eva Zabka
Eine neue „Zeit der Wirren"?
Der spät- und postsowjetische Systemwandel 1985-2000 im Spiegel russischer gesellschaftspolitischer Diskurse
Mit einem Vorwort von Margareta Mommsen
ISBN 978-3-8382-0161-0

103 Ulrike Ziemer
Ethnic Belonging, Gender and Cultural Practices
Youth Identitites in Contemporary Russia
With a foreword by Anoop Nayak
ISBN 978-3-8382-0152-8

104 Ksenia Chepikova
,Einiges Russland' - eine zweite KPdSU?
Aspekte der Identitätskonstruktion einer postsowjetischen „Partei der Macht"
Mit einem Vorwort von Torsten Oppelland
ISBN 978-3-8382-0311-9

105 Леонид Люкс
Западничество или евразийство? Демократия или идеократия?
Сборник статей об исторических дилеммах России
С предисловием Владимира Кантора
ISBN 978-3-8382-0211-2

106 Anna Dost
Das russische Verfassungsrecht auf dem Weg zum Föderalismus und zurück
Zum Konflikt von Rechtsnormen und -wirklichkeit in der Russländischen Föderation von 1991 bis 2009
Mit einem Vorwort von Alexander Blankenagel
ISBN 978-3-8382-0292-1

107 Philipp Herzog
Sozialistische Völkerfreundschaft, nationaler Widerstand oder harmloser Zeitvertreib?
Zur politischen Funktion der Volkskunst im sowjetischen Estland
Mit einem Vorwort von Andreas Kappeler
ISBN 978-3-8382-0216-7

108 Marlène Laruelle (ed.)
Russian Nationalism, Foreign Policy, and Identity Debates in Putin's Russia
New Ideological Patterns after the Orange Revolution
ISBN 978-3-8382-0325-6

109 Michail Logvinov
Russlands Kampf gegen den internationalen Terrorismus
Eine kritische Bestandsaufnahme des Bekämpfungsansatzes
Mit einem Geleitwort von Hans-Henning Schröder und einem Vorwort von Eckhard Jesse
ISBN 978-3-8382-0329-4

110 John B. Dunlop
The Moscow Bombings of September 1999
Examinations of Russian Terrorist Attacks at the Onset of Vladimir Putin's Rule
ISBN 978-3-8382-0388-1

111 Андрей А. Ковалёв
Свидетельство из-за кулис российской политики I
Можно ли делать добро из зла? (Воспоминания и размышления о последних советских и первых послесоветских годах)
With a foreword by Peter Reddaway
ISBN 978-3-8382-0302-7

112 Андрей А. Ковалёв
Свидетельство из-за кулис российской политики II
Угроза для себя и окружающих (Наблюдения и предостережения относительно происходящего после 2000 г.)
ISBN 978-3-8382-0303-4

113 Bernd Kappenberg
Zeichen setzen für Europa
Der Gebrauch europäischer lateinischer Sonderzeichen in der deutschen Öffentlichkeit
Mit einem Vorwort von Peter Schlobinski
ISBN 978-3-89821-749-1

114 Ivo Mijnssen
The Quest for an Ideal Youth in Putin's Russia I
Back to Our Future! History, Modernity, and Patriotism according to Nashi, 2005-2013
With a foreword by Jeronim Perović
Second, Revised and Expanded Edition
ISBN 978-3-8382-0368-3

115 Jussi Lassila
The Quest for an Ideal Youth in Putin's Russia II
The Search for Distinctive Conformism in the Political Communication of Nashi, 2005-2009
With a foreword by Kirill Postoutenko
Second, Revised and Expanded Edition
ISBN 978-3-8382-0415-4

116 Valerio Trabandt
Neue Nachbarn, gute Nachbarschaft?
Die EU als internationaler Akteur am Beispiel ihrer Demokratieförderung in Belarus und der Ukraine 2004-2009
Mit einem Vorwort von Jutta Joachim
ISBN 978-3-8382-0437-6

117 Fabian Pfeiffer
Estlands Außen- und Sicherheitspolitik I
Der estnische Atlantizismus nach der wiedererlangten Unabhängigkeit 1991-2004
Mit einem Vorwort von Helmut Hubel
ISBN 978-3-8382-0127-6

118   *Jana Podßuweit*
       Estlands Außen- und Sicherheitspolitik II
       Handlungsoptionen eines Kleinstaates im
       Rahmen seiner EU-Mitgliedschaft (2004-2008)
       Mit einem Vorwort von Helmut Hubel
       ISBN 978-3-8382-0440-6

119   *Karin Pointner*
       Estlands Außen- und Sicherheitspolitik III
       Eine gedächtnispolitische Analyse estnischer
       Entwicklungskooperation 2006-2010
       Mit einem Vorwort von Karin Liebhart
       ISBN 978-3-8382-0435-2

120   *Ruslana Vovk*
       Die Offenheit der ukrainischen
       Verfassung für das Völkerrecht und
       die europäische Integration
       Mit einem Vorwort von Alexander
       Blankenagel
       ISBN 978-3-8382-0481-9

121   *Mykhaylo Banakh*
       Die Relevanz der Zivilgesellschaft
       bei den postkommunistischen
       Transformationsprozessen in mittel-
       und osteuropäischen Ländern
       Das Beispiel der spät- und postsowjetischen
       Ukraine 1986-2009
       Mit einem Vorwort von Gerhard Simon
       ISBN 978-3-8382-0499-4

122   *Michael Moser*
       Language Policy and the Discourse on
       Languages in Ukraine under President
       Viktor Yanukovych (25 February
       2010–28 October 2012)
       ISBN 978-3-8382-0497-0 (Paperback edition)
       ISBN 978-3-8382-0507-6 (Hardcover edition)

123   *Nicole Krome*
       Russischer Netzwerkkapitalismus
       Restrukturierungsprozesse in der
       Russischen Föderation am Beispiel des
       Luftfahrtunternehmens "Aviastar"
       Mit einem Vorwort von Petra Stykow
       ISBN 978-3-8382-0534-2

124   *David R. Marples*
       'Our Glorious Past'
       Lukashenka's Belarus and
       the Great Patriotic War
       ISBN 978-3-8382-0574-8

125   *Ulf Walther*
       Russlands "neuer Adel"
       Die Macht des Geheimdienstes von
       Gorbatschow bis Putin
       Mit einem Vorwort von Hans-Georg Wieck
       ISBN 978-3-8382-0584-7

ibidem-Verlag

Melchiorstr. 15

D-70439 Stuttgart

info@ibidem-verlag.de

www.ibidem-verlag.de
www.ibidem.eu
www.edition-noema.de
www.autorenbetreuung.de